The Turkish Arms Embargo

The Turkish Arms Embargo

Drugs, Ethnic Lobbies, and US Domestic Politics

James F. Goode

Paperback edition 2022

Scholarly publisher for the Commonwealth, serving Bellarmine University, Berea College, Centre College of Kentucky, Eastern Kentucky University, The Filson Historical Society, Georgetown College, Kentucky Historical Society, Kentucky State University, Morehead State University, Murray State University, Northern Kentucky University, Spalding University, Transylvania University, University of Kentucky, University of Louisville, University of Pikeville, and Western Kentucky University.

Editorial and Sales Offices: The University Press of Kentucky
663 South Limestone Street, Lexington, Kentucky 40508-4008
www.kentuckypress.com

The Library of Congress has cataloged the hardcover edition as follows:

Names: Goode, James F., 1944– author.
Title: The Turkish arms embargo : drugs, ethnic lobbies, and US domestic politics: understanding the crisis in US-Turkish Relations, 1974–1978 / James F. Goode.
Other titles: Drugs, ethnic lobbies, and US domestic politics : understanding the crisis in US-Turkish Relations, 1974–1978
Description: Lexington : The University Press of Kentucky, [2020] | Series: Studies in conflict, diplomacy, and peace | Includes bibliographical references and index.
Identifiers: LCCN 2020013486 | ISBN 9780813179681 (hardcover) | ISBN 9780813179704 (pdf) | ISBN 9780813179711 (epub)
Subjects: LCSH: United States—Military relations—Turkey. | Turkey—Military relations—United States. | Military assistance, American—Turkey. | United States—Foreign relations—Turkey. | Turkey—Foreign relations—United States. | Cyprus—History—Turkish Invasion, 1974. | Drug traffic—Turkey. | United States—Politics and government—1974–1977. | Greek Americans—Political activity—20th century.
Classification: LCC E183.8.T8 G66 2020 | DDC 973.923—dc23
LC record available at https://lccn.loc.gov/2020013486

ISBN 978-0-8131-9591-9 (pbk. : alk. paper)

This book is printed on acid-free paper meeting the requirements of the American National Standard for Permanence in Paper for Printed Library Materials.

Manufactured in the United States of America

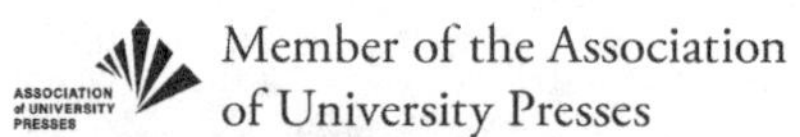

Member of the Association of University Presses

To Ginny, with whom I have shared fifty years of happy memories of the Middle East and much more.

Contents

Illustrations

Abbreviations

AHEPA	American Hellenic Educational Progressive Association
AHI	American Hellenic Institute
AIPAC	American Israel Public Affairs Committee
ARF	Armenian Revolutionary Federation
CIA	Central Intelligence Agency
DCA	Defense Cooperation Agreement
DEA	Drug Enforcement Administration
EC	European Community
EU	European Union
MFC	Minnesota Friends of Cyprus
NAMSA	NATO Maintenance and Supply Agency
NATO	North Atlantic Treaty Organization
NSC	National Security Council
PLO	Palestine Liberation Organization
SALT	Strategic Arms Limitation Talks
UHAC	United Hellenic American Congress

Preface

Scholars have written much about the Cyprus crisis of more than forty years ago and the resulting arms embargo that Congress imposed on Turkey. The crisis lasted more than four years (July 1974–October 1978) and strained US-Turkish relations to the breaking point. Most experts agree that it marked a turning point. The Turkish government would never again depend so completely on American support, and Ankara would pursue a more independent foreign policy in which Turkey's interests were paramount.

Many of those earlier scholarly works are now more than a generation old, and since their publication, new archival materials have become available at both the Gerald R. Ford and Jimmy Carter Presidential Libraries in Ann Arbor and Atlanta, respectively, as well as in the holdings of the National Archives. In addition, scholars have access to many new private collections of both individuals and organizations. Thus, it seems an appropriate time to revisit this crisis, incorporating new evidence and a broadened perspective.[1]

The current crisis in US-Turkish relations is arguably the worst in more than forty years. The two allies are espousing radically different policies regarding relations with the Syrian Kurdish militia and ties with Russia. Thus, it seems worthwhile to revisit the last occasion when bilateral relations deteriorated so markedly, as I believe that history can offer some guidance in addressing the current situation.

Although this study is rooted in US domestic politics, I have taken great care to elaborate on the contemporary situations in Turkey and Cyprus and, to a lesser extent, Greece, to make them understandable to readers.[2] Ultimately, developments there were as important to the continuation of the crisis as those on Capitol Hill, in the White House, or among the many ethnic lobbying groups across the country.

My research has led to a number of new and, I believe, important insights that are set out in detail in the following pages. One of the most significant led me to assign enhanced importance to the role of heroin in the deterioration of US-Turkish relations. The dispute over drugs preceded the Cyprus crisis and exacerbated tensions between the two allies, feeding a growing US exasperation with Ankara. Previous accounts viewed heroin as a subsidiary concern, whereas I have concluded that for many members of Congress and much of the American public, it was the central concern. As we find ourselves confronting rising levels of opioid abuse in the United States today, readers can readily appreciate how such an issue could undermine harmonious relations.

Earlier accounts centered almost exclusively on the Ford administration because the crisis originated at that time, as did the embargo itself. In addition, relevant archival records for the Ford years (1974–1977) became available to researchers much sooner than did those of his successor. And yet, the embargo and its legacy continued to trouble US-Turkish relations throughout the Carter administration. It also influenced support for that administration within the Greek American community. Therefore, approximately, one-third of this study focuses on the years 1977–1981, when the Democratic administration took up the challenge it inherited from its Republican predecessor.

When we compare the handling of this issue by the Ford and Carter administrations, some little-noticed facts come to the fore. Although the Carter administration enjoyed substantial majorities in both houses of Congress, while Ford had majorities in neither, Carter faced considerable congressional opposition from his own party on this issue. In fact, he never got a majority of Democrats to support lifting the embargo. Thus, to achieve victory, he relied heavily and repeatedly on the support of the Republican opposition. When questions arise today about the wisdom of depending on minority party support to pass key pieces of legislation, as they did during the speakerships of John Boehner and Paul Ryan, we would do well to examine the effective roles played by House minority leader John Rhodes and Senate minority leader Howard Baker in lifting the embargo, as well as the lobbying efforts of former president Ford and his secretary of state, Henry Kissinger. In that era of bipartisanship, cooperation could achieve significant benefits for the country. Republicans were active and effective participants under the Democratic administration.[3]

Whereas earlier accounts focused broadly on the struggle between President Ford and Congress, this study provides substantially more detail on the inner workings of the White House and Congress. For Congress, I was able to draw on a broad array of rarely used personal papers of key individuals, including Congressmen John Brademas, Donald Fraser, Lee Hamilton, Wayne Hays, Tip O'Neill, John Rhodes, Benjamin Rosenthal, and Paul Tsongas and Senators Robert Byrd, Thomas Eagleton, Robert Griffin, and Walter Mondale.[4] They stood at the political center of the crisis. Although diplomatic historians often overlook these records, they are valuable because they reveal the constant interaction and complex maneuvering involved in fashioning strategies related to foreign policy outside of either chamber. I came away much impressed with this behind-the-scenes activity that is so vital to the legislative process in a democracy. I should emphasize that although many of these actions took place out of the public view, they were nevertheless in the public interest; they provided opportunities for difficult political issues to be discussed, understood, and eventually resolved through compromise.

Much attention has centered on the large national lobbying groups such as the American Hellenic Educational Progressive Association, and they were, of course, important. But here, using the records of local lobbying groups, I have been able to show how rank-and-file members organized to encourage grassroots support for Cyprus and opprobrium for Turkey. With access to records from Minnesota and California (just two examples from a nationwide movement), I have pieced together the process by which these groups carried out their mission. This turned out to be one of the most important and interesting aspects of the entire project.

One less attractive element of the Save Cyprus movement was the slanderous characterization of Turks as barbarous and uncivilized, claims that were repeated vehemently in public and even more caustically in private correspondence. Admittedly, such criticisms came largely from traditional foes —Armenians, Greeks, and Greek Cypriots—but occasionally they became weapons in the hands of politicians associated with none of these communities. Turkophobia has a centuries-long history, but I was surprised at the extent of it and by the fact that so little of it had appeared in earlier studies. I emphasize this element not due to any particular preference for one party or another but because its pervasiveness helps us understand why this crisis repeatedly eluded so many well-meaning attempts at resolution. The presence of so much invective and misleading charges and countercharges makes it difficult to separate fantasy from fact. Some statements are blatantly inaccurate and easily dismissed, but plausible claims require more careful analysis. Researchers must pick their way through the evidence with the utmost care to arrive at sound conclusions.

In this volume I also reflect on the conflicted response of the American Jewish community and the government of Israel to the extended crisis. Many of the Greek American lobbying groups modeled themselves on the American Israel Public Affairs Committee, a very successful organization that pressed US politicians of both major parties to support Israel. But Israel itself had a number of concerns that led Tel Aviv to turn against the embargo, and many members of the American Jewish community turned with it.

Many issues analyzed in this study still concern us today, the most central being the proper role of Congress in making foreign policy. Then there are questions of civility in political campaigning, the propriety of ethnic Americans lobbying on behalf of their "beloved homelands," and the role of minority parties in policymaking. These are a few of the issues addressed in the following pages.

1

Background to Crisis

We usually associate arms embargoes with countries that are perceived as enemies of the United States, such as Iran, Cuba, and North Korea, or that stand accused of violating human rights, such as Argentina, the People's Republic of China, and the Republic of South Africa. Rarely has the United States imposed such sanctions on one of its closest allies, as it did with Turkey in 1974. An examination of how this happened and why it lasted so long provides the focus of this study.

Turkey is one of only a few friendly nations that the United States has subjected to such harsh public retribution. Certainly, no other member of NATO has come close to such a fate. Other allies have violated the spirit if not the substance of the Foreign Assistance Act of 1961, which proscribes the use of American weapons except for purposes of national self-defense. During the Six-Day War of June 1967, Israel struck Egypt and Syria without warning, using an arsenal of weapons largely supplied by the United States. Indonesia likewise waged a brutal war in East Timor, beginning in 1975 and lasting a quarter century, without any punishment from either Democratic or Republican administrations in the United States until almost the end of the conflict. Greece, under a military junta (1967–1974), transferred American-supplied weapons to Cyprus, also in violation of the arms agreement with the United States. None of these nations faced immediate American sanctions. In each case, the violations were well known. In the case of Israel, lawmakers often worried that if Ankara were to be punished, Tel Aviv might suffer a similar fate for the occupation of the West Bank, the Golan Heights, and the Gaza Strip beginning in 1967 or possibly for some future preemptive military action. (Their argument was that neither country should be sanctioned.) In the case of Indonesia, a few congressmen questioned the attack in East Timor at the outset, but their interest quickly waned, perhaps because the tiny island lay so far away, beyond the consciousness of most Americans. One-third of the East Timorese population would die before the United States cut off arms to Jakarta in the 1990s.

Why, then, did Turkey alone experience a complete arms embargo almost immediately after its invasion of Cyprus? The complex answer involves a unique set of factors both foreign and domestic. Taken together, they made the Turkish republic an inviting target for much of the American political establishment.

In Ankara, Prime Minister Bulent Ecevit (1925–2006) took two decisive steps in the summer of 1974: he reintroduced the cultivation of opium poppies, and he supported the invasion of Cyprus. Although the Turkish government offered justifications for each, many US lawmakers viewed these actions as malicious. They might have seemed unrelated, but taken together, these moves helped poison American public opinion toward Turkey. Turkish authorities had misjudged the political temper in the US Congress, perhaps focusing too much on the perceived weakness at the White House end of Pennsylvania Avenue. Summer 1974 turned out to be the worst possible time to carry out an attack on Cyprus. The movement on Capitol Hill to check executive overreach, especially regarding foreign policy, was gaining strength. Had the invasion of Cyprus taken place a short time earlier or later, the congressional response might have been much less robust.

To make matters worse, Turkey experienced a troubled period of weak national governments from the fall of 1974 until September 1980. Successive coalitions were unable to reach any compromise on sensitive issues such as the future of Cyprus. At critical times, Turkey had virtually no lobby in Washington; for example, its most effective spokesman, Ambassador Melih Esenbel, spent most of the period from November 1974 to April 1975 away from the embassy, serving as acting foreign minister in Ankara.

In the United States, the timing was perfect for congressional activists to challenge White House domination of foreign policy. After executive violations related to the war in Vietnam and the Watergate scandal, legalists on Capitol Hill could make a strong case against allowing Turkey to break the law with impunity.[1] There was already a great deal of animosity toward Turkey due to the poppy decision, which violated a 1971 agreement with Washington. Furthermore, Cyprus, with its majority-Greek population, had strong advocates in Congress and among the US public. All this transpired at a time when the US presidency had suffered a diminution of power and influence and Gerald R. Ford, the first unelected president, occupied the executive mansion. Each of these factors—and there were lesser ones as well—worked against the interests of Turkey, culminating in a foreign policy crisis that no one had foreseen and no one seemed able to resolve.

American ties to the Republic of Turkey and earlier to the Ottoman Empire have a long history. Yankee traders first appeared in Ottoman ports, especially Smyrna (Izmir), in the late eighteenth century. American Protestant missionaries followed in the early decades of the nineteenth century, establishing schools and colleges, as well as medical facilities, in many parts of the empire. Robert College, perched high above the Bosporus on the European side of Istanbul, represented one of the missionaries' most important educational achievements. From its founding in 1863, it graduated many Turkish students, who would become notable figures in their nation's history. These included Prime Minister Ecevit, who would take center stage in Turkish politics in the 1970s.

These missionaries often conveyed disparaging attitudes toward Turkish Muslims as well as Christian minorities, such as the Armenians, who resisted their attempts at proselytization. The American public generally held negative views of the Turks, especially in the later years of the nineteenth century, when reports of massacres of Armenians became more common. It was widely believed that the Turks were not to be trusted. When General Lew Wallace, author of *Ben Hur* and former American consul general to the Ottoman Porte, challenged that stereotype in front of American audiences, he was repeatedly shouted down amid a stream of abuse.

Events in World War I exacerbated such sentiments. Especially significant were the Ottomans' decision to join the Central powers in October 1914 and the Armenian genocide in eastern Anatolia beginning in 1915. In early postwar America, stories abounded of supposed Turkish massacres at Smyrna after the Greek army withdrew in September 1922. Such censorious claims were easily transferred from the dying empire to the early Turkish republic of Mustafa Kemal (Ataturk, 1881–1938). Competing with these views, however, was a grudging respect for the transformative and modernizing policies of the Turkish republic, established in 1923. American archaeologists working in Turkey between the world wars shared many positive observations about the new regime, as did US diplomats. They lauded the absence of corruption and the determination to create a modern, democratic, Western state.

The nationalist government, based in its new capital of Ankara, took control of most of the foreign educational institutions. This aspect of society was too important to be left in the hands of foreigners. Education provided an effective means of implementing a nationalist curriculum to produce proud, patriotic citizens of the new republic.

After the bitter experience of World War I and its aftermath, Turkey declared its neutrality in the Second World War. Only when the conflict was almost over, on February 23, 1945, did the Turkish government declare war on Germany. This allowed it to become a charter member of the United Nations.

In the early postwar years, as the United States and the Soviet Union drifted apart and the US government took steps to contain the Soviets, the Truman administration moved slowly to strengthen ties with Turkey, which had assumed new strategic importance. The Soviets pressed Turkey to relax control over Russian naval vessels moving through the straits that separated the Black Sea from the Aegean, and as Greece descended into civil war, the Truman administration decided to support Ankara's resistance to Soviet demands. In March 1947, after Britain had withdrawn from the area, Truman gave a landmark speech promising American economic and military assistance to both Greece and Turkey to counter communist aggression.[2]

Three years later, the Democrat Party swept to power in Ankara following free elections. It ruled for a decade. Moving away from many of the statist policies of Ataturk and the Republican People's Party, the Democrats opened the Turkish economy to foreign investment and international capital. Washington found these reforms appealing. Prime Minister Adnan Menderes also continued to seek membership for his country in the newly formed North Atlantic Treaty Organization. The Scandinavian members argued that Greece and Turkey were neither Atlantic nor democratic and opposed their admission. To neutralize this opposition, and to show Turkey's commitment to the Free World, Menderes sent a large contingent of 5,000 Turkish troops to aid the UN military effort in Korea. Turkey's considerable contributions led to battlefield losses of more than 700 soldiers killed. Although American and European diplomats duly noted this sacrifice, it was insufficient to achieve the desired objective. Ultimately, Turkey (and Greece) gained NATO membership in February 1952 due to changing strategic considerations in Washington, not to events in far-off Korea.[3]

In 1955, with US encouragement, Turkey, Iraq, Iran, Pakistan, and Great Britain formed the Baghdad Pact to maintain regional security. When Lebanon faced civil disturbances in 1958, American forces en route to Beirut used Turkish bases. By the end of the decade, the alliance with the United States had become the cornerstone of Turkey's foreign policy. Yet this extremely important relationship would soon be challenged in dramatic fashion.

The greatest threat to harmonious relations between Turkey and the United States during the Cold War began in the early 1960s, shortly after the establishment of an independent Cyprus in 1960. Almost 20 percent of the island's population was ethnically Turkish, a legacy of more than 300 years of Ottoman rule (1571–1878). Historically, this minority looked to the Republic of Turkey to defend its interests. Turkey, along with Greece and Great Britain, served as a guarantor of the 1960 Cypriot Constitution.[4]

Almost as soon as the Cypriot government in Nicosia commenced operation under its new president, Archbishop Makarios III, problems arose between the Greek majority and the Turkish minority, dispersed in informal enclaves around the island. Intercommunal tensions became so great that Ankara seriously considered military intervention in 1964. The infamous Johnson letter, familiar to all Turks, temporarily halted any such plans. The bluntness of LBJ's message stunned Turkish officials. He denied Turkey's right to use American weapons in such a venture and warned that NATO might not be obliged to defend Turkey if, in response to the Cyprus invasion, the Soviets moved against it. Prime Minister Ismet Inonu (1884–1973) sent a pained reply, challenging much of the American president's statement. He especially took issue with Johnson's interpretation of the NATO pact, which he declared showed a "wide divergence of views as to the nature and basic principles of the North Atlantic Alliance."[5]

Deeply enmeshed in the Vietnam War, President Johnson had no intention of being distracted by another crisis, this one in the Mediterranean. In fact, a transcript of Johnson's conversation with Secretary of State Dean Rusk a few days later indicated just how reluctant the president was to get involved in the crisis. His letter had invited Prime Minister Inonu to Washington for further discussions. Johnson now regretted that offer, saying plainly to Rusk, "Now what the hell is Lyndon Johnson doing inviting this big mess right in his lap? . . . I have no solution. I can't propose anything. He'll come over here looking for heaven and he'll find hell."[6]

Although most Turks were angered by the lack of American support in June 1964, recent evidence suggests that Inonu had been hoping for just such an American ultimatum to help him resist those elements of the Turkish military that favored an invasion. Apparently, he believed his own military was untrained and unprepared for a landing on the island, and Soviet leaders had already announced their support for Makarios against any foreign incursion. By sharing his plans with Washington and eliciting a sharp US response, Inonu could blame his ally for forcing the cancellation of the attack. If this was his scheme, he succeeded too well. The Johnson letter led many Turks to question their alliance with the Americans.[7]

The issue of Cyprus did not disappear, but for a short time, the situation on the island quieted down. During the years 1964–1967, a succession of senior American diplomats—George Ball, Dean Acheson, and Cyrus Vance—tried to broker an agreement. Ball warned Makarios that if he did not settle the disturbances, Turkey would invade one day, and no one would come to his rescue. Acheson seemed to accept the idea of partition or "double enosis." Secret negotiations between Greece and Turkey continued, but rising tensions on the island put any immediate compromise out of reach.[8]

As a young American Peace Corps volunteer serving in Iran, I visited Cyprus during this period of relative calm. I can testify to the ongoing tensions. Along with two fellow volunteers, I visited several countries in the eastern Mediterranean region during my annual leave. We did not travel to nearby Turkey, but the reason for this omission did not become clear to me until many years later. My friend who organized our itinerary had grown up in a Greek American home, where he commonly heard lurid tales about the "Terrible Turk." Given his background, he was unlikely to include a stopover in Istanbul or on any of the Turkish islands in the Aegean.

Our service in the Peace Corps did not guarantee that we were well informed about the political and social conditions in the countries on our itinerary. Although I had a vague sense of what we might encounter in Israel only two years after the Six-Day War and the occupation of the West Bank, Gaza, and the Golan Heights, nothing prepared me for the realities of Cyprus. Fresh from a few carefree days on the golden beaches of several Greek islands, we arrived in Nicosia expecting more of the same.[9] We headed to Paphos, an ancient city at the western end of the island, near the spot where, according to Greek mythology, Aphrodite sprang fully formed from the sea foam. On the way, we passed through the British Sovereign Base of Akrotiri, allotted to London in the negotiations that created the independent Republic of Cyprus in 1960. What a contrast to the surrounding parched, late-summer landscape! We saw long stretches of green grass and carefully manicured playing fields, flower beds, and trees, with neat bungalows stretching along the roadside. It seemed so unreal, as if a piece of England had dropped from the sky.

While traveling on a Greek Cypriot bus, I noticed that whenever we passed through a Turkish Cypriot enclave, only sullen faces stared up at us. At one point, I noticed (with some amazement) the long barrel of a dug-in, camouflaged artillery piece pointing in our direction from a nearby hillside. No sooner had we arrived at our destination and checked into the hotel than several plainclothes detectives, Greek Cypriots, visited us. They checked our passports and asked why we had come to Paphos, which was not a common tourist destination. A short time later, we strolled into the center of the city and recognized a number of blue UN sentry boxes strung out along an ancient wall. The wall, we were told, separated the Turkish Cypriot enclave from the surrounding Greek Cypriot sector of the city. The UN contingent included a small marching band that played at sunset, but it did little to lift the tension we felt. We departed the island several days later and, with a sense of relief, headed back to Tehran.

Eastern Mediterranean region

Mediterranean
Sea
Kyrenia
Turkish Republic of
Northern Cyprus
NICOSIA
Famagusta
Republic of Cyprus
Dhekelia
(U.K. Base)
Paphos
Akrotiri
(U.K. Base)
Mediterranean
Sea
0
25
miles

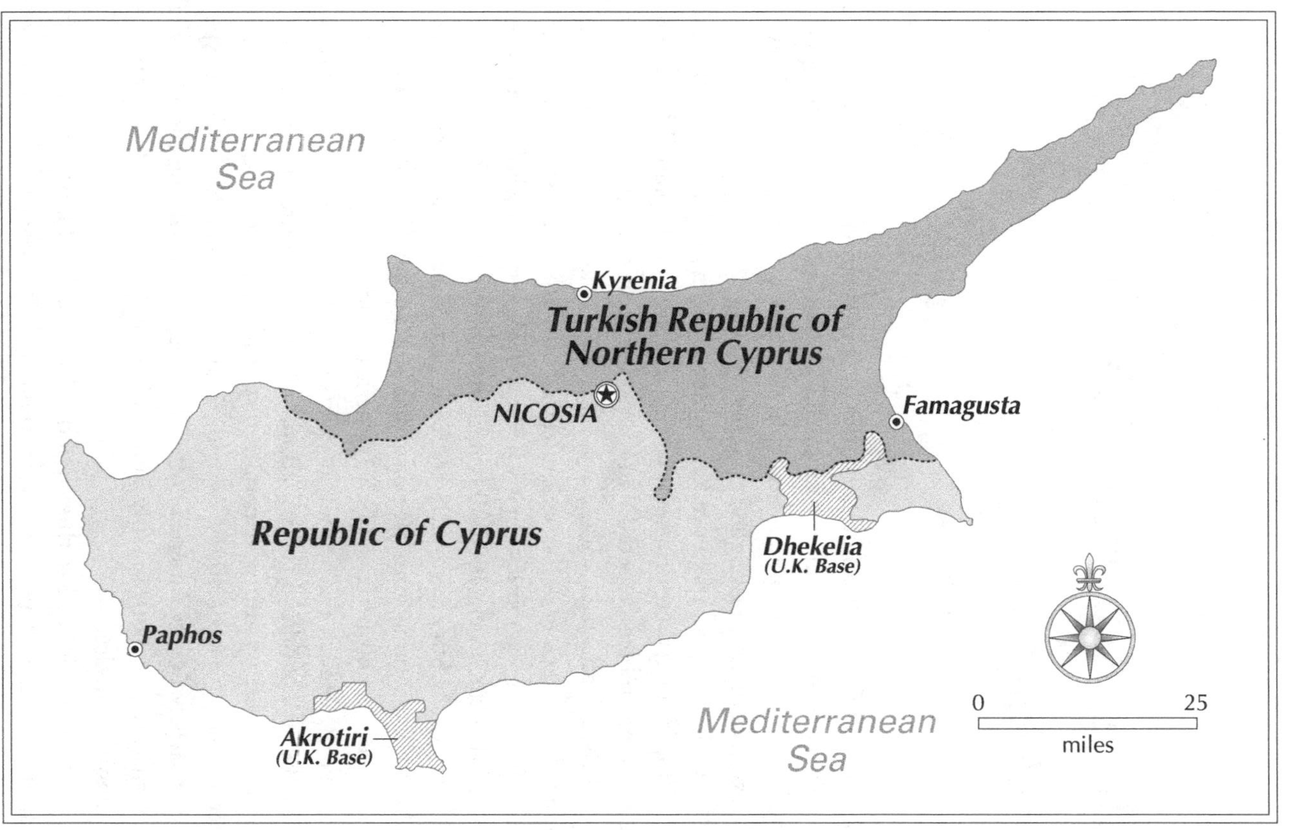

Cyprus, 1983

2

Killing America's Children

The Heroin Crisis

Conditions on Cyprus did not cause the next crisis in US-Turkey relations. Rather, it was American concern about the renewed cultivation of the opium poppy that set the two nations on a collision course. For many members of Congress, this threat outweighed all others.

The United States experienced an epidemic of illegal drug use in the late 1960s. Chief among these drugs was heroin, a derivative of opium. This proved to be a serious problem, especially in the poorer areas of major urban centers. One of the worst affected locations was Harlem in New York City, dubbed the "drug-trafficking center of the nation." Drug sales there, it was reported, constituted the major economic activity. In New York City as a whole, it has been estimated that there were 160,000 heroin users in the early 1970s.

It was widely but erroneously assumed that most of the heroin entering the United States came from the poppy fields of Turkey. Repeatedly, authorities claimed that 80 percent of the American supply originated from that source via the French connection in Marseilles, a major processing center. Despite the lack of official confirmation, this figure appeared prominently in the speeches and warnings of community leaders and politicians. No one seemed to question its accuracy. According to a US diplomat with long experience in Turkey, "every American official . . . became a walking encyclopedia on the subject and both socially and professionally their Turkish contacts heard about little else."[1]

Hollywood bookended this period with two blockbuster films about drugs, displaying Turkey in the worst possible light. *The French Connection* (1971), winner of the best-picture Oscar, showcased two New York City detectives determined to intercept a large shipment of heroin from Marseilles before it reached the streets. Filmgoers likely suspected that most of the raw material came from Turkey. *Midnight Express* (1978) detailed the harrowing experience of American Billy Hayes, who was imprisoned in Turkey under horrendous conditions for attempting to smuggle hashish out of the country. During his trial, he makes an impassioned attack on the Turkish people in general. In his review of the film in October 1978, well-known critic Roger Ebert argued that it was hard to feel much pity for Hayes, who took his chances and lost. But then Ebert went on to say, "It is possible, however, to discover the irony in the fact that Turkey, *whose economy is richened by an opium poppy crop that supplies much of the world's heroin,* should have such draconian drug laws at home."[2] All this illustrates the difficulty of abandoning long-held (mis)understandings.

The Nixon administration wanted a victory in the war on drugs, and the president's Ad Hoc Committee on Narcotics focused its attention on Turkey because, of all the opium producers in the world, including Mexico, the Golden Crescent (Afghanistan, Pakistan, and Iran), and the Golden Triangle (Burma, Laos, and Thailand), it seemed the most susceptible to US pressure. As a member of NATO, Turkey received large amounts of American military equipment and economic aid, and there was much talk in Washington in 1969–1971 of using a carrot-and-stick approach to obtain the desired result: the banning of poppy cultivation. The area in Turkey where the poppies grew was relatively compact and easily accessible, unlike the mountainous and isolated areas of Afghanistan, Pakistan, Southeast Asia, and even neighboring Mexico. In addition, the government in Ankara had better control over its countryside than did any of the other producing nations' governments. Thus, the campaign continued despite the fact that, at the time, there was no reliable way of identifying the foreign source of American heroin. Nevertheless, committee members claimed publicly that Turkey supplied most of the heroin in the United States, and the media and politicians, including congressmen representing poor urban districts, repeated this statement. The crusade continued through 1970. Washington constantly urged US Ambassador William J. Handley (1969–1973) in Ankara to take a more forceful approach with the civilian government, which continued to resist American efforts to end opium production.[3]

After the Turkish military took control in March 1971 in the so-called coup by memorandum, Washington found it easier to work out an agreement. The Nixon administration, which would soon establish the Drug Enforcement Administration (DEA), negotiated with the Turkish generals and worked out a complete ban on cultivation of the opium poppy in return for a $35 million subsidy for Turkish farmers. Urban leaders in the United States applauded. It would be easier, they thought, to restrict foreign supply than to control domestic demand.

The ban lasted three years, or until the Turkish military withdrew from power and called for democratic elections. The new civilian government became subject to increasing pressure, especially from rural areas, to allow poppy cultivation again, which had a long history in Turkey. Peasant farmers found many culinary uses for the plant; especially prized was oil from the seeds, which was used for cooking. They fed their cattle the harvested stalks and other leftovers, making for very contented cows. Opponents of the ban argued that no foreign country should tell Turkish farmers what they could grow. The issue assumed nationalistic overtones.[4]

By the spring of 1974, rumors abounded that the government of Prime Minister Bulent Ecevit was preparing to rescind the ban, raising concerns in both houses of Congress. Representatives from major cities welcomed the decline in the availability of heroin in their districts since 1971 and warned of dire consequences for America's urban youth should production be resumed.[5] Among these congressmen were Lester Wolff, representing New York's Sixth Congressional District and chair of the Subcommittee on International Narcotics Control of the House Foreign Affairs Committee, and Charles Rangel, also of New York City, who represented Harlem and served as chair of the Congressional Black Caucus (1974–1976). Rangel and Wolff, both Democrats, undertook a junket to Turkey in March 1974 to familiarize themselves with the local situation and to express their concerns directly to the Turkish government.

On their return, Rangel spoke out about the likelihood of this issue leading to a confrontation between Turkey and the United States, and he criticized the State Department for ignoring rumors rather than seeking to negotiate a better arrangement that would satisfy Turkish demands. Rangel explained that the Turks did not consider the poppy a poison, and the idea of its misuse was foreign to them. For centuries, farmers had grown the poppy as a staple. Thus, if the ban continued, the State Department would have to devise a program to improve the quality of life for Turkish poppy growers. The two congressmen declared their intention to meet with President Nixon and Secretary of State Henry Kissinger to discuss this very serious issue.[6]

The thirteen members of the Congressional Black Caucus, all of whom represented poor, urban districts, supported their colleagues' complaints, as did other big-city congressmen such as Joseph Addabbo (D-NY) of Queens, Edward Roybal (D-CA) of Los Angeles, and Morgan F. Murphy of Chicago (D-IL). More surprising, perhaps, was the attitude of Otto Passman of Louisiana, the powerful Democratic chair of the House Foreign Aid Appropriations Subcommittee. He recommended taking a hard line with Ankara, reminding the Turks that they owed their independence to US assistance following World War II and threatening to cut off military aid "if Turkey violated its understanding with the United States over poppies."[7]

In the Senate, too, there were angry bipartisan protests against a possible end to the opium poppy ban. Senators Walter Mondale (D-MN) and William Buckley (R-NY) introduced a concurrent resolution, calling on the administration to enter into immediate negotiations with the Turkish government. If they failed to reach an agreement, the president should terminate all economic assistance to Turkey. At a press conference called by concerned congressmen and senators, Wolff charged that Turkish officials had ties to organized crime, and Rangel noted that their own House resolution to cut off aid to Turkey already had thirty-two cosponsors.[8]

The US embassy in Ankara quickly recognized the seriousness of the issue. Writing to provide background information for the secretary of state's upcoming meeting with Turkish foreign minister Turan Gunes, Ambassador William Macomber (1973–1977) counseled, "While we have a range of US-Turkish bilateral problems to deal with here, only one, the Turkish threat to rescind the ban on the growing of opium poppies, is of sufficient potential consequence to require your personal attention in any depth at this time."[9] Three days later, at their meeting in New York City, Kissinger raised the thorny issue, indicating its importance "in terms of American public opinion." Gunes replied that he was "fully aware of the implications of the opium problem" and firmly suggested that they must find a solution that satisfied both American and Turkish public opinion. As he so often did, Kissinger ended the discussion on a jocular note, observing that he had learned more about opium in recent weeks than he really wanted to know. "I may go into the business myself," he remarked lightheartedly to the Turkish diplomat. Kissinger proved adept at using humor to relieve tension and increase the sense of collaboration with his opposite number.[10]

As these talks suggested, there was a good deal of pushback from Turkish officials. Gunes himself was noncommittal in his meeting with Kissinger. "I cannot say categorically," he stated, "that we are not going to grow opium poppies." Following this diplomatic double negative, Gunes assured the Americans that his government would exercise "the fullest control possible."[11]

Barely three weeks later, Prime Minister Ecevit took a less evasive position, announcing to the Turkish press that "poppy cultivation is a domestic affair of Turkey. Turkey itself decides what to cultivate and what not to cultivate on its territory." He made much of the fact that his was a democratically elected government and responsible to the people, unlike the military government that had signed the 1971 ban.[12]

The issue captured the attention of the American press, and major newspapers featured articles and editorials on the subject. A column in the *New York Post* advocated "bombing of the poppy fields by the United States Air Force." On a more realistic note, a May 4 *New York Times* editorial called for a de-escalation of the confrontation between the United States and Turkey, its NATO ally, over this sensitive issue. The editorial suggested a revision of the poppy ban, with the United States providing small-scale industrial projects for families that had abandoned their poppy crops.[13]

It was too late, however, to apply such measures in the hope of resolving the crisis. On July 1 Prime Minister Ecevit publicly announced the end of the poppy ban. Turkish nationalism had won out over American threats.

Staff at the US embassy thought Ecevit had been moving toward the US position, and Ambassador Macomber expressed his "bitter disappointment." In a midnight meeting with the prime minister, Macomber used some very undiplomatic language, barely managing to control his anger. He complained that American diplomats had learned of this key development through a public broadcast. He asked Ecevit to reconsider this decision, which would do enormous damage to the US-Turkish security relationship. This decision, he warned, would bring relations to their lowest point since World War II and increase the odds that "US military assistance to Turkey was finished." Congress, rather than the executive branch, would take action now. In parting, Macomber revealed that his government was considering recalling him to Washington for consultation to show its concern.[14]

Confronted by the ambassador's uncharacteristically strong language, Ecevit did not flinch. He stated boldly that "reconsideration was out of the question. He thought US-Turkish relations were deeper than the ambassador suggested. Although the decision was final, his government would be prepared to discuss effective methods of controlling the crop with the United States." Turkish civilian leaders believed that a basic principle of Turkish independence was at stake, and they would take action regardless of the impact on their relations with the United States.[15]

In Washington, the legislative campaign to punish Ankara made progress, much to the dismay of the National Security Council (NSC) staff. In the Senate, Mondale hoped to bring to the floor his amendment cutting off aid to Turkey; in the House, hearings on the Wolff resolution, which also called for President Nixon to suspend aid to Turkey, were scheduled before the Committee on Foreign Affairs. The latter took place on July 16, and many of those testifying used the occasion not only to challenge the recent Turkish decision but also to raise broader questions about Turkey and the US-Turkish relationship. The sponsor of the resolution, Congressman Wolff, spoke first. He claimed that there would be "100 to 200 tons of excess production that will find its way into the veins of the kids of this Nation." He went on to say, "Gentlemen, which is more important, our commitment to Turkey or your commitment to your constituents?"[16]

When asked why the United States had approved an increase in India's opium production, committee member Robert Steele (R-CT) explained that India could control its production because of the British origin of its bureaucracy, which made it more efficient and effective than the Turkish bureaucracy, which was a legacy of the Ottoman Empire. He observed that Indian officials were eager to track down even the smallest amount of leakage into the illicit market, whereas Turkish officials just did not seem to care. No one questioned his superficial and misleading analysis, which fit prevailing stereotypes.[17]

Representative Rangel used the occasion to raise doubts about the entire US-Turkish relationship. He believed that the security benefit the United States derived from its bases in Turkey had been exaggerated. "We are doing them a favor by being there," he argued. "The strategic value of Turkey to the United States is a myth," especially when Turkey reciprocates by bringing "human suffering and misery upon the American people." Rangel and his colleagues accused the Nixon administration of failing to respond adequately to this threat from Turkey. The New York City congressman then reflected on a recent meeting with Brent Scowcroft, Kissinger's assistant at the NSC. Scowcroft, he remarked, appeared to be completely ignorant of the fact that Ankara was considering lifting the opium ban, even though "it was on the front page of all of our major newspapers." The hearings allowed for all kinds of criticism, some of it well reasoned, but much of it misguided.[18]

In light of these developments, the NSC staff urged Kissinger to act immediately to forestall congressional action. Such punitive steps, they believed, would seriously weaken the ability to work with Turkey to prevent heroin smuggling into the United States. Senator Mondale agreed to revise his amendment to the DEA budget bill, calling not for an immediate cutoff of aid to Turkey but rather the suspension of aid after January 1975 unless the president could certify that the Turks had taken effective safeguard measures. This version of the amendment passed the Senate by a lopsided vote of 81 to 8.[19]

Thus, only days before the Cyprus crisis, key members of Congress were considering punishing the Turks for their unhelpful behavior. The groundwork had already been laid for a strong response. Ecevit's decision to resume poppy cultivation had antagonized many in Congress, and it seemed likely that his critics would judge Ankara's future actions with this most recent unpleasant experience clearly in mind.

Although historians have generally considered the opium issue a minor one in US-Turkey relations in the 1970s, one can reasonably argue that without it, the Turkish arms embargo would not have been imposed. A considerable number of legislators were willing to punish Turkey solely for its reckless and defiant policy on cultivation of the opium poppy. It required the twin issues of drugs and the illegal use of US weapons in Cyprus to persuade a greater number to vote for an embargo. Had members of Congress been faced with only a single challenge from Ankara, they might have been less likely to oppose the White House.[20]

3

Making Turkey Pay

Concurrently with the opium crisis came the Cyprus imbroglio. On the morning of Monday, July 15, 1974, Cypriot National Guardsmen, led by their Greek officers, attacked the presidential residence in Nicosia. The objective was to kill the president, Archbishop Makarios III, and establish a new government under Nikos Sampson, a champion of enosis, or union with Greece; Sampson was also a known terrorist who had personally killed Turkish Cypriots. Makarios narrowly escaped and eventually made his way to London. The Sampson government lasted only eight days before local and international criticism—and a Turkish invasion—forced him from office. Glafkos Clerides, a more moderate Greek Cypriot and the speaker of the House of Representatives, became acting head of state. Sampson's fall triggered a backlash against the military junta in Athens, which had instigated the coup (code-named Aphrodite) in the mistaken belief that a successful takeover of Cyprus would restore its tarnished image at home. Instead, the Nicosia debacle led to collapse of the Regime of the Colonels and restoration of popular rule after seven years of a harsh right-wing dictatorship in the birthplace of democracy. Exiled conservative political leader Constantine Karamanlis (1907–1998) was invited home from exile in Paris to form a government, pending parliamentary elections.

International Responses

Although the coup proved a dismal failure, it set in motion larger events that could not easily be reversed. The Turkish mainland lay only 65 kilometers from the northern shores of Cyprus, whereas Greece was more than 800 kilometers away. The Turkish government kept a careful eye on developments on the nearby island, where approximately 20 percent of the population (180,000) was Turkish. This Turkish minority had established enclaves across the island, where residents lived largely walled off from their Greek Cypriot neighbors.

In cities such as Paphos in the southwestern part of the island, the Turkish community lived behind a wall topped by blue UN watchtowers. The United Nations Peacekeeping Force in Cyprus had been established in 1964 during a time of increasing tensions between the Greek and Turkish communities. Turkish Cypriots taxed themselves and maintained their own education system. Young Turkish and Greek Cypriots grew up almost completely separated from each other. Groups of Turkish men and boys ventured into the Greek part of the city only on Fridays to purchase necessities not available on their side, but they did not linger there. The Makarios government in Nicosia had shown little interest in reversing this informal separation between the two communities. In fact, it had contributed to the situation by steadily whittling away at the minority guarantees provided in the 1960 constitution.[1]

Along with Greece and the United Kingdom, Turkey was a guarantor of the 1960 constitution, which had established an independent Cyprus and provided many safeguards for the rights of the Turkish minority. Thus, when the coup took place and Sampson became head of the post-Makarios government, Turkey's prime minister, Bulent Ecevit, believed he must act. Furthermore, Ankara determined that as a guarantor power, it had a right to take action to protect the Turkish Cypriot minority.

Flare-ups of intercommunal violence had taken place repeatedly since 1960, most notably in 1964 and again in 1967. The Turkish government came close to launching an invasion in each of those years, but the Americans intervened, including the infamous Johnson letter of 1964. The soldiers remained in their barracks, but the Turks were bitter about the lack of support from Washington.

Ten years later, in the summer of 1974, the Nixon administration was in disarray due to the Watergate scandal, and the president was edging toward resignation. Ankara knew that this time, there would be no Nixon letter. This seemed to be the perfect moment to secure the future of the Turkish Cypriot minority. Both Athens and Washington were in a confused and weakened state, and Greek Cypriot forces could hardly resist a Turkish onslaught.

Hurried talks took place in London from July 16 to 20, but it was clear that Prime Minister Ecevit was in no mood for compromise. On July 20, after Turkish demands had not been met, the Turkish army invaded Cyprus. Having received the coded message "*Ayse tatile cikti*" (Aisha went on holiday), the Turks seized territory around the port city of Kyrenia, a center for tourism on the northern coast of the island and home to a large number of Turkish Cypriots.[2] The army seized the city and its hinterland and a narrow corridor to the inland capital, Nicosia, amounting to less than 5 percent of the island. On July 22 a cease-fire negotiated by Britain and the United States took effect, and talks were scheduled to resume two days later in Geneva under British sponsorship. Both the Greek junta and the Sampson government collapsed on July 23.

The explosion of violence on Cyprus surprised the Americans, whose eyes had been fixed on a brooding President Nixon, who had withdrawn to his retreat in San Clemente, California. During a meeting of the Washington Special Action Group on July 17, chaired by the secretary of state, officials had concluded that the Turks were unlikely to invade. Kissinger could not understand why the Turks were insisting on returning Makarios to power, for he had been their archenemy. In any case, the United States had to make its position known to Turkey as quickly as possible: Washington would support an acting government under Glafkos Clerides for six months, followed by elections. Undersecretary of State Joseph Sisco, one of Kissinger's top aides, made a hurried call to the Turkish ambassador to present the American thinking, and then he left for London to explain to Makarios and Ecevit in person the US proposal.[3]

From the British capital, Sisco proceeded to Athens and Ankara. In the Greek capital, the collapsing junta agreed to a number of compromises to stabilize the situation on Cyprus, including the acceptance of a single Turkish enclave on the island. But these concessions came too late. The proponents of enosis had made a colossal blunder, opening the door for a Turkish invasion in the name of restoring the 1960 constitution. In Ankara, Sisco was waiting outside the meeting room of Turkey's National Security Council on July 20, while inside, Ecevit was making the decision to invade.[4]

Subsequent talks in Geneva made little progress. Neither the Greeks nor the Turks would shift their position, and British Foreign Secretary James Callaghan became increasingly frustrated. Kissinger rated Callaghan's chances of success as very slim. Perhaps Kissinger hoped the feuding parties would eventually turn to him to work out a settlement. Meanwhile, the meetings in Geneva dragged on into August.[5]

The embassy in Ankara reported general agreement between the military and the Ecevit government on the policy toward Cyprus. Furthermore, most

Turks believed they should gain all they could from the current situation. They would not return to the status quo ante. According to one observer, "there was no other issue, domestic or foreign, on which there was such unanimity in Turkey." Ecevit was a tough negotiator, as he had proved earlier during the opium crisis. As it turned out, he was not the moderate that his former Harvard University professor, Henry Kissinger, might have expected. The Turks made it clear that they wanted two separate communities on Cyprus, each with full autonomy. There could be a central government in Nicosia, but with limited powers. Callaghan wanted negotiations to take place between Glafkos Clerides and Rauf Denktash, the Turkish Cypriot leader, but the government of Turkey thought that would be a waste of time. Ecevit wanted the guarantor powers—Greece, Turkey, and the United Kingdom—to make the important decisions at Geneva, with the details to be worked out later. Ambassador Macomber was not hopeful.[6]

Turkey had been building its force on Cyprus since the first invasion, and by August 14, it numbered 40,000. On that day, having exhausted his patience in Geneva, Ecevit gave the order to recommence Operation Attila to gain by force what had eluded Turkey in the negotiations. Facing little opposition, the superior Turkish forces seized almost 40 percent of the island, including the important city of Famagusta in the east and the international airport at Nicosia. The Turks took more than they had planned to retain as part of the Turkish Cypriot sector, perhaps taking a page from the Israelis after the 1967 Six-Day War—that is, use land as leverage to achieve acceptance of a new status quo. (Whatever their original intentions, the boundaries have remained fixed since that time.)

Many more thousands of Greek Cypriots became refugees. Large numbers of Turkish Cypriots, who lived on the wrong side of the front lines were uprooted as well. Some of the latter ended up seeking shelter on the British air bases at Akrotiri and Dhekelia. This was a sad fate for an island population that had enjoyed a higher standard of living than either the Greeks or the Turks prior to the coup d'etat and the Turkish invasion.[7]

The Karamanlis government immediately withdrew Greece from the military structure of NATO, much as Charles de Gaulle had done with France in 1966. The prime minister was protesting an apparent lack of support by the members of the military alliance, including the United States. He had expected them to take firmer action against Turkey for its invasion of Cyprus.

The Turkish government seemed to agree with Karamanlis that the United States supported its attempt to resolve the Cyprus problem. Even the Turkish media praised the United States for following "the wisest policy among the Western powers despite the opium issue." The United States took Turkey's side, it was said, because it recognized Turkey's greater importance relative to Greece. One major paper, *Cumhuriyet,* announced that the United States understood the Turkish point of view.[8]

In private, Turkish leaders admitted that the United States had tried to be evenhanded, in contrast to the anti-Turkish sentiments expressed by most Western governments. This sensitivity was appreciated in Ankara, and the newly installed Ford administration might have been able to negotiate with the Ecevit government and actually be listened to.[9] Unfortunately, American policymakers did not take advantage of this opportunity in the interim between the initial invasion on July 20 and the dramatic expansion twenty-five days later.

Kissinger's response puzzled observers at the time and has confounded scholars ever since. It seems that he misjudged the Turkish prime minister, who proved to be more of a risk taker than any of his recent predecessors. How else can we account for the secretary of state's apparent lack of preparedness to engage the looming crisis with his arsenal of diplomatic skills? At other points in his tenure, Kissinger might have taken control and set out in person for the eastern Mediterranean, rather than sending a deputy. His sudden appearance in Athens or Ankara would have conveyed a sense of urgency to the respective parties. He was, of course, facing a major crisis at home as the Nixon presidency unraveled. With the US government in disarray—Nixon was holed up in California when the first invasion took place, and Gerald Ford had been in the White House less than a week when stage two of Attila was launched—perhaps he felt that he could not leave Washington.

Historians reflecting on these developments have concluded that the United States—that is, Henry Kissinger—could have done more to forestall the Turkish attack. Perhaps he underestimated the influence Washington could exert on Ankara or feared that the Turks would leave NATO altogether if Washington pressed too hard. Although the secretary of state might have leaned on Athens to be more flexible or could have joined the British at Geneva, the Americans were unwilling to tip too much in either direction, lest they destroy their bona fides if they were asked to mediate the dispute.

One cannot dismiss the possibility that Kissinger welcomed Turkey's cutting of the Gordian knot, ending once and for all the troubled island's periodic eruptions. After all, Dean Acheson, for whom Kissinger had the greatest respect, had concluded in 1964, after his failed mission to resolve an earlier crisis, that partition of the island might be the only long-term solution. He proposed the Acheson plan, of which his biographer Robert Beisner writes, "Acheson's visibly pro-Turkish recommendations shaped Washington's approach to Cyprus for a generation."[10]

Greek Americans to Arms

Although Turkey had strength of arms in the Aegean and eastern Mediterranean region, the Greeks and Greek Cypriots quickly attracted international sympathy and support. Nowhere was this more evident than in the United States, for Americans had a long history of championing the Greek cause. This began in the early nineteenth century, when the Greeks struggled for independence from the Ottoman Empire. An American journalist at the time referred to American support as "Greek fever." Rooted in the mistaken belief that modern Greeks were the direct descendants of ancient Greeks and that success against the Turks would restore the glory of Athens and the Greek city-states, many Americans supported the Greek war of independence in the 1820s. At that time, the American press "focused exclusively on Turkish abuses," feeding sympathy for the Greek side while ignoring the massacre of Muslim civilians during the war.[11]

More recently, American activists had opposed the rule of the military junta (1967–1974) in Greece. Several members of Congress, including Representatives Donald Fraser (D-MN), Ogden Reid (R-NY), and Donald Edwards (D-CA) and Senator Vance Hartke (D-IN), served on the board of the US Committee for Democracy in Greece. They worked to encourage Congress to cut off military assistance to the Regime of the Colonels in Athens. This passion for Greece would be rekindled in the Cyprus crisis of 1974.[12]

Greek American associations had been active from the first days of the Cyprus crisis in mid-July. They represented an influential community of an estimated 2 million immigrants and their descendants, most of whom had come to the United States from rural areas of the Ottoman Empire and the Peloponnesus in the late nineteenth and early twentieth centuries. Predominantly single men arrived at first; they became laborers on the railroads or factory workers on the East Coast, especially in Boston, New York, and Baltimore, and in Detroit and Chicago in the Midwest. Soon they established

Poster showing a Turkish soldier on Cyprus, with Ecevit to the left (English comments by an unknown source). (Courtesy Paul Tsongas Papers, Center for Lowell History, University of Massachusetts, Lowell)

themselves in small businesses, grocery stores, bakeries, and so forth. A second wave of immigrants came directly from Greece after World War II to escape the devastation and civil war. Members of the Greek American community became quite prosperous and expressed a considerable interest in politics. In the late 1960s they participated in the revival of ethnicity common to other immigrant groups in the United States, encouraging strong attachment to Greek traditions.

Influential associations, such as the American Hellenic Educational Progressive Association (AHEPA), responded even more vociferously once Turkish forces crossed the cease-fire lines on August 14. Unlike the initial invasion, it was difficult to justify the expansion of Operation Attila, and this new offensive was being carried out with US-supplied weapons. One flyer captured the mood at the time. It paired a description of Attila the Hun with a description of this new "Scourge of God"—the Turkish army—which was allegedly committing so many crimes on Cyprus that "the conscience of all civilized men shudders." How appropriate, wrote the author, that the campaign was named after the king of the Huns. The Turks were likely unaware that, to many Americans, the name "Attila" conjured ancient images of death and destruction. From the American perspective, the Turks could not have chosen a more inappropriate name for their offensive, and by doing so, they provided a propaganda advantage to their enemies.[13]

The Turks' opponents frequently presented them as the "Other" and cherry-picked their way through history to make facts conform to strongly held beliefs. In countless letters to government officials, they expressed the depths of their bitterness. In one example, Dr. Daniel Kavadas, a dentist who headed the Columbia, South Carolina, chapter of AHEPA, wrote to Congressman Floyd Spence (R-SC): "What the government of Turkey is striving to achieve today in Cyprus is exactly what Hitler's Third Reich strove to achieve—and achieved—in the annexation of the whole of Czechoslovakia some thirty-five years ago by using the minority problem as an excuse." Comparisons with the Nazis appeared repeatedly in flyers and various other publications.[14]

These characterizations might have seemed tame compared with the telegram from one activist referring to "the Turkish insane animals." In a letter to President Ford, another concerned American, Basil Rodes, noted that history was replete with examples of "the death and destruction visited upon peoples in Asia Minor, Europe, and North Africa by the Turks. The Turks are repeating the same practice of death and destruction in Cyprus today. The Turks had contributed nothing to the human race and its civilization, but they have spread death and destruction throughout the ages." Another wrote to Secretary Kissinger, emphasizing a common theme: "The major portion of Turkey today is a barren wasteland . . . buildings and monuments created by their 'restless minorities' now lie in ruins, further desiccated by the indolent and feckless peasants [Turks] who carry off pieces of building stone as needed, to reinforce their own dilapidated, shanty-like dwellings."[15]

Occasionally, such vitriol made its way into the publications of the major Greek American organizations. An article in the *Ahepan* stated, "From the very first day that the battle started, the Turks displayed that they are still the same savage people." A recounting of Greek-Turkish relations recalled all the harm done to the Greeks in World War I, including the massacres of Greeks and Armenians and the forced resettlement of Greeks from Asia

Minor to Greece. The article was silent on the Greek invasion of Anatolia after the war (1919–1922) and on the repatriation of a smaller Turkish population from Greece to the Republic of Turkey.[16]

One of the most troubling developments was repeated charges of atrocities on both sides. These were more numerous coming from Greek Americans, who had more outlets to present their arguments to the American public. There were tales of looting, rape, and intentional destruction of churches in the area under Turkish army control. The Cypriot embassy in Washington circulated an information sheet in mid-November 1974, claiming to provide "factual evidence" that the Turks were guilty of the greatest crime of all, "GENOCIDE," against the Greek population, murdering in cold blood hundreds of innocent women and children and crippled and old men. They had allowed "repeated and continual rapes of women from the age of twelve onwards on an organized basis by the officers and men of the Turkish army, reminiscent of Nazi concentration camps." Even Archbishop Iakovos added to the charges. In a letter to Congressman John Brademas (D-IN), the archbishop's office claimed that, among other crimes, "priests have been beaten to death, one priest attempting to rescue his daughter from being raped was savagely beheaded."[17]

Yet there was little incontrovertible evidence to support these lurid tales. When an AHEPA delegation to Cyprus met with Dr. Vasos Vasilopoulos of the Ministry of Health, he disputed reports that Cypriot women's breasts had been cut off or that boys had been emasculated. There were enough real problems, he explained, resulting from the destructiveness of modern warfare. Still, the exaggerated accounts did not subside.[18]

The government of Turkey also publicized questionable claims of atrocities, in spite of advice from the US embassy not to do so. A UN report concluded that, after an investigation of thirty alleged cases of so-called Greek atrocities against Turkish Cypriots, none had been verified. The UN did verify, however, a massacre of Turkish Cypriot civilians at the village of Tokhni, between Limassol and Larnarca, and also at Maratha. The US embassy in Nicosia reported that 90 percent of Turkish Cypriots released as prisoners of war or detainees chose to head north, even though their families were often in the southern part of the island. Turkish Cypriots were gathering in the area controlled by the Turkish army, quickly "Turkifying" the northern sector.[19]

Even responsible spokesmen sometimes wandered into this murky landscape. Such was the case when notoriously outspoken Congressman Ed Koch

(D-NY) recalled Ottoman barbarities toward the Armenians and suggested that "Turkish events in Cyprus today may yet warrant similar distinction." More surprising were statements by Congressman Brademas printed in the English-language *Turkish Daily News.* "The government of Turkey has in my opinion acted in a very uncivilized way," he observed. He followed this with a reference to Hitler's attempt to outgun everyone, noting, "might is right." The usually cautious congressman might not have understood how much the Turks resented such unfavorable comparisons, which had a long history.[20]

Throughout the last decades of the Ottoman Empire and into the early years of the Turkish republic, foreigners repeatedly made claims about the Turks' barbarity, their animal-like natures, and their lack of any civilizing qualities. These outrageous allegations seemed endless. It was in part to end such derogatory assertions by supercilious Europeans and Americans that Ataturk launched his movement to transform the Turkish nation, to make all Turks proud of their heritage and ethnicity. Symbolic of this goal was the founder's widely publicized statement, "Happy is the man who calls himself a Turk." This was not mere chauvinism; it was an attempt to encourage a new and necessary confidence among his fellow citizens. In this, he appeared to have remarkable success. Ataturk also positioned Turkey closer to Europe, distancing it from the Middle East.[21] Now, in the mid-1970s, many of the former stereotypes were resurfacing among foreign observers.

The Greeks and many of their Greek American supporters argued that the Turkish Cypriot minority had been treated well in Cyprus and got on well with their Greek Cypriot neighbors. They claimed that a minority of extremists, acting in accord with the Turks in Ankara, was forcing the Turkish Cypriots to live in isolated enclaves throughout the island. Father Evagoras Constantinides, a Cypriot by birth and a member of a delegation meeting with Secretary Kissinger and his deputy Robert Ingersoll on August 26, 1974, asserted that "he was not aware of any oppression of the Turks by the Greeks in Cyprus" and claimed that "insurrectionist Turks always held at least one member of a family hostage to ensure the return of the others." These seem, at best, only partial explanations for the continuing tension and violence between the two communities throughout the 1960s and early 1970s.[22]

Of the Greek American organizations actively pursuing justice for Cyprus, none surpassed AHEPA. Founded in 1922, it had thousands of members in all fifty states and possessed an effective structure for activating the larger community. On July 22, just two days after the initial Turkish invasion, AHEPA announced a July 24 press conference in Washington, where leaders of twenty Greek American societies would demand the withdrawal of Turkish forces from Cyprus. AHEPA would continue to be one of the leading critics of Turkish actions on the island and of the Ford administration's policies toward the crisis as well.[23]

Although AHEPA was the oldest and best known of the Greek American associations, there were others that took on important roles. The American Hellenic Institute (AHI) limited its membership of approximately 200 individuals to professionals and academics. Headquartered in Washington, DC, it was led by Eugene Rossides, who had served in the Treasury Department under Nixon and was a law partner of William Rogers, former secretary of state and attorney general. Rossides knew how to get things done in the capital. He became a leading spokesman on Cyprus and was often called to testify before congressional committees on behalf of Greek Americans. His model for AHI was the highly successful American Israel Public Affairs Committee (AIPAC). According to political scientist Paul Watanabe, who has studied the organization closely, "whenever any key votes were in the offing, AHI-PAC reviewed its congressional profiles in order to determine the most effective strategies to persuade individual congressmen. Armed with this information, AHI-PAC dispatched at least two influential Greek American constituents, who were carefully preselected, to contact, in person if possible, each congressman."[24]

The third of the "big three" organizations—those whose representatives were regularly invited to testify at congressional hearings—was the United Hellenic American Congress (UHAC) in Chicago, a center of Greek American activism. Andrew Athens, president of Metro Steel Corporation and a close ally of Senator Charles Percy (R-IL), headed this organization. It was said to be the creation of Archbishop Iakovos, and it maintained close ties to the Greek Orthodox Church. UHAC organized large public protests to support the arms embargo and aid for Cypriot refugees.[25]

Archbishop Iakovos, primate of the Greek Orthodox Archdiocese of North and South America, exercised an equally powerful voice. He was born Demetrios Koukouzis on the Aegean island of Imbros in the Ottoman Empire in 1911 and came to the United States when he was twenty-eight years old. He was ordained a priest in 1940 and became archbishop in 1959; he would serve in that post until his resignation in 1996. A strong supporter of the civil rights movement, Iakovos joined hands with Martin Luther King

Jr. at the Selma march in March 1965. He appears next to King in the iconic photo at the Edmund Pettus Bridge.

On Friday, July 26, the archbishop telephoned Congressman John Brademas, one of only five Greek Americans in the House of Representatives. Brademas, a Rhodes scholar, had become the first Greek American member of Congress when he was elected to the House in 1958, and he was now the spokesman for this small group of representatives. The archbishop expressed his concern about the buildup of Turkish forces on the island. Iakovos seemed to be out ahead of the Indiana congressman, who knew few details and initially argued that Turkey's actions were justified, given the coup against Makarios. Iakovos told Brademas that the Greek Orthodox Church could not look the other way when humanitarian issues were involved. From the outset, he also believed that the United States had encouraged the Turks to invade Cyprus. Brademas promised to contact the archbishop again on Monday, after his meeting with the other Greek American congressmen and a possible briefing at the State Department.[26] That same day (July 26), Brademas and his Greek American colleagues—Skip Bafalis (R-FL), Peter Kyros (D-ME), Paul Sarbanes (D-MD), and Gus Yatron (D-PA)—sent a congratulatory note to Prime Minister Karamanlis, praising Greece's return to free and democratic political institutions.[27]

In recent years, the Greek American community had split over how to relate to the military regime in Athens. Those who opposed the junta and wanted to cut US arms to Greece organized groups such as the US Committee for Democracy in Greece to lobby the US government. Others tolerated the junta and seemed content to carry on business as usual, just as the Nixon administration had done. With the junta's disappearance, they could all unite in their criticism of Turkey's actions in Cyprus.[28]

As arranged, Brademas spoke again with Iakovos and shared what he had learned at the State Department about the situation on Cyprus. He assured the archbishop that he and the other Greek American congressmen would work together on behalf of Cyprus. He suggested that Iakovos and other Greek American leaders write to officials in Washington to protest the continuing Turkish buildup on the island.[29]

Iakovos was one step ahead of the Indiana congressman, having called an important meeting for Tuesday, July 30, in New York City, where he resided. He convened the Archdiocesan Council and the presidents of many Greek American federations and societies at the St. Moritz Hotel in Manhattan. The gathering's purpose was to organize and take immediate action to bring relief to the people of Cyprus. The archbishop was clearly in charge. After much discussion, it was unanimously decided that he would appoint members to a committee to coordinate assistance. He would also select a representative in each state to organize a local committee to expedite the national program's work. The attendees decided to ask Congress to cut off all aid to Turkey if that nation had not complied with the UN cease-fire resolution within thirty days.[30]

Kissinger struggled amid the rising chorus of ethnic protest. On August 21, 20,000 Greek Americans marched in Chicago's Grant Park. AHEPA sent circulars to all its chapters instructing them to send telegrams asking their congressmen to cosponsor House Resolution 1319, calling for an aid cutoff. On August 18 AHEPA's annual convention opened in Boston, and over the next week, delegates representing the organization's 50,000 members focused on Cyprus and what they considered the failed policies of the Nixon and Ford administrations. On August 21 a delegation visited UN headquarters to meet with Undersecretary-General Frank Bradley Morse to express their concerns. Two days later, AHEPA supreme president William P. Tsaffaras and two other delegates met with the secretary of state in Washington to hear his defense of US policy. They reported a subdued Kissinger who blamed the US failure to respond to the threatened Turkish invasion on the disordered situation in Washington, with one president on the point of resigning and another unelected president about to take office. The delegates told him that if justice for Cyprus were not forthcoming, AHEPA members and Greek Americans in general would turn their anger against the president. "We will know what to do in the next election," they warned.[31]

Kissinger introduced the delegates to the new US ambassador to Greece, Jack Kubisch. On the spur of the moment, in response to an invitation from the delegates, Kissinger told the ambassador to go to Boston immediately and speak to the convention. He did, and for a moment, Kubisch became a symbol of the new administration's good intentions.[32]

On August 24, the final day of the conference, AHEPA took two important steps. It voted to raise $100,000 through its many chapters to continue to seek justice for Cyprus. It also approved the creation of an ad hoc Justice for Cyprus Committee to lead the campaign.[33]

It is little wonder that the Ford administration often seemed overwhelmed at the extent and vociferousness of these lobbying efforts. Activists seemed to be everywhere, sending postcards and telegrams; placing ads in local, regional, and national newspapers; and sponsoring rallies for Cyprus. Gerald Ford had assumed the presidency in the middle of the Cyprus crisis, and he had no time to ponder this issue or any of the others he had inherited from his predecessor. He had little choice but to retain most of Nixon's appointees, even if their personalities clashed with his own, such as that of Secretary of Defense James Schlesinger. In time, these awkward relationships would be resolved. Fortunately, Ford worked well with Kissinger, who was delighted to continue his tenure as secretary of state and national security adviser.

President Ford, Secretary of State Kissinger, and other top State Department officials met on numerous occasions with the AHEPA committee, Archbishop Iakovos, and delegations of congressmen who supported an embargo. The administration tried to be patient, but increasingly it came to view the Greek American activists as representing a special interest, to the detriment of the broader American interest. The executive needed to have a relatively free hand to negotiate with foreign countries, and the White House believed that an embargo would make the Turks less amenable to compromise. President Ford liked to tell visitors that he was a member of the AHEPA chapter in his hometown of Grand Rapids, Michigan, and that he counted a number of Greek Americans there as his friends. But these connections were of little help to him in Washington.

When President Ford appeared on television and stated that "our foreign policy cannot be simply a collection of special economic or ethnic or ideological interests . . . the executive must have flexibility in the conduct of foreign policy," AHEPA responded with a challenge. "One can only assume," it said, "that the President believes that Americans of Greek descent need to be 'put in their place' and that we should be reprimanded for voicing our opinions on the Cyprus matter! . . . Is foreign policy the sole possession of one, two, or twenty men?"[34]

In part, the president was grappling with a new phenomenon spawned by the civil rights movement: an ethnic revival that exhibited nationalist fervor whenever issues related to the homeland cried out "for emotional involvement." For many, ethnicity had become a social good. As historian Salim Yaqub recently wrote, "By 1970, it was much safer and more acceptable for people with dark complexions, strange names, and in some cases foreign accents to criticize the United States . . . boasting their own long heritage of stable and industrious ethnic communities in America." This movement was a protest against "the very fabric of WASP culture," and in this case, President Ford, Vice President Nelson Rockefeller, and even Secretary Kissinger represented the WASP establishment, which was trying to dictate how Greek Americans should behave. But that minority was not going to be shamed into silence.[35]

At the local level, too, new activist groups sprang into existence around the country to pursue goals similar to those of the national organizations. In Minneapolis–St. Paul, for example, a group calling itself the Minnesota Friends of Cyprus (MFC) actively engaged these issues in the Twin Cities, seeking funds, raising consciousness, lobbying the state's congressmen and senators, and urging its members to write letters to federal officials. The MFC remained active until the end of the 1970s. Another example was the Save Cyprus Council of Southern California, chaired by Professor Theodore Saloutos (1910–1980) of UCLA, the noted historian of the Greek immigrant community.

Saloutos left a detailed diary of these early days of organization and protest, providing an intimate look at the inner workings of the Greek American lobbying effort. It covers his various activities on both coasts during the critical period from August 30 to September 17, 1974. He eagerly assumed his new role, helping to organize meetings and protests against the Turkish invasion. He corresponded regularly with the offices of Congressmen Edward Roybal (D-CA) and Thomas Rees (D-CA) and Senator Alan Cranston (D-CA). He also established contact with Mike Minashian, an Armenian activist; they shared an antipathy toward the Turks, and their respective organizations cooperated in the defense of Cyprus. Representatives of their two groups met with Congressman Roybal at his Los Angeles office on September 4. They had been advised beforehand that the congressman was particularly concerned about Turkey's cultivation of the opium poppy, having traveled to Turkey with a group of his colleagues to study the problem. Thus, Saloutos and the others emphasized that issue in their meeting. Roybal, who served on the House Appropriations Committee, thought that opposition to poppy cultivation provided the best point of attack for curtailing aid to Turkey. A number of committee members already supported such a move, and others could be persuaded, he thought. Roybal urged them to publicize their activities. Saloutos came away with a view of Roybal as "a modern, unassuming man of integrity who speaks for the common people."[36]

Of course, not everything went as planned. On September 3 Saloutos complained about an atrocity story, accompanied by a picture of slain Turkish

Cypriots, that appeared on the front page of the *Los Angeles Times.* He viewed this as an unfair allocation of space and a form of "yellow journalism." A rally on September 6, on the south lawn of city hall, turned into a fiasco. It was poorly organized; there was no spokesman to meet with the media, and prominent personalities had never been invited. It was a disaster, according to Saloutos. That evening, however, things began to look up. Saloutos participated in a meeting at St. Sophia Cathedral, where John Brademas was the principal speaker. The congressman was visiting California to raise money for his reelection campaign. The Cyprus committee also raised $600 at the event. Brademas impressed Saloutos with his sophisticated presentation.

Four days later, Saloutos arrived at AHEPA headquarters in Washington, DC. There, he met with Eugene Rossides, who was then in the process of creating the American Hellenic Institute "to serve as a round-the-clock office on all legislation present and future dealing with the Cyprus question." Rossides planned to send information to AHEPA and church-based organizations, hoping to line up their public support. Saloutos read over the draft proposal and made a few suggestions. He recommended that, for academics at least, the AHI membership fee should be reduced from $500 to $100. He also met Rossides's assistant, a Cypriot who told him that most Greek Cypriots opposed enosis. The Greeks, he said, could not govern themselves, so "why should they seek to govern Cyprus 500 miles away." It seemed that no one knew for certain how many Greek Cypriots favored union with Athens and how many wanted to maintain independence.[37]

On September 11 Saloutos lunched with his good friend George C. Vournos, a Washington-based lawyer and former supreme president of AHEPA (1942–1945). Vournos asked Saloutos to read a draft article he had written for a scholarly journal in which he criticized the *National Herald* of New York, a leading Greek American paper; AHEPA leadership; and even Archbishop Iakovos and the Greek Orthodox Church for their earlier support of the junta, which, he argued, had contributed to the Cyprus tragedy. Vournos also suggested that academics should do more research and publish more work on internal Turkish issues such as the opium trade, the Armenian genocide, and Turkish militarism. Saloutos told him that it was a good piece of writing but too polemical.

On Friday, September 13, Saloutos met with Dr. Hratch Abrahamian, an associate professor at the Georgetown University School of Dentistry and a leading Armenian activist. He also served as head of the Armenian Revolutionary Federation (ARF). The two men had lunch together, and Abrahamian shared his family history, telling Saloutos how his parents had fled to Iran from Smyrna to escape the violence and chaos there in 1922. Later, Saloutos took Abrahamian to AHEPA headquarters and introduced him to the organization's executive secretary, George Leber, who arranged for them to visit AHEPA's Cyprus committee, which was meeting at a nearby hotel. When they arrived, the ambassador of Cyprus, Nicos G. Dimitriou, was speaking, and he left the impression that Archbishop Iakovos was the head of the Cyprus relief program in the United States. A number of AHEPA members took exception to this interpretation, explaining that the church had played a very limited role in Greek war relief during World War II. "Iakovos seems to think he is an ethnarch," wrote Saloutos, "and more or less operates as such." Former supreme president John Plumides, who served on both the AHEPA committee and the Archdiocesan Council, was not clear on the dividing line between their different spheres of activity.[38]

Finally, Saloutos introduced Abrahamian to the committee. He had earlier mentioned to Rossides that it would be a good idea to join with the Armenians in commemorating the upcoming sixtieth anniversary of the Armenian genocide of 1915. The Cyprus committee voted unanimously in favor of this recommendation. Saloutos then spoke individually with some committee members about happenings on the West Coast and the role of actor Telly Savalas in supporting their cause. Saloutos was very satisfied with the day's work.

On September 15 Saloutos was pleased to read two editorials that were favorable to Cyprus in leading newspapers, one in the *New York Times* and the other in the *Washington Post.* Another brief visit to AHEPA headquarters brought more criticism of Iakovos's attempt to take command of Cyprus relief. AHEPA would not disband its efforts to follow the archbishop.

After almost a week in Washington, Saloutos traveled to New York City on September 16, where he discovered a number of groups willing to aid Cyprus. He talked at length with representatives of the Emergency Food Aid Committee for Cyprus at Cyprus House; they were collecting and shipping food and clothing under the auspices of the seventeen clubs of the Cyprus Federation of America, founded in 1951. They too expressed strong suspicions of Iakovos, noting that the archbishop "had never displayed great concern over Cyprus in the past. Why now?" They also questioned whether sending relief funds to the Cypriot embassy in Washington was a good idea.

They wondered aloud whether such donations went to refugees or toward the operating costs of the government of Cyprus. On his last day in New York, Saloutos visited the Cyprus mission to the United Nations.[39]

This trip provided Saloutos with ideas about how his committee in Los Angeles could best contribute to the relief effort. He returned to California well informed about the various movements—and tensions—within the Greek American communities on the East Coast.

Congress Becomes Engaged

During the brief hiatus between the two Turkish incursions (July 20–August 14), Congressman Brademas focused more intently on the crisis. He continued his frequent contacts with Iakovos. At a State Department meeting on August 2, he expressed his deep concern to Undersecretary Sisco about Turkish troops on Cyprus and later introduced a resolution in the House urging the immediate withdrawal of foreign troops, both Turkish and Greek, from Cyprus. He and his four Greek American colleagues considered introducing an amendment to the foreign aid bill that would cut off aid to Turkey unless it removed its troops from the island. He knew the State Department would not be pleased, but Senator Walter Mondale had already proposed an amendment aimed at doing the same thing owing to Turkey's decision on the opium poppy. Reasoned Brademas, "An amendment to cut off aid to Turkey given the opium and troop build-up on Cyprus might well be successful."[40]

On the day of the second attack, the five Greek American congressmen sent a letter to their House colleagues urging them to support a resolution to cut off aid to Turkey. Here, a new argument began to emerge. "It is an outrage," they stated, "that American taxpayers should be supplying arms to Turkey that are used in attacks upon a friendly country in violation of NATO commitments."[41] This view would become the basis for a broad legalistic and persuasive argument capable of attracting widespread bipartisan support in Congress. Arms agreements forbade the use of weapons in such a manner and prescribed an arms cutoff in the event of a violation. Turkey was therefore breaking the law, and the administration must punish Ankara as the law stipulated. Coming on the heels of the Watergate scandal and the chief executive's bold violation of the law, this argument resonated with members of Congress. They were being called on to defend the basic principle of upholding the law—a principle for which they had struggled in recent months. If they failed

Cartoon published in the *Denver Post,* October 16, 1974, showing President Ford fondly cradling a diminutive Turkish pasha wielding a bloody sword and a hypodermic needle. (©2019 Patrick Oliphant/Artists Rights Society, New York)

to act now, all they had achieved could be lost. This approach lifted the debate from a narrow ethnic concern to a legal imperative. Also in play were humanitarian concerns for the displaced Cypriots, which coincided with rising support in Congress for human rights in general, an issue that received a cold reception from the secretary of state. This combination of principles would surely attract the interest and support of most members of Congress.[42]

The day after the attack, the five congressmen met with Kissinger and his senior staff to discuss the situation on Cyprus and US policy to address the crisis. The secretary tried to put a good face on developments, arguing that, in hindsight, the United States might have done things differently, but "anything constructive that had developed during the crisis in Cyprus had been the result of US pressure." Brademas, the most senior of the five, attacked the State Department's failure to speak out at key moments about the coup, the

Turkish invasion, or the Geneva talks. The United States, he claimed, had remained virtually silent. They were not blaming President Ford, he told Kissinger, "but rather . . . we place the blame squarely on you, sir." Private diplomacy had failed, and they expected an end to US military sales and grants to Turkey until its armed forces left the island. Kissinger indicated that he could live with a sense-of-Congress resolution but not with any kind of mandate. He did not want to take action that would "mortgage our long-term relations with the Turks." He favored a cantonal arrangement for Cyprus. Brademas ended by assuring Kissinger that he and his colleagues were not acting out of any sense of ethnic chauvinism.[43]

In this one long meeting, the two sides set out their basic arguments, which they would repeat many times over the following months. Kissinger knew that Brademas was a skillful tactician and fully conversant with the legislative intricacies of the House of Representatives. Brademas had served in Congress for fifteen years and would soon become the Democratic majority whip; he was thought to aspire to an even higher position in the House hierarchy. In fact, on another occasion, Kissinger would say to Brademas, "They tell me that one day you will be Speaker. Help me now with the new members of the House." The secretary knew he could not trifle with the Indiana congressman.[44]

As protests large and small unfolded across the country, embargo forces were organizing in both houses of Congress. Theirs was no easy task because they faced intense pressure from the White House, which warned of dire consequences to US-Turkish relations should an arms cutoff be mandated. Nevertheless, new champions of censure arose in both the House and the Senate, and they were not Greek Americans; thus, they were unlikely to be accused of pursuing parochial interests. In the House, Benjamin Rosenthal (D-NY), a senior member of the Foreign Affairs Committee, became a leading spokesman for the embargo, based on the principle that the invasion violated American law. He and Pierre DuPont (R-DE) introduced an amendment to the continuing appropriations bill that would suspend aid to Turkey until the president certified that a satisfactory agreement had been reached regarding military forces on Cyprus. On September 24 the House passed the amendment by a vote of 306 to 90. But that was far from the end of the legislative battle. Over the next three weeks, Rosenthal was in the forefront of successful attempts to reject weaker Senate language and to respond to two presidential vetoes. Success came at last on October 17. Paul Sarbanes (D-MD), another strong supporter of the amendment, had feared that a failure to override the veto might cost them the whole battle; he sensed that the House was losing patience and that its members were eager to leave the capital for the fall recess.[45]

During these tense days, while the measure was making its way slowly through the House, Brademas attended a swearing-in ceremony in the White House Rose Garden, where he engaged in an impromptu conversation with President Ford. The president teased Brademas for giving him a hard time. Brademas responded that he was only trying to help Ford obey the law. The congressman also told the president that, "quite frankly, we simply could not believe much of what Kissinger told us."[46]

In the Senate, Thomas Eagleton (D-MO) became the fourth member of the so-called Gang of Four, joining Brademas, Sarbanes, and Rosenthal. Eagleton had gained public attention in 1972 when Democratic presidential candidate George McGovern chose him as his running mate and then quickly dropped him from the ticket when he learned that Eagleton had received psychiatric treatment for depression. Brian Atwood, the senator's senior adviser on foreign policy and defense issues, believed the incident had only enhanced his influence in Congress, making him a national figure. "He was probably the most sane person in the US Senate," remarked Atwood. After his rejection by McGovern, Eagleton turned his attention back to Capitol Hill, where he continued to oppose the Vietnam War and the so-called imperial presidency.[47]

Atwood had recently met with a young State Department lawyer who revealed that he had written a brief for the secretary of state concerning the legality of the Turkish invasion of Cyprus. The lawyer had concluded that Turkey violated its agreement when it used American weapons offensively. His report had been shelved on the advice of Kissinger's former personal lawyer and current State Department counselor Carlisle Maw. Troubled by this information, Atwood wrote a speech for Senator Eagleton that took a cautious line, indicating that "unnamed bureaucrats were not informing the president of his legal responsibilities. . . . That got front-page headlines in the [*Washington*] *Post* and the *New York Times*. It was really big because the press had already been asking about it [the legal question]. Eagleton's speech gave everybody on that side of the issue a boost."[48]

Atwood became worried, however, about the growing tension between Congress and the executive branch. As a former diplomat, he was also concerned about the harmful effect of a cutoff on US-Turkish relations. With Eagleton's permission, Atwood met with Maw and "suggested to him that if

State could indeed get something going on the diplomatic front, perhaps through the UN, perhaps just directly, to get the Turks to agree to come to the table to talk about the issue, then they could legitimately ask the Congress to hold off." He got nowhere.[49]

Later, Kissinger called Senate majority leader Mike Mansfield (D-MT) and asked whether there were going to be any problems with this issue. Surprisingly, Mansfield reportedly said, "I don't think you'll have a problem as far as I know but why don't you come down to the Senate and you can address the Democratic caucus, and we'll see." So Kissinger made arrangements to speak to each caucus separately.[50]

When the secretary of state met with the Senate Democratic caucus on September 19, he faced considerable hostility. Eagleton questioned him about the State Department's legal memorandum "claiming [that] Turkey's August actions could not be legally justified." Kissinger acknowledged that his lawyers agreed with the senator but added that Eagleton did not understand "the foreign policy priorities." The senator replied, "Mr. Secretary, you do not understand the rule of law." This confrontation only a month after President Nixon's resignation "shocked some senators and convinced them that Congress was compelled to take extraordinary measures."[51]

Eagleton led the embargo campaign in the upper house during this time, making a number of powerful speeches. He reminded his fellow senators of recent events. "We have just emerged from a trying period of American history," he remarked, "a period when laws were winked at and rationalized to fit the concepts of policymakers. By and large, we have learned that policies created in ignorance or in spite of the law are doomed to failure." And in response to the secretary of state's concerns, he argued, "We are told to ignore the law, we are told that Henry [Kissinger] does not like the law; that Henry will have his hands tied, just as Henry said we would tie his hands if we terminated the Cambodian bombing . . . our distinguished Secretary of State is famous for his tilts. He tilts toward the junta in Chile. He tilts toward Thieu in Vietnam. His most famous tilt was the pro-Pakistan tilt. His current tilt, his Turkey tilt, is no wiser than the other tilts."[52]

At first, Eagleton seemed to be acting on his own, without any input from concerned members in the House of Representatives. On September 9 he sent a letter to his Senate colleagues, asking them to support a sense-of-the-Senate resolution he had introduced three days earlier. He reminded them that in 1964 LBJ had warned Prime Minister Inonu that using American weapons to intervene in Cyprus would violate the bilateral agreement on military assistance and sales to Turkey. Now there could be no doubt that Turkey had crossed that line, and US policy must hold the Turks to account. This resolution passed the Senate with strong bipartisan support (64–27) on the same day that Kissinger met with the Democratic caucus.

Eagleton returned later that month with a much stronger proposition, demanding a cutoff of all military aid to Turkey. By this time, the leading pro-embargo congressmen and the senator and their staffs had met to coordinate strategy. The administration gave insufficient attention to this significant development, as it was rare for members of the two chambers to work together so closely.

Senator Eagleton was not entirely satisfied with the House and Senate amendments, which allowed for a presidential determination that if progress were being made toward resolving the Cyprus crisis, aid would not be suspended. This provision obscured the fact that Turkey had violated US law and that Congress must ensure that military aid is not "subject to the vagaries of the policy choice at the moment." "It is not the 93rd Congress," he argued, "it is the law which calls for a cut-off of aid to Turkey." The presidential waiver, however, remained part of the embargo amendment.[53]

After their initial success in Congress, it was time to express thanks. Brademas understood the importance of Senate support, and he thanked Eagleton for his "splendid leadership," and as the "Dean of the Greek bloc," he expressed the gratitude of all Americans of Greek origin. For his part, Eagleton sent a letter to AHEPA in late September congratulating Hellenic Americans across the country who had worked so hard to get his resolution adopted by the Senate. This, said Eagleton, was an even greater accomplishment "because of the fact that Secretary of State Kissinger lobbied so strongly against it."[54]

Just three days after final passage of the embargo bill by both houses of Congress, Brademas served as master of ceremonies at an event in New York City commemorating the fifteenth anniversary of the enthronement of Archbishop Iakovos. It was attended by a wide array of political and religious leaders, and Brademas used the occasion to reflect on their recent success in Congress. He and his colleagues had entered into a "lengthy but determined effort to compel the president of the United States and the Secretary of State to obey the law and halt further US military aid or sales to Turkey." President Ford and Secretary Kissinger did not like the bill, but it had succeeded because of the extraordinary leadership and teamwork in Congress. Here, he singled out for praise Eagleton, Sarbanes, Rosenthal, and Kyros. He also praised the groups whose representatives sat in the audience. "We really saw, 'Greek power' mustered with unity and speed at a time when it was essential," he said. Although Brademas was always careful to explain that this campaign was not solely a Greek American affair, he made it clear in his speech that night that the bill might not have passed without the wholehearted support of that community. "Now we have proven," he continued, "that no man is above the law and in conducting the foreign policy of the United States both President Ford and Secretary of State Kissinger must obey the law. Congress is no longer willing to sit quietly by while the nation's laws and ideals and yes, even our national security interests are trampled on by the Executive Branch of the Government." US foreign policy could no longer be based solely on economic and military power, he said. "We must learn anew to give heed in our foreign policy—as in our policy at home—to the ideals of freedom and justice."[55]

Brademas delivered, in essence, a victory speech. And what a welcome offering it must have seemed to the archbishop on his anniversary. Iakovos had earlier marched alongside civil rights demonstrators in the South; now he marshaled Greek Americans for their own righteous cause.

Assessing Tactics and Strategies

Congress was pushing back against what many members considered executive overreach. And activists had the support of well-organized and wholly motivated ethnic groups. This proved to be a powerful coalition, one that the Ford administration found impossible to overcome.

From late September to early December 1974, the embargo law received much attention. Presidential vetoes necessitated some amendments to the original legislation, but the fundamental principle remained. Eventually, President Ford had to admit the inevitable: supporters of the embargo possessed a veto-proof majority in both houses of Congress. As Brademas could have explained, advocates for human rights, drug control, and respect for the law had come together in a grand alliance that overwhelmed the administration.

Supporters of the embargo had more to do, however. They became actively engaged in the off-year elections of November 1974, with mixed results. In Los Angeles, a group comprising Greek, Armenian, and Syrian Americans campaigned for Long Beach City College professor Mark Hannaford, who promised his support on the Cyprus issue. In contrast, Hannaford's Republi-

California campaign poster from 1974 supporting Democratic House candidate John Dalessio. (Courtesy Theodore Saloutos Papers, Immigration History Research Center)

can opponent, Bill Bond, did not respond to the group's questions on the subject. Believing that Democrats "are more responsive to our sentiments regarding Greece, Turkey, Cyprus, genocide, and the Armenian question," they supported the Democratic candidate Hannaford, who won the open congressional seat. Another group tried to unseat popular Republican congressman Alphonzo Bell, who represented the West Side of Los Angeles. He had broken his promise, they said, to vote for the cutoff of military aid to Turkey. They campaigned for John Dalessio, who vowed to support the embargo. Bell won easily, even in the year of Democratic landslides. Brademas, Sarbanes, and Kyros wrote to "Greek Friends in Utah," urging them to support Congressman Wayne Owens's campaign for the US Senate. He, too, had voted for the embargo bill, but Owens lost to his Republican opponent, Jake Garn.[56]

There were some bright spots for Greek American candidates. Four of the five congressmen won reelection; only Kyros of Maine lost his seat. He had been outspoken about the need for Kissinger to find a new job, and perhaps his more moderate constituents thought he had gone too far. This was also the year when Paul Tsongas and Michael Dukakis of Massachusetts won election to the House of Representatives and the governorship of the Bay State, respectively.[57]

Overall, the Democrats won a major victory, picking up forty-nine seats in the House (291) and four in the Senate (60), guaranteeing that the Ford administration would face difficulties not only over Cyprus and Turkey but also over other foreign and domestic policy issues. In a special election held in February, Gerald Ford's former seat in staunchly Republican Grand Rapids, Michigan, had already fallen to the Democrats. The Republicans had not lost there in sixty years.

To make matters worse, when Kissinger met with the new congressmen at the State Department in late December 1974, before their swearing in, he apparently antagonized several of them. He reportedly lectured to the group and treated them in a condescending manner, as if he were conducting a graduate school seminar. This did not bode well for future relations.

These so-called Watergate freshmen were not only more likely to confront a Republican administration but also less likely to respect their party elders, especially the long-serving committee chairs in the House of Representatives. Old-timers such as Otto Passman (D-LA), chair of a subcommittee on foreign aid appropriations, and Thomas "Doc" Morgan (D-PA), chair of the House Committee on Foreign Affairs, faced new challenges in their committees, which they had formerly run with a firm hand.[58] Initially, even the Republican congressional leadership could not ensure that a majority of its caucus would back the administration. In two critical votes in October and early December, a majority of House Republicans supported the embargo. Even in minority leader John Rhodes's Arizona delegation, the other two Republican congressmen voted for the punitive measure.[59]

One has to question how effectively the administration responded to the Cyprus issue throughout the fall of 1974. Certainly, Kissinger underestimated Congress's determination to take action if the executive did not. He may have thought he had time to resolve the crisis, but the situation quickly moved beyond his control. In late August the White House thought the protests by Greek Americans had died down, but September brought renewed lobbying in support of the congressional resolutions. Although Brademas was the moving force behind the embargo amendment, "because of his Greek heritage and leadership post [deputy whip]," he did not offer the motion in the House. That privilege went to Rosenthal and DuPont. President Ford had telephoned DuPont and tried to convince him to back off, arguing that passage would harm delicate negotiations. However, the bill with the amendment attached—and with the Delaware Republican's support—sailed through the House.[60]

Next, the White House called in the bipartisan leadership to discuss the situation in Congress and to recommend what action could be taken. Views were scattered, and no clear solution emerged. Congressman Peter Frelinghuysen (R-NJ) remarked, "We don't have an ideal solution and the House vote shows what the sentiment is." The sense of this group seemed to be that the Senate should try to water down the House amendment through either a conference committee or a separate amendment. (Both would be tried, and both would fail.)[61]

Congressman Rhodes urged the president to meet with Archbishop Iakovos, who might be prevailed on to issue a friendly statement and call off the Greek American protests. Ford met with Iakovos on October 7 and explained that the Greek American attacks were counterproductive to US policy toward Cyprus. Not surprisingly, he made little headway.[62]

The administration seemed to be lost, uncertain what policy to pursue. President Ford wistfully reported that the leading Greeks of Grand Rapids understood his Cyprus policy, unlike those in Washington. The president railed against "a new generation of wildass Democrats." The old guard, such as Carl Albert (D-OK) and Tip O'Neill (D-MA), were through, he thought, so he did not know who to deal with. Secretary of Defense James Schlesinger thought they might get Rosenthal to back off if they gave Congress some sort of concession on Cyprus. Kissinger thought they would be better off fighting back and recommended going to the people to turn them against Congress. "I will go to the people, too, and talk about the executive and legislative relationship. In the name of human rights, they will undermine national security." He was, of course, referring to broader issues that went beyond Cyprus.[63]

The strength of opposition in Congress seemed to take the administration by surprise. Administration officials did not understand that key senators and congressmen had joined forces, and by the time they did, it was too late. Secretary Kissinger failed to use the time between passage of the amendment in mid-October and its implementation in early February to leverage Turkish action, which might have defused the situation.[64] Kissinger did, however, make a last-minute attempt in late December to encourage Greece and Turkey to compromise over Cyprus. He chose to act through an intermediary, Congressman Wayne Hays (D-OH), who traveled to Ankara and Athens to meet with the leaders there. They knew Hays well owing to his membership in the North Atlantic Assembly, an organization over which he would preside on three separate occasions, including in 1975. Hays made little headway, however, for the coalition government in Turkey was weak, and Karamanlis was waiting for the embargo to take effect.[65]

Hays's colleagues John Brademas and Paul Sarbanes also traveled to the area, making a brief fact-finding visit to Cyprus in January 1975. They went to refugee camps and met with Archbishop Makarios, newly returned to the island. At the president's office in Nicosia, Makarios agreed to accept a cantonal arrangement but said that all Greek Cypriots should be allowed to return to their homes as quickly as possible. Although he made some "mildly acerbic remarks regarding Secretary Kissinger," he agreed that the United States must take the lead in finding a solution. The fact that Democrats now had a big majority in Congress should expedite matters, he thought.[66]

As the date of the embargo (February 5, 1975) approached, the Gang of Four sent a letter to Kissinger to remind him what the law required. They expected a total cutoff, they said, including weapons that were already in the pipeline but not yet delivered to Turkey. The secretary responded that in such cases, the State Department usually informed the leadership of Congress that arms in the pipeline would continue. Now, however, the problem was that the leadership did not control the rank and file.[67]

John Brademas and Paul Sarbanes in a Cyprus refugee camp kitchen, January 1975. (Courtesy Brademas Papers, New York University Archives)

John Brademas and Paul Sarbanes in a Cyprus refugee camp, January 1975. (Courtesy Brademas Papers, New York University Archives)

John Brademas, Paul Sarbanes, and Archbishop Makarios in Nicosia, January 1975. (Courtesy Brademas Papers, New York University Archives)

Four days later, the congressmen met with the secretary and two of his top aides for a general discussion of the Cyprus situation. The two sides were clearly far apart. Kissinger argued that the threat of a cutoff had not been helpful. There had been a good chance of reaching an agreement with Ecevit in October, but now that his government had fallen, the weak interim government that ruled in Ankara was incapable of making important decisions on Cyprus, pending new elections. Although Congress might have acted with honorable convictions, the result was a foreign policy disaster. Here, Kissinger interjected that other countries such as China were beginning to rethink their relations with the United States, and his influence in the Middle East had become decidedly weaker because of what Congress had done.[68]

If Kissinger hoped to elicit sympathy from the Gang of Four, he had badly misjudged the situation. Brademas, not easily intimidated, denied that foreign policy was a disaster. The law had been violated, and the United

States had to react. Sarbanes said that Turkey must make a substantial concession. The others agreed that a deep-seated principle was involved, and a pragmatic solution was unlikely. Rosenthal told Kissinger that without the agreement of the individuals in the room, "you will not get congressional action." Brademas warned that it was "a whole new ballgame in Congress. If you try to get this overturned, you will be clobbered and it will not contribute to a Cyprus solution, and it could worsen your relations with the Congress." Senator Eagleton told the secretary he would report that "they had an amicable discussion but that we are in basic disagreement." Again, Brademas assured Kissinger that they were acting on principle. "I want you to understand that this is not anti-Turk." He was always concerned that they might be perceived as acting solely out of a narrow ethnic interest.[69]

One wonders whether Kissinger had ever encountered such blunt language from US lawmakers. Speaking to top administration officials in such an uncompromising manner indicated the depth of feeling over the Cyprus crisis. This encounter seemed unprecedented, unlike any foreign policy confrontation between Congress and the White House—except for Vietnam—since the end of World War II. Ironically, this was taking place during the presidency of a man whom everyone in politics knew as "Jerry," someone who had apparently made no enemies during his twenty-five years in the House. On Capitol Hill he had acted as a negotiator and a peacemaker, but those skills failed him now.

Although the three congressmen and the senator seemed supremely confident in their discussion with the secretary of state, as the cutoff date neared, they expressed some concern about how a negative reaction from Ankara would reflect on Congress in general and on them in particular. On February 3 Eagleton telephoned Brademas and suggested that they give Kissinger an extra two weeks to negotiate some concessions. This, he thought, would take some of the pressure off Congress. Brademas thought this would cause more problems than it solved, leading the Turks to believe that Kissinger could turn Congress around at the last minute. Brademas was able to quiet Eagleton's concerns, at least for the moment.[70]

Thus, act one of this great political drama finally came to an end. After months of tense negotiations, made more dramatic by intense foreign and domestic lobbying, the improbable arms embargo had become law. And it appeared unlikely that Congress would reverse itself anytime in the near future.

4

Turning Congress

Once the embargo went into effect on February 5, the administration began a long and determined counteroffensive to make it disappear. It would take most of 1975 to achieve this goal, and even then, the White House could claim only partial success. Antagonism in Congress, especially toward Kissinger, remained deep and widespread. The "Watergate freshmen" had now taken their seats in the House of Representatives, and they were determined to seek a more active role in the foreign policy–making process.

The day after the embargo took effect, President Ford met again with a bipartisan group from Capitol Hill that included Senators Clifford Case (R-NJ) and John Sparkman (D-AL) and Representatives William Broomfield (R-MI), ranking minority member of the Foreign Affairs Committee, and Doc Morgan. Ford pointed out all the difficulties that had arisen due to the cutoff of aid to Turkey. Sarbanes and Brademas would not admit they were wrong, he declared, and they had seriously weakened NATO. Referring to the origin of the crisis, the president remarked, "The Greeks have to remember they started it . . . Turkey moved because the Greeks moved."[1]

Then Kissinger took over and presented the view that Turkey was very important to the United States in the Middle East and that even Greek prime minister Karamanlis realized the embargo would not work. The secretary remarked, with some exaggeration, that between 1960 and 1974, "Makarios had reduced the Turks to ghetto status and had torn up the laws." Kissinger believed that Rosenthal and Brademas wanted to be able to back away from this issue and that Sarbanes, who had a lot of Greeks in his district, was the only rigid one. Clearly, Kissinger saw this very much as an ethnic issue, despite his earlier comments to the contrary. Congressman Broomfield thought they should enlist the aid of the Jewish community, which could be helpful if it saw the Turkish embargo as harmful to Israel. They talked about the influence of the press, especially the *New York Times.* They appeared to consider Senator Eagleton a difficult case because, they said, "he's taking it as a legal moral issue."[2]

They ended by agreeing that some kind of waiver from the president might work. The president could have the embargo lifted if he could declare to Congress that substantial progress had been made. Ford had been reluctant to "finagle," as he called it, but he agreed with the congressmen that perhaps they should "finagle" together.[3]

The following day, Broomfield suggested that the president appoint former secretary of state Dean Rusk as special negotiator on the Cyprus issue. He knew that Kissinger would find such a proposal offensive, but without a new negotiator, Congress was unlikely to lift the ban. As he remarked, "The Greek community has developed such a hostile attitude toward Secretary Kissinger that his involvement has become counterproductive."[4]

Ford met with yet another bipartisan group on February 20, including Senators Mike Mansfield (D-MT) and Hugh Scott (R-PA), the majority and minority leaders, respectively, and Representative John McFall (D-CA), the majority whip. Again, he laid out the harm that was being done. "The victim of this is not Turkey but Greece," he warned, because Turkey would not proceed with negotiations while the embargo was in place. The president commented that concessions would never be enough for Brademas and Sarbanes. They could get two-thirds of what they wanted, but only at the end of the process, not at the beginning.[5]

Concerned Voices

White House discussants repeatedly raised the possibility of support from the Jewish community, the supposition being that the weakening position of the United States in the Middle East and its worsening relations with Turkey would be harmful to the interests of Israel.[6] Kissinger decided to inform Jewish leaders of the dangerous situation being created in the Middle East by the embargo. Vice President Rockefeller approached Israeli ambassador Simcha Dinitz to determine whether he could help with Rosenthal. The initial effort proved fruitless, however, when word got out that the administration was pressing the diplomat to speak with the congressman.[7]

As far as Israel was concerned, the administration could not easily persuade the government in Tel Aviv to speak out against those who supported the embargo. Brademas, for example, had always been a strong supporter of

Israel, voting consistently to send US arms to Tel Aviv. He even wrote to one constituent that he objected to the sale of Hawk missiles to Jordan and to efforts to expel Israel from the United Nations.[8]

Brademas received two long letters from Elliott Green, a supporter in Philadelphia who set out the position of many Jewish Americans. Green criticized dishonest journalists like Rowland Evans and Robert Novak, who attacked both American Jews who supported Israel and American Greeks who supported the Greek people. Greeks and Jews needed to help each other, he wrote, especially against the machinations of the "treacherous Dr. Kissinger." Several weeks later. Green wrote again, complaining about the administration's intent to sell weapons to Saudi Arabia. In a generalization about all Muslim peoples, Green stated, "Turks, Arabs or Pakistanis have a cult of conquest, male vanity and military glory, [and] arming them would only increase their appetite for more war." Greeks and Jews should work together, he thought, "to expose the arrogant barbarism of Turkey and Arab Muslims." As much as supporters of Ataturk had worked to distance Turkey from the Islamic Middle East, detractors lumped the coreligionists together, without hesitation.[9]

At the same time, Yale professor William A. Creasey wrote to Rosenthal criticizing Turkey as an untrustworthy ally. As evidence, he cited the fact that Ankara had refused to allow the United States to use its bases to resupply arms to Israel during the 1973 Yom Kippur War. Jews and Greeks, he wrote, had long been targets of Turkish hatred and atrocities.[10]

There was, however, growing concern within the Jewish community that the governments of Greece and Cyprus might not be adequately supportive of Israel. Jewish congressman Ed Koch sent a strong letter to Archbishop Iakovos, complaining that Cyprus had sponsored a UN resolution condemning Israel. He asked Iakovos to address this matter with Archbishop Makarios. "It would be a tragedy," he wrote, "if defending their own liberties, Cyprus or Israel sought to stifle each other's." After a lengthy interval, Iakovos finally responded, saying that he had been deeply pained by the UN resolution equating Zionism with racism and that he had asked the ambassadors of Greece and Cyprus to explain their support of the resolution.[11]

The government of Cyprus took note of this concern and issued a confidential statement to supporters in the United States, explaining its position. It had recognized the Palestine Liberation Organization (PLO) in order to outmaneuver Turkey and retain the support of Arab states in the region. It needed support from all sides, it stated. Cyprus had not changed its policy toward Israel and would not break off relations, as some Arab states had pressed it to do. Yet the government in Nicosia believed, as it always had, that Israel should abide by UN resolutions regarding the Occupied Territories.[12]

One of Congressman Rosenthal's constituents raised a different concern. He warned that supporting an arms embargo against Turkey might establish a dangerous precedent that could be used against Israel for taking similar actions. Additionally, he pointed out, Turkey was one of only a few Muslim countries with trading and commercial links to Israel. "And what of the Greeks," he asked, "where do they stand on Israel. Their foreign minister Dimitrios Bitsios recently declared in parliament that his country supports the Palestinian quest for independence and stands with the Arabs in this struggle." Rosenthal had to admit that the question of whether Greece or Turkey was more important to Israel was a complicated one.[13]

By mid-1975, Tel Aviv had concluded that the arms embargo and continuing impasse with Turkey were harmful to Israeli interests. The embassy warned Rosenthal "with much feeling" that his leadership of the pro-embargo forces had caused Ankara to threaten a break in diplomatic relations with Tel Aviv. The Israeli embassy's counselor reported that its diplomats had failed to convince Rosenthal or his colleague Sidney Yates (D-IL), but they had succeeded with others. At the same time, the Israeli ambassador invited Senator Eagleton to lunch to try to convince him of the harm being done.[14] Brademas and his colleagues had reason to worry that they might lose the votes of some of the twenty-one Jewish congressmen, most of whom had initially supported the embargo.[15]

The Israeli concern would outlast the Ford administration (as did the embargo issue itself). In July 1977 the Israeli Foreign Ministry provided information to Rosenthal that he had requested during his last visit to Tel Aviv. In the communication, Israeli officials urged Rosenthal, Brademas, and Sarbanes to speak to the Greek ambassador about the deterioration of Greece's official stance toward Israel. Greece had voted in the United Nations to allow the PLO to take a seat on the Economic and Social Council not as an observer but as a member state. The Cyprus representative had joined in the condemnation of Israeli policies in the Occupied Territories, citing "a number of analogies with Nazi crimes." The Cyprus foreign minister had stated that the ultimate solution must involve Israel's withdrawal from the Arab territories occupied after the Six-Day War, and the Palestinians' right of return must be respected. Cyprus had also granted the PLO diplomatic status in Nicosia.[16]

Rosenthal dutifully wrote to Ambassador Menelaos Alexandrakis of Greece to express his "profound disappointment" at the position taken by Athens. The Greeks had given recognition, he said, to "a terrorist body [PLO] whose primary mission is the violent and total destruction of a United Nations member state [Israel]."[17] The gap between Israel on the one hand and Greece and Cyprus on the other was gradually widening.

Although Jewish Americans might be conflicted over the Turkish embargo, the smaller Armenian American community had no such doubts. From the earliest days of the crisis, Armenian leaders and organizations had voiced strong support for Cyprus. Armenians had settled in large numbers in only a few urban centers—Los Angeles, Boston, and New York City—but they could exercise considerable influence in several congressional districts, especially when voter turnout was low. The Committee for the Defense of Cyprus, organized in the fall of 1974, was a political action group made up of concerned citizens of Greek and Armenian origin who endorsed and campaigned for those candidates that favored their respective causes. They helped plan a massive rally on Friday, September 6, at Los Angeles City Hall to protest both the Turkish invasion of Cyprus and the oppression of Christians in Turkey.[18]

In March 1975 the Armenian National Committee called for broad community support to commemorate the sixtieth anniversary of the Armenian genocide on April 24. To increase their numbers, they invited the local Greek community to participate as well. Likewise, Armenians would join in the celebration of Greek Independence Day on March 22. This would take the form of a day of protest against what they considered the pro-Turkish policy of the US government.[19]

On the anniversary of the Armenian genocide, Saloutos's Save Cyprus Council placed a large ad in the *Los Angeles Times* under the heading "After All, Gentlemen, Who Remembers the Armenians (Adolph Hitler)," suggesting that the failure to hold the Turks responsible for the earlier genocide had emboldened Hitler to treat the Jews in a similar manner. It also included a list of Turkish massacres of Armenians and Greeks over the previous century. To avoid similar violence in Cyprus, it urged citizens to tell their congressmen to maintain the embargo and warned that the Kissinger-Ford policy on Cyprus would backfire, as did their policy on Vietnam. "Have we forgotten," it asked, "that a president's violation of the law led to the tragedies of Vietnam and Watergate?"[20]

On Armenian commemoration day, Dr. Gregory Adamian, a leading member of Boston's Armenian community and the president of Bentley College, gave a public address in which he cited US Ambassador Henry Morgenthau's damning words from 1918: "They, the Turks, were lacking in what we may call the fundamentals of a civilized community. They have no alphabet, and no art or writing, no books, no poets, no art, and no architecture. They built no cities and established no lasting state. They know no law except the rule of might and they had practically no agriculture and no industrial organization. They were simply wild and marauding horsemen whose one conception of tribal success was to pounce upon people who were more civilized than themselves and plunder them." Although these sentiments from the First World War era ignored a mountain of contradictory evidence, many Greek and Armenian Americans in the mid-1970s would have nodded their heads in agreement.[21]

Far more serious was a series of deadly attacks carried out by Armenian terrorists against Turkish diplomats around the world. They began in 1973 and lasted for more than a decade. There were assassinations in Australia, Spain, France, and many other countries. In the United States alone, four diplomats were killed between 1973 and 1982. Each administration from Nixon to Reagan received its share of concerned letters from Ankara regarding the protection of Turkish officials and the hunt for terrorists.[22]

White House Counteroffensive

In the midst of marches and protests and a flood of constituent letters, the maneuvering between the White House and Congress continued. As a result of the earlier White House meetings, Senators Scott and Mansfield introduced a bill to lift the arms embargo in conjunction with a presidential waiver stating that progress was being made to resolve the Cyprus crisis. Opponents quickly challenged the move. Brademas warned Assistant Secretary of State Robert McCloskey that there would be a fight, although he hoped it could be avoided while Kissinger was "laboring on the delicate Middle East situation." Kissinger had agreed not to press for action in the Senate, but President Ford was unhappy with that arrangement. This led Brademas to observe that he understood why any president might be annoyed at seeing his internationally famous secretary of state get all the attention "and might feel it necessary from time to time to wrap [*sic*] his knuckles in order to let him know who was top man." But in this case, the arrangement stood. According to Lawrence Eagleburger, executive assistant to the secretary of state, and Undersecretary

Oval Office discussion regarding Turkey and Cyprus, March 21, 1975. President Ford (behind the desk) with (left to right surrounding the desk) Congressmen John Brademas, Paul Sarbanes, and Benjamin Rosenthal and staff members Brent Scowcroft, Jack Marsh, and Max Friedersdorf (back left). (Courtesy Ford Presidential Library)

Sisco, Kissinger truly wanted to avoid a confrontation with Brademas. However, administration officials were always probing for any weaknesses within the opposition. McCloskey wondered how committed Senator Eagleton was on this issue. Brademas reported that the senator was deeply committed and, in any case, was now too involved to withdraw.[23]

As the president prepared for another face-to-face meeting with the Gang of Four, Kissinger, who was not scheduled to attend, sent a memo reminding Ford that Brademas was prepared to fight any effort by the administration to push for Senate action on the Scott bill. Brademas reiterated this point after the president's opening remarks, saying, "We think Kissinger has focused more attention on turning Congress around than to turning Turkey around." Sarbanes noted that telling the Turks that the administration was trying to get the embargo reversed would only encourage Turkish intransigence. The four members of Congress had talked with Ambassador Macomber and read his cables from Ankara. He "has acted as an agent for Turkey," concluded Sarbanes. They knew the Turks held most of the cards, but they had to give up something—perhaps the city of Famagusta—to allow some movement toward a settlement.[24]

The discussion continued, and although much of it concerned what would happen in the Senate, Eagleton did not join in. They ended with an agreement to keep searching for a solution. Brademas had the last word for the lawmakers, telling the president, "Kissinger is a little impatient with us now." A few days later, Kissinger informed the president that he probably could not get Turkish concessions that Sarbanes would accept. He complained again about "the constant intervention by Congressmen in our ongoing negotiations when they don't know what is going on." For the secretary of state, this was the heart of the matter.[25]

The president refused to take the easy way out—that is, announcing that adequate progress had been made and issuing a waiver. He reminded his visitors of the difficult internal political situation in Turkey. Because all the important leaders were outside the government, compromise was next to impossible as elections approached. This seemed to be a constant refrain where Turkey was concerned.[26]

During the years 1973–1980, politics in Turkey was chaotic. There was a rising tide of violence in the major urban centers between extremists on the left and the right, and in successive elections, no political party gained a clear majority, allowing it to rule without entering into a coalition (both major parties rejected the idea of a grand coalition). The two largest parties were the Republican People's Party, headed by Bulent Ecevit, who had reshaped it as a social-democratic party, and the moderately conservative Justice Party, led by Suleyman Demirel (1924–2015). Neither party received enough support to govern without at least one of the minor parties. Of these, the two most important were the National Salvation Party, which was a conservative religious party, and the National Movement Party, which favored a strong state and an expansionist foreign policy. Ecevit and Demirel alternated back and forth, both of them leading weak coalitions throughout this period. They were unable to take strong positions on the Cyprus issue for fear of losing essential minority party support in parliament. From September 1974 through March 1975, Turkey had a caretaker government when neither Demirel nor Ecevit could establish a ruling coalition. The timing could not have been worse for Turkey's interests in Washington. It was at the end of this period that President Ford remarked on the fragile nature of conditions

Ecevit campaign poster touting Turkey's peaceful mission on Cyprus, circa late 1974 (English comments by an unknown source). The poem at the bottom right, which became a popular nationalistic song in the late 1970s, reads as follows: "My race is joyful in the Mediterranean now / My homeland extends beyond Mersin / We have connected the road from Kyrenia to Anatolia / My glorious army is victorious in Cyprus." (Courtesy AND Company, Istanbul)

in Turkey. This uncertainty and weakness at the center continued until the military finally took control in September 1980.[27]

Fortunately for President Ford, the US media, observing the deterioration in US-Turkish relations, began to shift its perspective in favor of administration policy. In a persuasive editorial, the *Chicago Tribune* stated that the force of law was on the side of Congress, but not the force of logic. The embargo would probably harm Greece more than it did Turkey, and Congress should listen to the president, wrote the editor, "before worse harm is done." Andrew Athens of the UHAC accused the *Tribune* of being brainwashed during its exclusive interview with Ford. Likewise, the *Baltimore Sun* ran a long article that was strongly critical of the Greek American lobby and its role in the Turkish arms embargo debate.[28]

Most of the communications received at the White House or by members of the Gang of Four from the letter-writing public, however, seemed to favor maintaining the arms cutoff. Brademas received many letters from his constituents as well as from the general public. Most of these writers seemed to have some connection with the Greek American community. For instance, Roxane Athanassiades of Atlanta, an American-born woman of Greek extraction, took issue with President Ford's recent statement about "ethnics" influencing US foreign policy. "In short Mr. Brademas, if the word 'ethnic' has become pejorative, I throw it back in their teeth. . . . We have . . . the same rights as the ethnic Anglo, of which, I presume, Mr. Ford considers himself a member." When the president extolled the glory of the Turks in his recent state-of-the-world speech, he showed a remarkable amnesia regarding history, she thought. "Do they teach American history in Grand Rapids, do you suppose?" she quipped. She urged Brademas not to be deterred until final victory had been achieved. "I submit that the only way this world can relax is to lie back in an easy chair with its feet on an Ottoman."[29] And a letter from an AHEPA chapter arrived at the White House in late April to remind the president that its authors would never tire of pointing out "the injustice your administration does by blindly supporting the Turkish side. Abraham Lincoln, certainly, would have handled this situation differently."[30]

AHEPA sent another delegation to the White House on April 25, 1975, that included Alex Demar, Ford's old friend from Grand Rapids. Kissinger told them that the administration needed flexibility to proceed, and he lamented the fact that their most effective card had already been played—"namely the cut-off of aid to Turkey." Another delegate, Mr. Plumides, complained that the president never spoke about Greece. "In your administration," he said, "Turkey is the star of US foreign policy." The president called on AHEPA members to support the Scott bill, which would remove the embargo; then he would make monthly progress reports to Congress. He refused to unilaterally issue a waiver, which in theory he could do, and which Sarbanes and Brademas had urged him to do. Ford thought that doing this would leave him too exposed, allowing Congress to "lower the boom" on him.[31]

Tempers were already fraying because of an inappropriate comment by Vice President Rockefeller. When a reporter asked Rockefeller how he would respond to the Turkish invasion using US arms if he were a Greek, the vice president said he would be thankful that, because of the blunders of the junta, the government in Athens had been overthrown. "I would be down on my knees praying to whoever they pray to." Lee Cusack, the Greek American mayor of Syracuse, New York, complained to Brademas that the vice president's remarks demeaned both Cusack's religion and his ancestry.[32]

Brademas chastised embargo supporters when he thought they had acted improperly. He became very angry, for example, when the United Hellenic American Congress published a circular containing information that its director had earlier agreed to omit. This concerned the February 1 meeting with Kissinger in which the secretary, apparently hoping to prove how active he had been in addressing the crisis, shared with Brademas and his colleagues some telegrams he had sent to Ankara. Brademas had been appalled to read the secretary's advice that Turkey should hold firm and that Ford and Kissinger "would bring Congress around." Now, the mention of these telegrams in the UHAC circular had breached the secretary's confidence, which would do nothing to improve relations with the administration.[33]

After much delay, the Scott bill finally came up for a vote in the Senate on May 19. It passed by the slim margin of 41–40, with more Republicans than Democrats in support of it (26–15). Senator Robert Byrd (D-WV), the majority whip, joined the Republicans to pass this measure, but he could not convince his own party members to do so. Byrd had originally supported the embargo, believing that the United States should register its disapproval of Turkey's illegal use of American arms on Cyprus, but he soon came to believe that the punitive action had become counterproductive.[34]

Now the battle moved to the other side of the Capitol, where Brademas had promised war. But it would be some time before the House took up the

President Ford, Turkish prime minister Suleyman Demirel, and Henry Kissinger at the US ambassador's residence, Brussels, Belgium, May 29, 1975. (Courtesy Ford Presidential Library)

measure. In fact, opponents delayed consideration of the Senate bill for more than two months, not sharing the administration's sense of urgency.

In the meantime, Ford and Kissinger traveled to Brussels for a NATO heads-of-state meeting. During this trip, the president planned to meet with Karamanlis and the newly elected Turkish prime minister, Suleyman Demirel. Karamanlis was in a strong position politically. His New Democracy Party had achieved an overwhelming victory in the elections the previous November, winning 219 of the 300 seats in parliament. In his meeting with Ford, the prime minister said that Greece was prepared to accept a geographic federation on Cyprus, as long as the territory assigned was proportional and refugees could return to their homes. When Kissinger mentioned that he had recently had a long talk in Ankara with his former student Bulent Ecevit, Karamanlis noted, "That's why we Greeks suspected you were pro-Turk." The secretary did not respond to the accusation. He went on with his general presentation, stating that there was no guarantee the Turks would negotiate a settlement even if aid were restored, but without it, nothing would be possible.[35] The Americans had briefly considered asking Karamanlis "to call off Brademas," but they worried that the congressman would leak that information. All they could do at present was stress to the Greek prime minister how difficult Congress was making their lives because of this issue.[36]

As the Scott bill slowly headed toward a vote in the House, the administration tried to avoid the war promised by Brademas. The House had become the focus of support for the embargo, and the White House organized several meetings in June with its leadership, trying to work out a compromise. Ford invited a mix of supporters and opponents of the embargo to the White House on June 19. The supporters still urged the president to use the waiver, but he demurred. Then Brademas and Sarbanes took a hard line, saying they could not back away from the embargo unless the Turks gave them something. It could not be forgotten that the Turks had carried out aggression against Cyprus. Lee Hamilton (D-IN), chair of the House Subcommittee on Europe and the Middle East, who opposed the embargo, indicated that the House lacked the votes to lift the ban without some reason for making the change.[37]

The group met again four days later and went through the same arguments back and forth. It was clear that everyone wanted a compromise, but neither side was willing to give enough to make it happen. Hamilton openly disagreed with Brademas and Sarbanes. He thought a carrot would work better than a stick with the Turks. Kissinger pointed out the danger of the crisis dragging on and undermining the conservative government of Karamanlis and opening the way for Andreas Papandreou (1919–1996) and the forces of the left to take power in Athens. Brademas reiterated that Congress had acted out of principle; this was not a "get Kissinger" action. (But in part, it surely was.) He warned again against forcing a vote in the House, saying, "I think we can defeat you." He wanted the president to use the waiver and get Turkish concessions by July; then they would see what could be done in the House. The president said he respected the congressmen's views and believed that he had done everything he could to work with them, but ultimately, he was disappointed. Finally, he commented, "I think we unfortunately have reached an impasse. I think the consequences will be tragic."[38]

On June 26 Ford hosted another meeting with a different group of congressmen; this time, none of the leading proponents of the embargo had been invited. The twelve congressmen represented the bipartisan House leadership and included Carl Albert, Tip O'Neill, Tom Morgan, and Robert Michel (minority whip). Most of them had opposed the embargo from the beginning or had since decided to vote for its repeal. Joining Ford and Kissinger were Brent Scowcroft, deputy assistant to the president for national security affairs, and Max Friedersdorf, assistant to the president for legislative affairs. Morgan revealed that he had received a letter from twenty-four Republican House members saying that they would change their position. Even Rosenthal was looking for a way out. "Brademas and Sarbanes will compromise if they see their support eroding." O'Neill said there were still insufficient votes to lift the embargo. Turkey had to make some concessions. Lee Hamilton and John Rhodes agreed that the administration could not yet count on the support of a majority, but the House was moving in the right direction.[39]

Rhodes had remained staunchly opposed to the embargo from the outset, despite experiencing considerable pressure from Greek American constituents to change his perspective. In replying to a May 1975 letter from six leaders of the Greek community in Phoenix, warning that he might face defeat in the next election, Rhodes remained obdurate. He responded to their "irrational diatribes" by reminding them that he had been in Congress for more than twenty-two years. "You can imagine the number of political threats I have received similar to the one you set forth in the last paragraph of your letter," he wrote. "They have never impressed me, and your latest effort is no more impressive. The only thing I know is that I must continue to do what I think is right and hope that the majority of my people will agree with me." In June the Republican Policy Committee decided to support a partial lifting of the embargo, confident that a majority of party members in the House would agree.[40]

On the Democratic side, Wayne Hays, the most outspokenly pro-Turkish representative, argued that the Greek lobby would not rest until the Turks had left Cyprus. The Greek dictatorship would have exterminated the Turks on Cyprus, he believed, if Turkey had not invaded. According to Hays's friends in the Turkish legislature, the Turks would probably wait until July 15 before taking action against US bases. The secretary of state observed that the Greek community in the United States was more radical than the Greek government.[41] Brademas and Sarbanes were trying to obtain more than what Athens would settle for. Dante Fascell (D-FL) and majority leader O'Neill were the only congressmen present who still supported the embargo, and Fascell argued that there had to be some flexibility to let people off the hook. He knew that AHEPA and other Greek American organizations were gearing up for a fight.[42]

The White House struggled to contain this threat. William J. Baroody Jr., Ford's liaison to ethnic groups, began telephoning leaders in the Greek American community to explain the administration's position. The president held two congressional breakfasts, where he tried to enlist support for the Scott bill. By July 15, the president was confident that he had the votes to ensure its passage. In a meeting with the president, Tom Pappas, a wealthy Greek American business magnate, political fixer, and friend of the CIA (according to journalist Tim Weiner), urged the president to avoid a vote, but Ford said he could not. He was obviously sensing that victory was within reach. A week later, John Reagan "Tex" McCrary, another Republican insider and major donor, commented to Jack Marsh, counselor to the president, "Your team is a tough one." The administration had shifted the vote of a friend of his in the House. McCrary urged the president to be magnanimous in victory because a victory for the Turks might be a loss for the president. He recalled the William Safire quip: "Kissinger is the first Secretary of State under whom two presidents have served." Ford, he thought, should reach out to Greece, whatever the outcome in the House.[43]

That same day, however, Marsh reported to the president that there had been some slippage, and Hamilton agreed that they were in trouble on the floor. Ford's last chance to pick up support would be at the congressional breakfast the following morning, one day before the long-awaited vote. In response to congressmen who complained that the president continued to veto measures they sent to him, Marsh counseled Ford to emphasize that this was a case of national security.[44]

The president might have gone too far in indicating that even the Greek government favored lifting the embargo. When the Greek ambassador heard this from several breakfast attendees, he issued a corrective that stated in part, "if such representations were made, they are absolutely erroneous and contrary to the well-known views of the Greek government."[45] Members of the House reported tremendous efforts by the Greek lobby, and Marsh himself noticed these lobbyists at work on the Hill. All this activity coincided with the first anniversary of the Turkish invasion of Cyprus. Greek American organizations had chosen to commemorate the "Day of Infamy," as they called it, and the United Hellenic American Congress announced a list of activities in Washington. These included a Congress appreciation rally on the west steps of the Capitol for approximately thirty senators and congressmen, a solemn church service with Archbishop Iakovos officiating, and a candlelight march to the Lincoln Memorial.[46]

President Ford lobbying a congressional breakfast group at the White House prior to the embargo vote, July 17, 1975. (Courtesy Ford Presidential Library)

AHEPA called on all its chapters to arrange suitable commemorations. Knowing that the House vote was only a few days away, leaders of AHEPA and UHAC urged each chapter to send representatives to Washington to lobby against the Scott bill. The executive committee of the Minnesota Friends of Cyprus decided to send two delegates to the nation's capital to participate in the memorial service on Sunday, July 20, and then to lobby Minnesota's congressmen, focusing on Republicans William Frenzel and Thomas Hagedorn and their Democratic colleagues Donald Fraser, James Oberstar, and Joseph Karth. The delegates received specific guidelines for lobbying at the Capitol. Each delegate should demand to see the congressman himself unless he was "a known supporter of our cause." They were instructed to insist on a commitment against the resumption of military aid or sales to Turkey. They were told to mention that this was an issue of "grave importance to Greek-Americans and that they are not likely to forget his position on this issue in the future." Finally, they should ask the congressman what message they should take back to his district. "Avoid becoming angry," they were advised, "and do not make any threats." They were directed to communicate the results of their visits by telephone to the organizers before leaving Washington.[47]

Minnesota Friends of Cyprus. Left to right: Professor Clarke Chambers, Mary Mantis, Father Anthony Coniaris, Congressman Donald Fraser, Father Parry Paraschou, Professor Kim Munholland. (Courtesy Immigration History Research Center)

The Minnesota lobbyists clearly made an impact on James Oberstar of the Eighth District. He sent a rather embarrassed note to the president the day after the vote, saying that although he appreciated the federal decision to fund the new water filtration plant at Duluth in his district, he had to vote his conscience. Having made a commitment to his Greek American constituents, Oberstar had joined the majority in a stunning rejection of the Scott bill by the narrow margin of 206 to 223 (the Republican vote was 103 to 39; the Democratic, 103 to 184).[48]

When it appeared likely that Donald Fraser would vote to lift the embargo, his old friend Homer Mantis, who was active in the Minnesota Friends of Cyprus, had written him a pained letter. Mantis reminisced about their earlier struggles against the war in Vietnam and the junta in Athens. "I am at a loss to understand," he confided, "your present position." If Congress lost this battle, where the moral issue was clear, then it might as well accept Nixon's view of the limited congressional role in foreign policy. If Fraser cast his vote in support of the Scott bill, Mantis would never be able to defend him to his friends in the Greek American community.[49] In spite of the pressure, Fraser voted to lift the embargo. He explained his reasons for doing so in a convoluted manner that left his friends confused and angry. Mary Mantis, longtime president of the MFC, drafted a strong letter (never sent) to Leon Schull, executive director of Americans for Democratic Action, criticizing Fraser's behavior.[50]

Mary Mantis was a force in the Twin Cities in support of Cyprus. She and members of her committee pressed editors of local papers to seek balance in their coverage of the Cyprus issue. In April she was one of only a handful of American women to go to Cyprus and participate in the Peace Walk organized by the Greek Cypriot community. A Palestinian representative spoke, and well-known Greek actress Melina Mercouri (whom President Ford had referred to as that "gal") led demonstrators through the streets of Nicosia. At a reception in Limassol, Mantis explained that her group lobbied Congress on issues related to the island nation. Activities of groups like the MFC were critical, she noted, to those in Congress who were opposing the administration's efforts to lift the embargo. As recent scholars have indicated, however, the number of Greek Americans or Armenian Americans in a particular district was less important than politicians' perception that even a small number of well-organized and vocal constituents could affect the outcome of elections.[51]

As the House vote approached, Brademas and his colleagues had left nothing to chance. His staff drew up a list of likely questions and provided detailed responses about the embargo and the administration's policies. Brademas himself compiled a long checklist of what needed to be done.[52] One item of special interest was a reminder for Brademas to call Charlie Rangel "and ask him to send a letter to all members of the House pointing out . . . the Turkish heroin aggression against a generation." This suggested that the drug issue might still be useful as leverage, especially with big-city Democrats, who could provide crucial votes to maintain the embargo.[53]

Retired army general James A. Van Fleet had come to the defense of the embargo, one of the few military men to do so. He had testified in Congress and sent a letter to House members in mid-July arguing that Greece, not Turkey, was "the strategic key to the Eastern Mediterranean" and of greater strategic importance to the United States and NATO. Retired admiral E. R. Zumwalt, who had opposed the administration's détente policy, seconded Van Fleet's conclusion about the relative importance of Greece and Turkey.[54]

Cartoon in the *Washington Star* critical of US policy toward Cyprus, summer 1975. (©2019 Patrick Oliphant/Artists Rights Society, New York)

Two foreign policy experts, George Ball and Cyrus Vance, had also testified before the House International Relations Committee, supporting the embargo. They argued that lifting it would send the wrong message to other nations that had acquired American arms under similar restrictions.[55]

There was, of course, fallout from all these pro-embargo activities. Brademas received letters critical of his actions after the vote. One accused the congressman of acting in the interests of the Greek American minority. "Please," the constituent wrote, "look at this from the point of what's good for America. Most of your constituents are AMERICANS FIRST and people of national origin second." Another began, "You ought to be ashamed of yourself for putting your personal feelings against the national security of our country." It went on to mention the threatened loss of bases in Turkey and the impact on NATO. "All you could think of was . . . your beloved Greece." Congressional newcomer Paul Tsongas received his share of letters as well. One medical doctor chastised him for his recent vote against arms for Turkey, pointing out that "American foreign policy, having been held in fiefdom by the pro-Israel lobby for so long now has another master in the pro-Greece group."

These were the kind of arguments that Brademas and the other Greek American representatives had worked so hard to discourage. They had urged non-Greeks such as Rosenthal, Eagleton, and others to take leadership positions in the struggle and always to emphasize the legal principles involved.[56]

This was an issue, however, that never faded. Just after the Senate vote in May, Senator Barry Goldwater (R-AZ), who supported the Scott bill, wrote a letter to a Greek American constituent in Phoenix explaining his vote. He wrote in part, "Is America more important to us or is the country of origin of our fathers and grandfathers more important, and, frankly, I think America should be considered supreme." George Kokalis, a philanthropist and entrepreneur, must have shared the senator's reply with Professor Saloutos, whose Save Cyprus Council was actively working against the Scott bill in Southern California.[57]

Saloutos was very concerned about the line of argument contained in the letters to Brademas and Kokalis. He wrote in August to an activist friend in New York City complaining about a letter from Andrew Athens of the UHAC, who said the recent vote in the House was a vote for the benefit of Hellenism. Saloutos took exception to this, arguing, "We have to think in terms of what serves the best interests of the United States," otherwise "we will be criticized by the American public for playing the kind of ethnic politics that Kissinger has been accusing the Greek-Americans of playing." Athens learned of this complaint and wrote directly to Saloutos, agreeing that "the problem involving Cyprus is an American problem."[58]

Saloutos went on to write a short piece entitled "Ethnic Politics: The American Hellenic Model," refuting the charge that a minority group like the Greek Americans enjoyed the kind of influence claimed by the Ford administration. Rather, leaders of the embargo movement appealed to broader issues, such as the use and abuse of executive power in foreign and domestic affairs, to gain enough support in Congress to thwart the administration. Second-generation Greek Americans, he explained, understood better than their parents how the political process worked, how to frame issues, and what techniques and methods to apply.[59]

Determined to Try Again

Several days after the defeat in the House, President Ford and Secretary of State Kissinger set off for Finland to attend the signing of the Helsinki Accords at the Conference on Security and Cooperation in Europe. Ford had already been criticized by eastern European groups in the United States led by a number of prominent individuals, including Soviet émigré writer Aleksandr Solzhenitsyn. These groups claimed that the Helsinki treaties represented a surrender to Soviet domination of eastern and central Europe.

Ford had also arranged separate meetings with the Greek and Turkish prime ministers, but he arrived with diminished credibility after his failed struggle with the House of Representatives. In the meeting with Karamanlis on July 30, Ford complained of actions taken by the Greek embassy in Washington to oppose administration policy. He took exception to the letter sent to members of the House refuting the administration's claim of Greek support for lifting the embargo. (Kissinger denied that the administration had ever made such a statement.) On the day of the crucial vote, the House galleries had been full of staff from the Greek embassy, and Ford believed the embassy had acted improperly. If this continued, the "American people will want to blame someone," he said.[60] The Americans also "complained about the activities of the Greek-American community, not known for its dispassionate analysis." According to the president, they had unrealistic expectations about what could be gained from Turkey. Members of his administration, he said in exasperation, had spent as much time on the Cyprus issue as they had on the entire Middle East.[61]

If Ford and Kissinger were hoping that the Greek government would weigh in on their side with the Greek Americans, they came away emptyhanded. Opponents of the embargo believed that as long as the embargo was in place, neither Greece nor the Greek Cypriots would negotiate seriously for a compromise with the Turkish Cypriots.

In a separate meeting with Foreign Minister Bitsios, Kissinger reiterated the complaints against the Greek American opposition. They had undermined his prestige and therefore his ability to conduct delicate negotiations, he said. Brademas would fail, he predicted; he had done "a stupid thing" by opposing the Scott bill.[62]

The day after the defeat of the Scott bill in the House, Turkey carried out its threat to close twenty-seven US installations, many of which contained sensitive listening posts aimed at the neighboring Soviet Union. To reassure Turkey that the administration was actively seeking a resolution of the crisis, Ford immediately had the defeated bill reintroduced in the Senate, where it narrowly passed 47–46 on July 31, the day after his meeting with Karamanlis. The president hoped it would receive speedy attention in the House, but due to parliamentary delays by opponents, the bill would not be considered until after the long summer recess.

Administration supporters in the Senate, led by Mansfield and Scott, had urged the president not to reintroduce the bill. They were not certain it would pass, and a defeat would strike a heavy blow to Ford's prestige abroad. But the president, working through Marsh, had insisted, and he was proved right.[63]

Despite his busy schedule at Helsinki, the president found time to send a thank-you letter to key supporters in the upper chamber, among them Senator Byrd. Ford praised the majority whip's strong support for the bill to lift the embargo. A few days later, Kissinger also wrote to Byrd, praising the senator's role in keeping a large number of senators on the floor for the late-night vote.[64]

In early September, both sides of the issue began to plan for another campaign in the House that might determine the fate of the embargo. Brademas and Sarbanes were busy meeting with representatives of Greece, Turkey, and the United Kingdom. They cautioned members of the Greek finance minister's delegation to remember that when they met with representatives of the State Department, they would be talking with their adversaries. They must avoid any linkage between the financial assistance they were seeking and the Turkish aid issue.[65]

One week later, the two congressmen met with a delegation of Turkish businessmen. The two Americans criticized Kissinger for being more interested in turning Congress around than in getting Turkey to negotiate. Despite what the visitors might think, Brademas and Sarbanes assured them that the vote in Congress was based on the principles of US foreign policy and the law, not on ethnic politics. They had won on the embargo issue because of Watergate, which had made both houses of Congress much more concerned with upholding the law. The Turkish representatives argued that the Greeks, too, had infiltrated Cyprus with US arms, but no ban had been imposed on them. They also observed that the Demirel government would fall if it compromised on Cyprus.[66]

Differences remained over three points. First, the Turkish visitors saw both the July 20 and the August 14 offensives as defensive actions warranted by events on Cyprus. Second, they believed that good relations between Turkey and the United States were more important than continuing the embargo. And third, they thought that too much emphasis had been placed on making progress in Cyprus before the embargo could be lifted. Progress would come, they assured the congressmen, once Demirel had strengthened his position.[67]

President Ford and Archbishop Makarios at the Helsinki conference, July 30, 1975. (Courtesy Ford Presidential Library)

Two days later, the congressmen met with Maeze Fort from the Cyprus desk at the British embassy. The British official believed that the problem had to be resolved soon, lest Turkey take more drastic action. The Turks were unreasonable and intransigent, and Kissinger would not compromise with Congress. Thus, London had concluded that it was up to Congress to find a way out of the crisis.[68]

These were interesting forays into the world of diplomacy. Neither Brademas nor Sarbanes served on the House Foreign Affairs Committee, but they had clearly attracted the interest and attention of the relevant foreign governments. Since the crisis began, they had taken it upon themselves to liaise with leaders and representatives of Turkey, Greece, Cyprus, and the United Kingdom. As early as the end of July 1974, Brademas had written to Prime Minister Karamanlis on behalf of the five Greek American congressmen, sharing their resolution calling for a halt to military and economic assistance to Turkey. He had assured the prime minister that many congressmen disagreed with the US policy on Cyprus and would make every effort to change it. Some of the results of this close relationship were apparent in the tense discus-

Left to right: Greek prime minister Constantine Karamanlis, President Ford, Secretary of State Kissinger, and Greek foreign minister Dimitrios Bitsios at Helsinki, July 31, 1975. (Courtesy Ford Presidential Library)

sions in Helsinki between Ford and Karamanlis. This amateur policymaking, as Kissinger would have described it, went against all the secretary's Metternichian principles regarding how foreign policy should be conducted.[69]

The embargo's proponents did not neglect the domestic front as the House moved closer to another vote. Over the ten days between September 8 and 18, they held at least four meetings to plan strategy and tactics for the upcoming battle. Brademas, Sarbanes, Eagleton's aide Brian Atwood, and staff from the House Foreign Affairs Committee met to discuss a particularly challenging article in the *Baltimore Sun* that raised some serious questions about the lobbying efforts of the Greek American community. In particular, it took aim at Eugene Rossides and his autocratic control of the American Hellenic Institute. "His Turkophobia is manic and irrational," it reported, "and he does not tame it for the quiet offices of the Hill. He regularly compares Turkish actions on Cyprus to what the Nazis did to the Jews." Brademas and Sarbanes met with Rossides, and it was decided that the AHI chief should respond to the article. Atwood reported on Senator Eagleton's recent trip to Greece, but most of the meeting was devoted to the Senate bill

(S 2230). The Speaker of the House had yet to decide which committee it should be referred to. Sarbanes and Brademas wanted to make sure the bill went to the Foreign Affairs Committee, which had many supporters of the embargo. They worried about the possibility of some "fast action" to avoid standard procedures and bring the bill to the floor sooner than expected.[70]

They were right to be concerned, for the administration was pressing hard for action. At the suggestion of John Rhodes, President Ford spoke with Speaker Carl Albert and Doc Morgan about having the Rules Committee act quickly to assign a date for a floor debate even before the Speaker had assigned the bill to a committee. (The administration considered the Rules Committee a friendlier body than the Foreign Affairs Committee.) Ray Madden (D-IN), chair of the Rules Committee, would not accede to this request. Madden, who supported the embargo, wanted no part in bypassing the Foreign Affairs Committee. He reminded Morgan that regular procedure must be followed, and he opposed any attempt "to take a short cut through the Rules Committee."[71]

Atwood reported that Secretary Kissinger would stay out of lobbying efforts this time, likely because of the antagonism he aroused among many members of Congress. The Pentagon would take the lead, tying the defense of Israel to the Turkish bases. This would press the Jewish congressmen to change their position.[72] But in a meeting on September 11, Dante Fascell, who had served many years on the House Foreign Affairs Committee, said they needed to offer something more constructive. Brademas suggested introducing an amendment that would allow Turkey to receive weapons purchased before the embargo's implementation if it met some particular requirement, such as allowing refugees to return or withdrawing a significant number of troops. Their aides would work on the exact language.[73]

On September 18 Sarbanes and Brademas met with freshman congressmen Paul Tsongas (D-MA), Eddie Beard (D-RI), Marty Russo (D-IL), and Norman Mineta (D-CA) to discuss tactics for the upcoming fight on the Turkish aid issue. Mineta reported that David Taylor, assistant secretary of the air force, had been arguing that the Turkish bases were vital to US security interests. Brademas suggested that the newcomers talk with Speaker Albert, majority leader O'Neill, and majority whip John McFall about postponing debate on the Turkish arms bill until after the October election in Turkey, when presumably the government in Ankara would be in a better position to negotiate. In the meantime, they would draw up lists for each of the freshman whips and draft a general letter to be sent to all members of the House. Finally, they would inform AHI and California state senator Nick Petris, who had considerable influence on the West Coast, what their strategy would be in the House.[74]

On the same day, there was discussion about participating in an NBC documentary being organized by Gene Diamond of the Free Cyprus Coalition to counter the bad publicity surrounding the Greek lobby. The documentary would stress that the lobby was composed of citizens conveying their views on an issue of importance to them and exercising a right available to all Americans.[75]

Opponents in the House were not idle. For some time, key representatives such as Clement Zablocki (D-WI), the second ranking member on the International Relations Committee, had been pointing out that Turkey was not the only recipient nation violating US law. At a House hearing in October 1974, he had reminded members that, "when in 1967, Israel invaded the territory of Egypt and Jordan . . . we did not cut off our military sales or other relations with Israel." He was quick to acknowledge that such aid was right and served the interest of justice and peace. And one year later, as the vote on a partial lifting of the embargo approached, he pointed out to one correspondent that Greece, too, had violated the international agreement by stationing more troops on Cyprus than allowed and by transferring weapons from its US inventory to the island.[76]

Lee Hamilton, who took the lead in welding together a majority on the committee to modify the embargo, joined with Edward Biester (R-PA) in July 1975 to send a letter to colleagues stating, "Both Turkey and Greece may have, at times, violated agreements concerning the uses and transfer of US military equipment." Two months later, he and Charles Whalen (R-OH) reiterated this point and noted that several Arab states and Israel had taken similar actions.[77]

In the September 17 hearing on the partial lifting of the embargo, Congressman Hays, always a strong supporter of Turkey and chair of the important House Administration Committee, stated that in 1967, "Israel violated the same law, used exclusively American weapons, and made a preemptive strike and undertook an invasion." And no one had introduced a resolution to cut off aid to Israel. Quickly affirming his support for Israel, Hays added, "If they had, I would have voted against it." One week later, at a meeting with Republican leaders, President Ford assured them that the Jewish community had promised to help the administration, knowing that Israeli leaders were unhappy with the embargo.[78]

To sum up the embargo opponents' arguments: (1) Turkey had been singled out for a variety of reasons that were not unique to that country. (2) The embargo had proved ineffective. (3) It should be relaxed to encourage Ankara to be more flexible in Cyprus negotiations.[79]

The White House kept pressing for action. Two days after their visit to the Hill, President Ford met with the same delegation of Turkish businessmen. His message would have sounded much more supportive to them and no doubt undermined any good Brademas and his colleagues had achieved. Ford told them that, from the beginning, Congress had been wrong on this issue. The great majority of the American people did not agree with Congress, he told them, and "we know that we can't expect movement in the negotiations [on Cyprus] until the embargo is ended." Ford emphasized, however, that once the embargo was lifted, there would have to be progress toward a settlement. The head of the delegation promised that they would take his words home to their government and the Turkish people.[80]

Although Kissinger had decided not to lobby actively, he clearly found it difficult to stay in the background. During a meeting in New York City with the Greek foreign minister, the secretary of state twice indicated that the administration did not want Greek help on the embargo vote, which must have left Bitsios with exactly the opposite impression. He assured Kissinger that the embassy would remain neutral this time.[81]

In Washington, Kissinger participated in a White House meeting with bipartisan House leadership, but Ford, Rockefeller, and Scowcroft did all the talking for the administration. Tip O'Neill asked the president to consider what would happen if he lost the vote in the House. "Wouldn't it be better to hold off for thirty days?" asked the majority leader. But Ford insisted that the vote must go ahead. The administration would do everything it could to ensure success. "Our national security is very much involved in this issue," the president reminded them.[82]

The Veterans of Foreign Wars, meeting at its annual convention, resolved that the bases in Turkey were vital to US security and that it was necessary "to reverse this congressional blunder." NATO secretary-general Joseph Luns also appeared on the Hill to explain that the embargo was having a generally negative impact on the alliance.[83] Earlier, Luns had met with President Ford and Secretary of State Kissinger to explain that the embargo was "becoming an obsession" to their allies. They were concerned that it was weakening NATO and wondered whether similar measures might be taken against them if they displeased Congress in some way. Luns also remarked that Turkish officials had been hinting that NATO installations in Turkey might suffer the same fate as American facilities if the embargo were not lifted soon. Kissinger emphasized that the more the secretary-general could talk on the Hill, the better it would be.[84]

The president had been anxiously awaiting the House vote since the bill's narrow defeat in July. He had received assurances from the Republican leadership that the whip check showed substantially more support than in earlier tallies. As they all knew, success depended on obtaining a large majority of the votes from members of the president's own party.[85]

John Rhodes had consistently criticized House action to withhold arms from Turkey. In a radio address to his constituents, he stated, "This is a complex foreign policy issue into which Congress had no business entering." Congress, he said, was usurping the place of the secretary of state, allowing itself to act emotionally "when deciding a purely *strategic issue.*"[86]

Senator Robert Griffin (R-MI), the minority whip, held similar views. In a letter to constituents prepared by his chief of staff Robert Turner, Griffin argued that the president was charged by the Constitution with the execution of foreign policy, and Congress "must allow him the necessary flexibility to negotiate with the parties involved." In editing the letter, Griffin praised that "excellent" point but suggested that Turner "soften a bit the pitch on Executive *control* of foreign policy." He explained that, "after Nixon and being a senator, I can't come down too hard."[87]

Gradually, Rhodes and the Republican leadership managed to shift doubtful caucus members, but not without a struggle. In late July, for example, Congressman Charles Mosher (R-OH) admitted to the minority leader how difficult the decision would be. "I just need more time to ponder all the evidence and arguments," he wrote, "and to squirm." Mosher finally decided to vote for the partial lifting of the embargo, along with a large majority of his Republican colleagues.[88]

The day before the House vote, Doc Morgan, chair of the newly renamed Committee on International Relations, issued a press release criticizing attempts to delay the vote by introducing a proposal that would change nothing. "The embargo has not worked," he argued. "If anything it has made things worse." In the face of so much determined resistance, the pro-embargo

Cartoon in the *Washington Star*, October 1975, following a partial lifting of the embargo. (©2019 Patrick Oliphant/Artists Rights Society, New York)

forces could stall no longer.[89] Morgan, like other long-serving committee chairs, had had enough of both bumptious Watergate freshmen and more experienced members who should have known better than to challenge his authority. According to one assessment, Morgan had shown little interest in international relations. "He considered the committee a subordinate partner to the executive branch, a view reinforced by his limited work ethic." Younger committee members assumed subcommittee chairmanships and hired new staff consultants, many from the peace movement. These developments weakened Morgan's power. Frustrated, he would finally retire in 1977 after thirty-two years in the House.[90]

The drama finally reached a climax on October 2 when the House voted 237–176 to partially lift the embargo. The minority Republicans supplied only one less vote in favor (118) than the Democrats (119). At last the administration could savor a victory. US military grant aid would remain suspended, but Turkey could access materiel in the pipeline before the cutoff and could make new purchases of US arms as well. This news, it was hoped, would warm relations with Ankara.[91]

A number of factors likely contributed to this victory. The harm attributed to the embargo had become more apparent, and the administration and the media had spread that message effectively. It also helped, no doubt, that this was only a partial lifting of the embargo, making it easier for congressmen to justify their support. Finally, the controversy over opium, which had troubled so many Americans, was finally nearing resolution.

President Ford immediately sent letters to Karamanlis and Demirel. To the Greek prime minister, he reiterated his belief that a partial lifting of the embargo would contribute to progress in the negotiations on Cyprus. To the Turkish leader, he remarked on the need for "early and visible movement toward a Cyprus settlement" and the reactivation of US military facilities in his country. Ambassador Macomber, who had been in Washington to lobby on the Hill, would now be returning to Ankara to talk with Demirel about rebuilding and revitalizing the US-Turkey relationship.[92]

President Ford could take considerable pride in this victory, which had seemed to be in question right up to the day of the vote in the House. Against the views of his advisers, he had insisted on immediately reintroducing the defeated bill in the Senate. He had also resisted attempts to postpone the House vote in September. The administration had organized as never before, opposing many skilled parliamentarians on the Hill. Now, the president could reasonably believe that the pendulum had shifted in his direction and that it would only be a matter of time before Congress lifted the embargo entirely. Ford had demonstrated considerable ability in delicate negotiations, thereby strengthening his own position.[93]

Opium Issue Resolved

Although the Cyprus crisis and the resulting arms embargo had become front-page news, and American diplomats had shifted their full attention to resolving these unexpected issues, the opium question lingered. After being recalled to Washington, Ambassador Macomber had returned to Ankara only a few days before the coup d'etat in Nicosia, with a directive to enter negotiations with the Turkish government on the opium issue. Cyprus had overshadowed this earlier concern.[94] Nevertheless, the battle against the opium poppy provided a companion argument for those who wanted to punish Ankara for its two-stage invasion of Cyprus in July and August 1974. It became a convenient weapon for those who wanted to present Turkey in the worst possible light.

Many anti-Turkish cartoons, articles, and broadsides presented the opium issue as another symbol of Turkish perfidy. Typical of this genre was a broadside from the files of the Minnesota Friends of Cyprus in the Twin Cities. One side showed a bloody dagger (made in the USA) plunged into the heart of Cyprus. In addition to the message about freeing Cyprus were the following cautionary words:

> American Taxpayers
> Do you know where your money goes?
> It goes to Turkish opium growers, who
> Turn your children into junkies.
> [The reverse side provided more detail:]
> SAVE OUR CHILDREN FROM DRUGS
> 90% of heroin into the U.S. originates in Turkey
> U.S. aid to Turkey brings in heroin in return
> Save your children from this scourge
> Help destroy Turkey's poppy fields
> Write your congressman to stop all aid to Turkey now!
> Napalm bombs on civilians in Cyprus, and
> Now heroin for America's children
> Halt heroin. Write your congressman now—
> No aid for Turkey![95]

The Ford administration, hastily inaugurated on August 9, 1974, after President Nixon's reluctant resignation, had shown ongoing concern over the Senate (Mondale) and House (Wolff) resolutions regarding opium poppies. Although differing in their language, both called for the suspension of all US aid should Turkey not take effective steps to control opium smuggling. The new administration was divided over the appropriate response. Some agencies, including the Office of Management and Budget, the Domestic Council, the Treasury, and the Agency for International Development, favored a hard line, imposing sanctions against Turkey at the outset of negotiations. This stance would find favor in Congress and show US determination to halt the narcotics traffic. Other agencies worried that the US-Turkish security

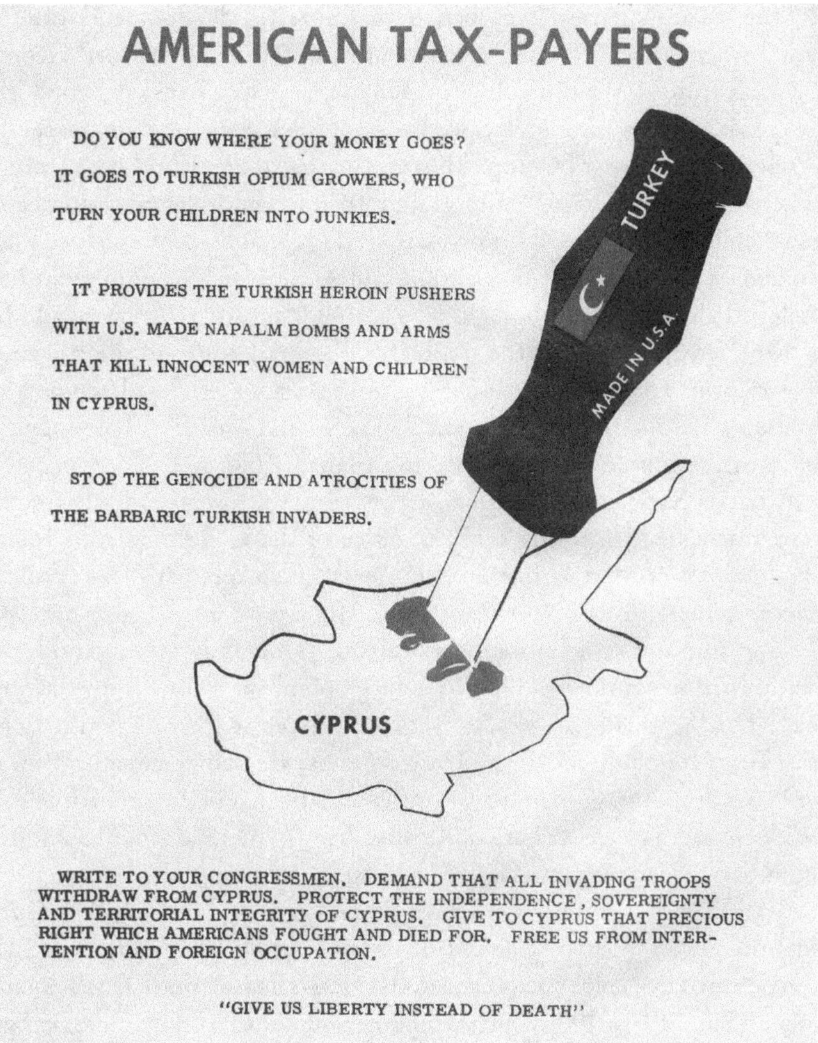

Broadside warning "American Tax-Payers" of the dual threat from Turkey. (Courtesy Immigration History Research Center)

relationship could be irreparably harmed by such steps. The State Department, the Department of Defense, the CIA, and the US Information Agency supported a more moderate approach that involved entering into negotiations and advising Turkey of likely future sanctions, as required by the Foreign Assistance Act, should adequate steps not be taken.[96]

The Turkish government had been following developments carefully. Early in September 1974 the foreign minister told Ambassador Macomber that aside from all the difficulties related to Cyprus, he had some good news: the Ecevit government had decided to adopt the straw processing method for 100 percent of its poppy crop. This meant that there would be no need to incise the plant to obtain opium gum; rather, the entire plant would be harvested and shipped abroad for extraction of the narcotic. This method made it much easier to control production and to keep opium gum from being smuggled abroad to be processed into heroin. And soon Turkey would have its own factory to process the poppies.[97] The Ford administration immediately informed key congressional committees and interested senators and representatives of this positive development. But would it be enough "to blunt further initiatives on the Hill to penalize Turkey?"[98]

Charles Rangel was skeptical. At his request, several officials from the Department of Agriculture and the office of the Coordinator for International Narcotics Matters in the State Department met with him to discuss the straw method of opium extraction. They tried to reassure him, even showing him a film of a straw processing plant, that this method could greatly enhance Turkey's ability to reduce opium smuggling from the poppy fields. During this meeting, Rangel again expressed his determination to keep Turkish opium out of the United States. He had personally witnessed too many deaths and too much sorrow caused by heroin. His constituents, he said, were more concerned about Turkish heroin than Cuban missiles (or, he might have added, the invasion of Cyprus).[99]

Rangel had introduced his own amendment to cut off aid to Turkey until the government cooperated in controlling opium production. It had been defeated in a voice vote. Instead, the House had supported the Rosenthal amendment, 201 to 190, which would cut off aid to Turkey unless progress were made on settling the Cyprus issue. Although the "opium firsters" could not muster majority support for their tough position, they continued to exercise considerable influence in the ongoing debate over Turkey. Their votes would prove indispensable to the veto-proof majority in the House of Representatives.[100]

In the late fall of 1974 the Turkish government was not entirely convinced that the threatened cutoff of US aid was not being driven by the opium issue rather than by its actions on Cyprus. According to the Turkish foreign minister, at a recent breakfast in London hosted by the Turkish ambassador for visiting parliamentary delegations, the US representatives had seemed far more worried about poppies than about Cyprus. The US political counselor in Ankara tried to convince Turkish officials that the invasion of Cyprus would be the primary cause of any aid cutoff. But even years later, in 1993, Ecevit told a television audience that he believed the embargo had been imposed because of his government's "decision to lift the opium ban, not its intervention in Cyprus."[101]

Although the Turkish government overestimated the significance of opium on Capitol Hill, it was not as insignificant as one official at the State Department claimed when he wrote, "Adoption of the Rosenthal amendment was not [repeat] not influenced by [the] narcotics issue." But of course, it was. Rosenthal and Brademas and their House colleagues had put together a coalition, and one bloc of votes came from representatives such as Rangel and Wolff, who were not yet convinced that Turkish poppies were no longer a threat to their constituents.[102]

Propaganda regarding Turkey and heroin continued into the new year. On Greek Independence Day, March 22, 1975, the *Hellenic-American Reporter,* published in Redondo Beach, California, ran a series of cartoons on its front page lampooning Kissinger and Ecevit and their supposed complicity in flooding America with heroin. One shows the Turkish prime minister handing the secretary of state an opium pipe in exchange for US arms. The caption reads: "Exported by Etsevit [*sic*] and Kissinger Corporation for Instant Death to Our American Boys and Girls." In another cartoon, Kissinger rests on a map of Cyprus, pipe in hand, and the caption reads: "New Land for Poppies."[103]

One group, Parents Concerned with Drug Abuse, placed an advertisement in the *New York Times* showing a hypodermic needle plunged into a map of the United States and bold letters announcing: "FROM TURKEY WITH . . . LOVE . . . HEROIN FOR OUR CHILDREN." It called on citizens to urge their congressmen to suspend aid to Turkey until that country restored the ban on poppy cultivation. One cartoon by Patrick Oliphant showed President Ford cradling a diminutive Turkish pasha who was brandishing an oversized heroin needle in one hand and a bloody sword labeled "Cyprus" in the other (see chapter 3).[104]

Rangel expressed his concern in a letter to the president in May 1975, charging that Turkey had not imposed effective controls on opium and that he would urge the House to continue to withhold aid to Ankara until it did

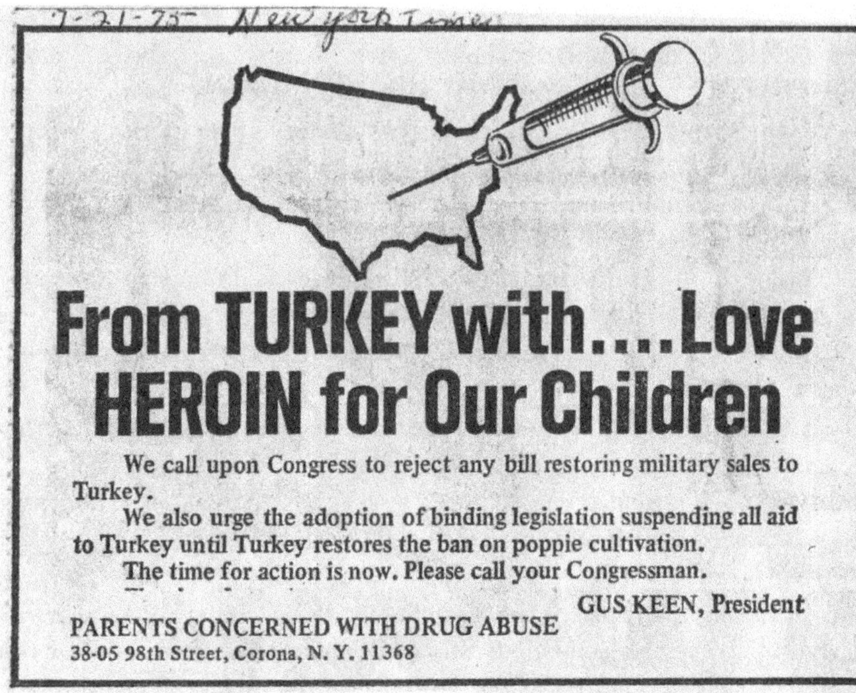

Notice placed in the *New York Times,* July 21, 1975, warning of drugs coming from Turkey. (Courtesy Immigration History Research Center)

so. He compared the drug threat to American youth with the danger faced by the crew of the *Mayaguez,* whom the administration had recently rescued with much fanfare. He encouraged the president to stay strong in dealing with the narcotics threat as well.[105]

Opponents of Turkey continued to manipulate the heroin issue, even when it seemed well on its way toward resolution. Admiral E. R. Zumwalt Jr., retired chief of naval operations, issued a statement marking the first anniversary of Turkey's invasion of Cyprus in which he reminded readers that Ankara had unilaterally rescinded the ban on growing opium poppies. "Thus, to Turkey's aggression against the Island of Cyprus, using American arms," he noted, "has been added her aggression against an entire generation of young Americans with opium grown in Turkish soil."[106]

As the date for the House vote approached, Brademas sought Rangel's help in arousing concern over the opium issue. Less than a week later, the

Drawing entitled "Seeds" to accompany Congressman Charles Rangel's editorial "The Poppy Whose Sap Is Anti-Life," *New York Times,* July 19, 1975. (Courtesy Brad Holland)

New York Times published a guest editorial by the Harlem congressman titled "The Poppy Whose Sap Is Anti-Life." Rangel wrote of Turkey's continuing failure to control opium production, the increased flow of Turkey's drugs into the United States, and the lackluster response of the Ford administration, which did not want to step on anyone's toes. No attempt to lift the arms embargo could succeed, he argued, without strong Turkish action to prevent drug trafficking. Apparently, neither administration officials in

Washington nor US Ambassador John Scali at the United Nations had been able to convince the New York congressman that the opium issue had been resolved.[107]

One wonders whether Rangel authored this piece out of genuine concern or because he hoped to increase his leverage on the administration. Shortly after it appeared, government witnesses testified before Congress that Turkey's control mechanisms were working and that "no significant narcotics diversion to U.S. markets is expected." After the hearings, Rangel indicated that he had been impressed by the testimony.[108]

On July 25, shortly after the administration lost the close vote in the House (206–223) to lift the Turkish arms embargo, Rangel told James Cannon, assistant to the president, that he believed at least fifteen congressmen had voted against lifting the embargo not because of Cyprus but "because of narcotics-related problems." He claimed that he could deliver these votes if the administration took steps "demonstrating high-level concern with the drug problem." He then offered a range of actions that could be taken on the domestic front, including a public presidential affirmation of the importance of the war on illicit narcotics and the appointment of a special assistant in the White House to keep the president up to date on the drug scene.[109]

President Ford and Secretary of State Kissinger heard about Rangel's proposition even in far-off Finland, where they had gathered with other world leaders to sign the Helsinki Accords. In a July 31 meeting with the new Turkish prime minister Suleyman Demirel, the Americans explained that they were working on lifting the arms embargo and hoped to pick up an additional ten votes if they could get Rangel's support. They pressed Demirel to provide a list of positive developments that they could put in a letter to the New York congressman, and the prime minister willingly complied. Kissinger was so impressed that he suggested that Ford telephone Rangel rather than waiting for a letter to be delivered to Capitol Hill. Ford made the call. In the letter that followed, the president emphasized how important the control of illicit drugs was to him, calling drugs "a threat to our national security." He and the secretary of state would make this clear to Congress upon their return, thus meeting Rangel's demand.[110]

Rangel initiated one last challenge. He succeeded in adding an amendment to the Scott bill calling for discussions with Turkey to prevent the diversion of opium poppies into illicit channels. Although this lacked any sanctions clause, the administration scrambled to assure the House and Rangel that this had been accomplished within the sixty-day period set out in the amendment. On December 8 President Ford was able to inform Senator John McClellan, chair of the Senate Committee on Appropriations, that, based on information from the embassy in Ankara, the DEA, and the United Nations, the government of Turkey had successfully established a system of effective control. US agencies would continue their discussions with Turkish representatives on this issue. He concluded by saying that he believed the desire of Congress had been met.[111]

Thereafter, the pressure from Rangel and his colleagues eased. The absence of any compulsion in Rangel's October 1975 amendment seemed to be a clear indication that the congressman was finally convinced that the menace of Turkish heroin had evaporated. Although Rangel had secured the president's support, he failed to deliver the votes he had promised. When the partial lifting of the embargo passed the House (237–176) on October 2, only Rangel, Shirley Chisolm (D-NY), and Barbara Jordan (D-TX) voted with the majority; none of the other members of the Congressional Black Caucus supported the measure.[112]

Three days after Gerald Ford's defeat in the 1976 presidential election, the embassy in Ankara confirmed that the end of the second year's poppy harvest in Turkey indicated continued success of the government's control system. "There has been no reliable evidence of any diversion whatsoever," it reported. This was good news on Capitol Hill. That announcement signaled the end of a particularly contentious issue in US-Turkish affairs.[113]

5

"They Have Made a Mess of Cyprus"

The administration had won the battle, but the struggle was far from over. Those who supported the embargo did not waver, and they kept a careful watch to see whether there would be any positive response from Ankara after the October vote. The administration had stated that unless there was some Turkish movement on negotiations, its position would become impossible. And yet, in spite of all the expectations of progress following the partial lifting of the embargo, the Turkish government failed to act. The ruling coalition in Ankara was weak and could not deal with contentious domestic and foreign issues. The ongoing congressional restrictions on Turkish military aid—said to be "a knife at the throat of Turkey"—hampered any movement on the Cyprus issue for fear that Prime Minister Demirel's opponents and the general public would perceive this as caving in to foreign pressure.[1]

Cyprus Becomes a Campaign Issue

Senator Eagleton took a series of steps to support the embargo. He continued to prod his colleagues to do the right thing. Outside the Senate, he asked the comptroller general to determine whether Turkish facilities were really as important as the Ford administration claimed for maintaining surveillance of the Soviet Union. He also questioned the Turkish foreign minister about his country's policies in Cyprus, including the number of troops on the island, the emigration policy for Turkish nationals, and the government's general policies in the eastern Mediterranean.[2]

Increasingly, Eagleton and others were thinking about the upcoming election year, 1976. In addition to other problems, both foreign and domestic, Ford's supporters wondered whether the president had paid too high a political price in getting substantial parts of the embargo lifted. There were early warnings. Tex McCrary, an important Republican donor with close ties to Greece, repeated his earlier warning that "the president might win for the Turks but lose for himself in November '76. . . . The Heritage vote could be lost, from Greeks and Armenians to Poles and all the rest who have been traditional Republicans." In a meeting with Ford and Kissinger, McCrary remarked that "the feeling of the Jews about Kissinger is deep [in opposition], so don't be misled by pledges of support." He advised the president to send a high-level mission to Athens right away to mollify the Greeks and Greek Americans.[3]

Warnings came from the Greek American community as well. Dennis Lavadas, the supreme counselor of AHEPA, wrote to Myron Kuropas, the new special assistant to the president for ethnic affairs, and urged the administration to act quickly with a grassroots campaign if it had any hopes of recapturing the ethnic vote in the upcoming election. Dr. Andrew Kopan, a professor at DePaul University and a spokesman for the Greek American community in Chicago, advised Kuropas to warn the White House that it should stop impugning the loyalty of ethnic American lobbyists. He noted that George Christopher, the Greek American former mayor of San Francisco, had already called on people of Greek descent "to repudiate the Republican leadership in Washington." The Greeks were only a small contingent in the total voting public, but they could play a crucial role, according to Kopan, in states such as Illinois and Massachusetts.[4]

The appointment of Kuropas in early 1976 was an indication that the White House realized it had work to do to restore good relations with various ethnic groups. This became clear in an "eleventh hour" memorandum that William J. Baroody Jr. sent to the president on May 7, 1976. The assistant for public liaison emphasized the need for Ford to reach out to the ethnic American community before Jimmy Carter, the likely Democratic candidate, could consolidate support among them.[5]

Four days later, Ford made a speech at the White House to Republican leaders of various ethnic groups, stating how anxious he was to learn their views. Kuropas would now provide a direct link between them and the administration. The president reminded these leaders that he had not cut the budget for the Ethnic Heritage Studies Program and had continued to support the bilingual education program. Three additional meetings had been scheduled over the next three months. Finally, in a reversal of the ideas put forward in a speech a year earlier, Ford now praised the involvement of ethnic groups in the political process, saying, "Good government in America requires a politics of participation and involvement on the part of all Americans." Baroody must have been pleased.[6]

The president could not recover lost ground so easily, however. In May, when Ford and challenger Ronald Reagan were locked in their furious battle for the Republican presidential nomination, activist George Christopher sent out a letter to the Greek American community reciting Reagan's words: "The present tragic situation in Cyprus is another example of the failure of the Kissinger-Ford foreign policy." Then Christopher added, "Compare it to the words of duplicity and malice by Mr. Ford, who is following the orders of his hate-filled Secretary of State Henry Kissinger."[7]

The annual AHEPA congressional banquet in early April had been an awkward affair for the White House, given the tense relations between the president and the Greek American community. There was some question whether Ford should even attend. Eve Griffin, who worked on Ford's reelection committee, urged the president to participate. The AHEPA leaders had great influence in their respective communities, she wrote, and the president had some fence-mending to do if he wanted to receive their backing. Kuropas also strongly recommended that Ford attend. To cancel just a few days before the event would only worsen relations. The supreme president of AHEPA, William Chirgotis, had assured him there would be no demonstrations at the banquet.[8]

Following a rousing reception for Congressman Dante Fascell and standing ovations for Congressman Martin Russo (D-IL) and Senator Eagleton, the attendees welcomed the Fords with "good, polite but withheld ovation." Mrs. Ford received the outstanding woman of the year award from the Daughters of Penelope. Her husband carefully avoided any mention of Cyprus in his brief remarks. The next day, Chirgotis sent Ford a frank letter, stating in part, "The applause . . . should not be misunderstood as implying approval of the policies of your administration toward Greece and Cyprus."[9]

Kuropas faced a nearly impossible task in trying to strengthen the administration's ties with various ethnic groups. In August, after Ford narrowly won his party's nomination at the Kansas City convention, Kuropas recommended that his first position paper should be on Cyprus. This, he thought, was especially important because the Greek American community was planning a massive voter registration drive to support the Democratic nominee, Jimmy Carter. A thoughtful statement from the president might give ethnic voters reason to reconsider their support for Carter.[10]

President Ford and former Turkish prime minister Ecevit at the White House, July 29, 1976. (Courtesy Ford Presidential Library)

Ultimately, such strategies proved ineffective. Brademas and Sarbanes worked closely with AHEPA and UHAC leaders to arrange a meeting with Carter on September 16 in Washington, where they exchanged views on Cyprus. Carter issued a clear statement criticizing the Ford administration's policy, which, he said, "failed to uphold either principle or the rule of law in the conduct of our foreign policy. American law requires that arms supplied by the United States be used solely for defensive purposes." As a result of the meeting, a Pan-Hellenic Committee was formed to support Carter's candidacy. Ford was losing the battle for the Greek American vote.[11]

As the election approached, the editor of the *Light*, an important Greek American paper on Long Island, New York, took an impassioned stand for Carter and against Ford. "Ford has sold out the Greeks to their longtime enemy the Turks," he wrote. He urged all Greeks to vote for the Democrat. Their motto should be: "Carter in the White House."[12]

Carter received some pushback from the small Turkish community. Under the heading "Cyprus: Another Greek Tragedy," the president of the American Turkish Association set out the chronology of events leading up to the original Turkish invasion of the island. He noted that the Turks had forestalled the movement for enosis on Cyprus and concluded, "Greeks blame the United States . . . Greeks blame NATO . . . Greeks blame Turkey . . . Greeks blame all but themselves." In the final days of the campaign, "You be the judge," he counseled.[13] Rauf Denktash sent Carter a letter setting out the Turkish Cypriot perspective. "It [the Turkish Cypriot community] would not offer itself, once again, as a sacrifice to 'Greek Gods'" (referring to the defunct 1960 constitution that inadequately protected minority rights). There should be intercommunal talks "*on the basis of equality.*"[14]

It is unlikely that either of these messages made an impression on Carter or his staff, for these voices were drowned out by the flood of Greek American endorsements. The Turks in the American electorate were politically insignificant. As Congressman David Bowen (D-MS) later reported to a Turkish journalist, "Before each vote I receive hundreds of letters from Greek origin Americans requesting that I should vote to keep the embargo. But until today I have not received one single letter from a Turk." To make matters worse, the Turkish ambassador spent most of the early embargo period (November 1974 to April 1975) in Ankara, waiting in vain for the new coalition government—in which he would become foreign minister—to form. Meanwhile, the embassy in Washington was left in the hands of a chargé d'affaires.[15]

Senator Eagleton took a prominent role in advising Carter on the Cyprus issue. Members of his staff drafted a long memorandum pointing out some of the pitfalls the candidate would need to avoid with regard to Turkey. The Ford administration had negotiated a four-year Defense Cooperation Agreement (DCA) with Ankara under which US bases and installations would be reopened in return for $1 billion in grants, credits, and loans. Congress had indicated its reluctance to take up the measure until after the election. The memorandum warned that if President Ford presented the DCA as a major American security interest, Carter might be forced to state his position. If so, the Democratic candidate needed to be cautious. Carter should advocate an interim agreement with Turkey that could be presented as a pro-NATO policy, leaving his hands free for further negotiation once he was in the White House.[16]

On September 1 Senator Eagleton presented the essence of the memorandum in a personal letter to Zbigniew Brzezinski, one of Carter's chief foreign policy advisers. The difficulty, he pointed out, was to "win over the Greek-Americans while guarding against alienating the Turks." Carter should stress the failure of the present administration's policy, while pointing out that his administration would provide the opportunity for a new look. It would be improper, Carter could argue, to comment at present on any particular agreement. He needed to keep his future options open.[17]

Despite all the challenges, Kissinger and Turkish foreign minister Ihsan Caglayangil had negotiated a new DCA in March, but opponents in Congress immediately threatened to block its approval. A group from UHAC expressed "shock and dismay" when they heard about the new DCA. Some of its members had been seeking a meeting with the president, but they notified Kuropas that they "would not be able to attend any meeting with President Ford" under these new circumstances. In Ankara, the prime minister responded to these outbursts by saying that US-Turkish relations could not be restored with threats from Congress hanging over the agreement. Should the DCA be rejected, he warned, such action "will unavoidably have fatal consequences on our already damaged relationship."[18]

Ford reassured the prime minister that the United States wanted to restore relations with Turkey and that a majority in Congress supported such a restoration. Congress also wanted to see "early movement toward a Cyprus solution," however. The administration would try to keep these two sentiments from coming into conflict, and Ford hoped Demirel would do all he could to help them attain both goals.[19]

The defense agreements for both Greece and Turkey became hostage to the Cyprus crisis. Greece stalled negotiations on its own agreement, fearing that its completion would serve as a green light for Congress to act on the Turkish DCA as well. Both were held over for the next administration.[20]

The Cyprus crisis and the resulting Turkish arms embargo proved to be one of the Ford administration's most difficult foreign policy issues. In his memoir, *A Time to Heal*, the president would write, "I considered this the single most irresponsible, short-sighted foreign policy decision Congress had made in all the years I'd been in Washington." Historically, foreign policy had not attracted a great deal of interest from the American public, and on those rare occasions when it had, the attention had usually faded quickly, leaving the executive largely in control of policymaking. In this instance, key elements of the public became deeply engaged, and their engagement lasted throughout the administration. Congress also seized on this issue, partly in response to the public outcry, but also due to other factors, such as questions about the legality of Turkish actions and the ongoing legislative-executive conflict rooted in the Vietnam disaster and the Watergate scandal.[21]

Surprisingly, Henry Kissinger's formidable diplomatic skills failed him in this crisis, as he and the administration suffered a string of defeats. The distracted secretary of state apparently failed to recognize the seriousness of the looming crisis in the eastern Mediterranean, and by the time he realized the scope of the threat, events had outrun his ability to control them. Domestically, he underestimated the strength and effectiveness of congressional and ethnic opposition.

President Ford had little foreign policy experience, and he was necessarily focused on the details of setting up a new administration at a time when the crisis required his full attention. He agreed with Kissinger that the White House should direct foreign policy and that Congress had a right to be consulted, but it could not make foreign policy. He worked with the established congressional leadership during this lengthy crisis, but leaders in both chambers often had difficulty controlling their own members. This became even more problematic following the so-called Watergate election in November 1974, when large numbers of "radical" freshmen won seats in Congress. The old guard had difficulty imposing its will. Republican votes became more predictable than those of the majority Democrats.

Unfortunately, successive Turkish governments were in an extremely weak political position and either could not or would not risk compromising on Cyprus to resolve the crisis. Supported by public opinion and reassured by periodic statements from the US embassy, Turkish prime ministers chose to wait it out.

Given all these complicating factors, it is difficult to suggest what else the Ford administration might have done to resolve the crisis once Congress imposed the embargo. It chose to pick away at the measure, achieving partial success in October 1975. The White House hoped that its views would eventually prevail on Capitol Hill, but time ran out for Ford. It remained for his Democratic successor, who would be working with a Congress controlled by his own party, to fashion a solution to the Cyprus problem and end the arms embargo.

How to Handle Cyprus?

Soon after the election, President-elect Carter reached out to the Republican leadership in Congress, meeting them at the Capitol on November 23. Initially, Rhodes and his colleagues were pleased with Carter, but when he made a clear threat "to use the mailed fist" if Congress resisted programs that he wanted enacted, the leaders quickly abandoned any thoughts of "sweetness and light." Rhodes saw Carter as full of self-assurance and absolute confidence in himself and in the power of the presidency. In a moment of candor, one leader remarked to the president-elect, "We Republicans may turn out to be your best friends from time to time." This would certainly be true with regard to the embargo, but that meeting of minds lay far in the future.[22]

As time went on, the arguments of opponents of the embargo began to gain traction. In spite of genuine concerns about violations of the law, it became increasingly clear that US security interests would be irreparably harmed if the embargo continued indefinitely. Initially, however, Carter seemed to favor the status quo.

Carter's victory on November 2, which turned out to be a closer race than anyone had predicted, filled the friends of Cyprus and supporters of the embargo with great optimism. James Cunningham, professor of history at the College of St. Catherine in St. Paul, told his colleagues in the MFC that with fellow Minnesotan Walter Mondale as vice president, they had good reason to be cheerful. Mondale, who would evidently have more than the usual impact on policy, was concerned about the plight of Cyprus, "a concern that our organization helped to develop and keep current." Cyrus Vance, who would serve as secretary of state, had been very involved with Cyprus in the 1960s. And, of course, John Brademas, whose concern for Cyprus was well known, would now serve as majority whip in the House of Representatives. (Cunningham might have added that Paul Sarbanes had now been elevated to the US Senate.) Groups like theirs must continually remind political leaders that the issue remained unresolved.[23]

At the MFC's January 5, 1977, meeting, Clarke Chambers, professor of history at the University of Minnesota, reminded members that their new senator, Wendell "Wendy" Anderson, "was in a critical position and would be open to MFC political desires." (As governor, Anderson had effectively nominated himself to serve the remainder of Mondale's term.) Anderson had to build a political constituency for the 1978 election, so he would be a "captive audience," and they needed to orient him on the Cyprus problem. It was agreed that Chambers should contact Anderson and all Minnesota "Congress persons" to remind them of the MFC's position.[24]

Brademas surely would have been pleased at the number of academics involved in the work of the MFC. He once wrote to a professor friend who had criticized his support of the embargo on Turkey, "I want to see much more sensitivity on the part of the academic community . . . to questions of the rule of law and all the more so after the experience of Watergate."[25]

The committee pursued its contacts with Senator Anderson, who helped arrange Mary Mantis's participation in President Carter's meeting with 100 Greek American leaders at the White House on June 22, 1978. Anderson informed her that he would continue to oppose lifting the embargo until there was a just settlement in Cyprus. In September, Paul Sarbanes visited the Twin Cities to campaign for the Minnesota senator, but Anderson would lose his bid for a full term.[26]

One of Eagleton's aides produced an interesting analysis following the 1976 presidential election. Andrew Manatos, soon to become assistant secretary of commerce for congressional affairs, pointed to the significant role of Greek American voters. Their switch to Carter in New York and Pennsylvania, he argued, had contributed to the Democrat's victory in those two key states. For the first time, the community "fully utilized their considerable assets for electoral purposes."[27]

In both Athens and Nicosia, there was great anticipation about the new administration. Archbishop Makarios was quoted as saying that "the opinions of Secretary Kissinger should no longer be considered." Kissinger told President Ford that Makarios had declared a public holiday when Carter won.[28]

Turkish officials worried that the incoming administration might succumb to the wiles of the Greek American lobby. Two weeks after the election, Foreign Minister Caglayangil sent a private letter to his friend, former US ambassador to Turkey George McGhee, urging him to use his influence within the Democratic Party "to dispel misunderstandings and misjudgments" about Turkey. Caglayangil had recently returned from a speaking tour in the United States, during which he had been the target of picketers who were protesting Turkey's actions in Cyprus.[29]

The Gang of Four sent a letter to the president-elect on December 14, setting out their positions with regard to Cyprus and the DCA with Turkey, which Kissinger had negotiated in March. They thought a new administration could make much more progress in urging the resumption of Cyprus negotiations, with an excellent prospect of success. A carrot-and-stick approach toward Turkey might gain Ankara's cooperation. They concluded that they believed Carter shared their "perceptions of the issue."[30]

Later in the same month, the Gang of Four met with incoming Secretary of State Vance to reiterate their position. The outgoing administration had never pressured Turkey to compromise, they charged. They also recommended changing ambassadors in all three countries—Turkey, Greece, and Cyprus. Clearly, they were most interested in having William Macomber removed. They also advocated sending an emissary to the region while they worked on a solution in Washington.[31]

On January 18, just two days before leaving office, the Ford administration resubmitted the Turkish DCA to Congress, without notifying the president-elect. Because that body had failed to take up the measure before the end of the previous session, it had lapsed and now had to be reintroduced in the new session. This could have been left to the incoming administration, but Ford and Kissinger clearly wanted to ensure that it received attention. No doubt, they took some satisfaction in knowing that its reintroduction in mid-January put Carter in an awkward position. As Ford had remarked regarding another policy issue in his final days, "It puts Carter on the spot, too."[32]

This did, in fact, cause problems for Carter because it brought the issue into the public arena, where positions would have to be taken. The new administration had hoped to take time to study all the questions relating to Turkey before approaching Congress. Ford's action forced Carter's hand, and the State Department asked Congress to withhold consideration of the DCA. This angered Ankara, which interpreted the delay as an indication that the Carter administration felt the need "to placate the Greek lobby in Congress."[33]

The Clifford Mission

Indeed, the new administration seemed to heed the wishes of the pro-embargo advocates. On February 3 President Carter announced that he was sending veteran foreign policy adviser Clark Clifford to the eastern Mediterranean as his personal representative to assess the situation. Clifford's selection would not have surprised anyone close to the new president. He was one of the grand old men of the party, and his views were frequently solicited by Democrats in Congress and the White House. Clifford had supported Carter for the Democratic nomination, prompting a handwritten note from the candidate in early May, expressing his appreciation for "your confidence in me and your continuing input into our campaign."[34]

In June 1975 Clifford had written to his friend Senator Edmund Muskie (D-ME), criticizing the Ford administration's handling of foreign policy and especially Kissinger's "personal style of diplomacy." With regard to the crisis in the Mediterranean, he claimed, "They have made a mess of Cyprus." Now he would have an opportunity to straighten out that "mess."[35]

Once his appointment was announced, Clifford met with members of the House Committee on International Relations to discuss his mission. He also met with Brademas and his associates to hear their views before he left. These discussions led him to conclude that Congress was "shockingly uninterested in the long-term Greek-US or Turkish-US relationship" or the loss of Turkish bases.[36]

Meanwhile, Greek American groups prodded the administration to uphold its campaign promises. In mid-February, even before the Clifford mission, members of the American Hellenic Committee to Elect Carter-Mondale met with Vice President Mondale to discuss ways to improve US-Greek relations. They told him that they would be monitoring administration policy carefully in the coming months.[37]

The vice president would take an unusually prominent role in the new administration, and individuals and groups regularly sought his assistance. President-elect Carter had made it clear that he wanted Mondale to play a key role in policymaking, and he made good on that statement after Inauguration Day. Carter told his cabinet and White House staff, "If you get a request from Fritz [Mondale], you treat it as if it were a request from me." The vice president occupied an office in the West Wing of the White House, unlike his predecessors, who had been located in the Old Executive Office Building next door. Carter and Mondale lunched together each Monday, and the vice president always participated in the Friday morning breakfasts with Carter and other top officials. Mondale and his staff oversaw agenda setting for the first year of the administration. Carter relied on Mondale's close links to Congress and his knowledge of foreign policy issues. The vice president would often represent the president abroad, just as Clark Clifford was about to do in the eastern Mediterranean.[38]

Prior to his departure on February 15, Clifford met with the top-ranking members of the administration, including Vance and national security adviser Brzezinski. Even at this early stage, differences emerged between the two top officials. Brzezinski thought Clifford should focus on Ankara and

Athens and avoid Nicosia; Vance thought Clifford should be free to pursue the course he thought best. They all agreed that the objective was for Clifford to return with enough evidence of Turkish flexibility on Cyprus to induce Congress to move on the Turkish DCA. They also agreed that the chances of achieving this objective were slim. Clifford stated that Cyprus had no economic or military significance for Turkey; it was purely an emotional issue, he thought, which they should work to diminish.[39]

Clifford seemed to be mistaken in this early assessment. Although there was an emotional element in the Turkish response, there were security concerns as well. Many Turks viewed the coup in Cyprus as an attempt to ring their country with Greek-controlled islands from the northern Aegean to the eastern Mediterranean, cutting it off from easy access to the Mediterranean. No one at the Policy Review Committee meeting on February 10, however, challenged his statement.[40]

On the day he was scheduled to leave for Europe, Clifford met with the president at the White House. Carter emphasized the importance of Greek and Turkish bases and the significance of the Greek American lobby. During his mission, Clifford should explain that the United States was prepared to help, but "we would not intrude."[41]

Clifford spent three days each in Athens, Ankara, and Nicosia. On his flight to the region, he stopped in Vienna to meet with UN Secretary-General Kurt Waldheim, and on his return, he stopped in London to brief British officials. He received a warm welcome from everyone, with the exception of Rauf Denktash, the Turkish Cypriot leader, who was under considerable pressure from Ankara to enter negotiations with Archbishop Makarios, which he opposed.[42]

In Athens, Ambassador Kubisch reported how pleased he was to see "the friendly waves and spontaneous applause" as he and Clifford moved around the city. This came, he said, "after two and a half years of living in an environment characterized by hostility, resentment and bitterness against Americans." He was more optimistic about future relations.[43]

On March 1 Clifford submitted his assessment to the president. In it, he reported that leaders in the area had been impressed by Carter's focus on regional issues so early in his administration. Former prime minister Bulent Ecevit, however, had emphasized how "disturbing" it was for a country in Turkey's difficult geographic situation "to observe that its security might be decided by the internal politics of foreign allies." Clifford had responded that, like it or not, Cyprus affected the US-Turkey relationship, and he hoped progress could soon be made toward settlement.[44]

In Nicosia, Clifford had cautioned Makarios that now was the best time to reach a settlement with Turkey. After the first year of the new Carter administration, US interest would decline, and its concern for restoring relations with Turkey would weaken Makarios's bargaining position. The following day, the Cypriot leader told Clifford that at the upcoming March 31 meeting with Denktash in Vienna, he would present a bizonal map of the island, indicating that he was considering a federal arrangement to resolve the crisis. Clifford saw this as a positive development.[45]

Clifford had acted wisely in counseling Makarios as he did, for the Carter administration faced a long foreign policy to-do list, including negotiating the Panama Canal treaties, expanding relations with China, finalizing SALT II, and pursuing Middle East peace, to name but a few. Many items were left over from the Ford administration, which had put a number of foreign policy matters on hold during the intense primary and general election campaigns, assuming that it could deal with them later. That task now fell to the victorious Democrats, who would soon have to take up other pressing issues. The focus on Cyprus would not last.

At this point, however, the administration was still prepared to link enactment of the DCA to substantial progress on Cyprus. The White House was engaged in a balancing act, hoping to calm its restive allies until a settlement could be reached. On March 4 Clifford met with Carter, Vance, and Brzezinski to review his report. The president indicated support for Clifford's recommendation to give Turkey some additional military credits ($50 million) but to withhold any military aid until the Cyprus problem was resolved. They thought the pro-Greek members of Congress would go along with this as long as the administration did not push the DCA.[46]

President Carter seemed well pleased with Clifford's effort. He sent Clifford a handwritten note, thanking him for his "superbly performed mission." Carter continued, "because of your good work, it may very well pay rich dividends for world peace."[47]

On the same day as the White House meeting, however, Paul Henze, the new desk officer for Greece, Turkey, and Cyprus on the National Security Council staff, advised Brzezinski that Clifford may have antagonized Turkish military leaders by his "ultimatum" that Turkey choose between Cyprus

President Carter (right), Secretary of State Cyrus Vance, special envoy Clark Clifford, and NSC staff assistant Greg Treverton, discussing Clifford's report on the eastern Mediterranean at the White House, March 4, 1977. (Courtesy Carter Presidential Library)

and the DCA. Henze was a Turkophile, having served for several years in Ankara as head of CIA operations there. Repeatedly, throughout the Carter administration, he would advise the national security adviser and others not to antagonize the Turks, emphasizing Turkey's unique strategic position in the eastern Mediterranean.[48]

Turkey's long-serving ambassador, Melih Esenbel, had finally returned to his Washington post and lost no time lobbying the new administration for quick passage of the DCA. Meeting with Vance in early April, he revealed that, based on his own soundings of senators and congressmen, there was much support on the Hill for moving forward. Although Clifford had expressed pessimism on this point, Esenbel urged the administration to endorse the DCA.[49]

Prime Minister Demirel made similar arguments to Carter and Clifford in May during a NATO meeting in London. The president explained why it was so difficult to proceed with the DCA without some movement on Cyprus. This reflected the sentiment in Congress, he said, not his own feelings. He would sign the agreement immediately if he could, but he needed time to change the attitude in Congress. Still, he observed, the US arms package for Turkey showed how much the United States valued its bilateral relationship. Demirel protested vigorously that relations were being damaged "for nothing." Passage of the DCA, he declared, would repair the relationship. He responded sharply when the president asked what he could do to help. "One thing," said the prime minister, "ratify the DCA!"[50]

Demirel's pointed response must have been influenced by the increasingly difficult situation he faced at home. The economy was in shambles, and violence perpetrated by extremist groups on the left and the right resulted in hundreds of deaths each year. Just two weeks before the NATO meetings in London, a left-wing rally in Istanbul's Taksim Square had ended in violence, leaving forty-two dead from snipers' bullets and the panic that ensued. Demirel needed some good news.

The Americans had assumed that once Turkish general elections took place in June, a more stable situation would emerge. In the June 5 polling, however, no party received a majority in parliament. Although Ecevit and the Republican People's Party won the largest number of seats (213), it was shy of the 226 needed for a majority. Furthermore, there were no suitable smaller parties on the left with which the would-be prime minister could create a coalition. Ecevit eventually pulled together a bare majority, but it did not hold. Demirel soon returned to office with a right-wing coalition.

With all this internal instability, the Turkish government was unlikely to make the difficult decision to compromise on Cyprus. Despite internal disagreements on most issues, almost all Turks supported the government's Cyprus policy, and many believed Turkey had finally resolved the plight of the Turkish Cypriot minority. Clifford's views notwithstanding, many Turks also believed that Greece had tried to encircle their country and that the 1974 invasion of Cyprus had forestalled that threat to Turkey's security.[51]

The honeymoon between Carter and the pro-embargo congressmen and senators lasted only a few months. The congressional leaders wasted no time in lobbying the administration. Over a four-day period (April 19–22), for example, they met with Vance, Brzezinski, Mondale, and finally Carter himself. In these meetings they took a firm position, characterizing the new administration's policy toward Turkey as "no real shift from the Ford-Kissinger policy." They claimed that Turkey had done nothing in the negotiations that warranted an increase in assistance from $125 million to $175 million, which the administration had proposed without consulting Congress. Nor, they argued, should the administration endorse in principle the Turkish DCA. Unlike Demirel, the group from Capitol Hill thought the administration had gone too far in allowing military transfers to Turkey, including the easing of government-to-government cash sales to allow Turkey to purchase Phantom jets. "Brademas was profoundly disappointed and characterized the recommendations as 'inconsistent' with the 'Holy Writ' of the president's campaign promises." He "believed that the administration had 'drawn a line in the dust.'"[52]

Based on his considerable experience in Congress and his initial support of the embargo in the Senate, Vice President Mondale often took the lead in meeting with pro-embargo lawmakers and with members of the Greek American community as well. In this instance, he took great care in countering the arguments of his former colleagues. He urged them not to challenge every tactic of the administration but to understand the strategy, which would put the United States in a position to insist on progress on Cyprus after the June elections in Turkey. To President Carter, he suggested that they emphasize the differences between their policy and that of the previous administration, saying, "We will insist on satisfactory progress on Cyprus before we enter a defense cooperation agreement with Turkey."[53]

The president and the secretary of state cautioned that they could no longer publicly link the embargo and Cyprus. Turkey was too sensitive on this point. Ankara knew the two were linked, but the US government could not make this connection officially. The administration claimed that giving aid to Turkey, without a linkage to Cyprus, would encourage Turkey to compromise. Opponents of these more lenient terms argued that there had been no substantive Turkish movement toward settlement, and Ankara had even begun to settle large numbers of Turks from Anatolia in northern Cyprus.[54]

Opponents would have been even more concerned if they had read a CIA intelligence memorandum issued at the end of March, suggesting that Ankara manipulated troop levels on the island to give the appearance of flexibility and to influence US and international opinion. In February 1976, when Foreign Minister Caglayangil had been scheduled to visit Washington to finalize the DCA, Turkey had announced that 2,000 troops would be withdrawn from Cyprus. Again, at the beginning of the Carter administration in January 1977, it had done the same thing. But, the report concluded, "more often than not, these announced cutbacks have been carried out incompletely or offset by subsequent, unannounced replacements." The total number of Turkish troops had changed very little.[55]

The Gang of Four lobbied Secretary of State Vance not to include the F-4 Phantom jets in any deal with Turkey, and the secretary agreed. He promised to speak with anti-embargo advocates such as Senator Hubert Humphrey and Congressman Lee Hamilton and tell them "it's ok to knock out the F-4 deal." But this had to be done very quietly so as not to embarrass Turkey. Congress refused to fund the jets, but the higher credit ceiling remained.[56]

On May 24, 1977, the House also defeated the Findley amendment by a vote of 150–256. This would have given the president discretion to lift the embargo completely under certain conditions related to US security. The Carter administration had actually opposed the amendment, so it was difficult to know exactly where members of the House stood on the embargo issue in mid-1977.[57]

Kostas Carras, a British businessman and political activist of Greek heritage, wrote to his friend John Brademas in June to congratulate him on the defeat of the Findley amendment. He wondered, however, whether someone in the administration had been working behind the scenes to make the point that "if the administration *had* officially got involved, it would have been a hard fight." Carras argued that the time was right to press the Turkish government for concessions on Cyprus, given its very weak economy made worse by military expenses on the island. He hoped the United States would not miss this opportunity.[58]

Plans Unravel

Events conspired to drown out Carras's advice. On August 3 US policymakers received a shock—news of the unexpected death of Archbishop Makarios at age sixty-three, following a heart attack. The Cypriot leader had worried American officials for years, cozying up to the Soviets and befriending Nasser of Egypt and other radical figures in the developing world. By the beginning of the Carter presidency, however, Makarios had seemingly altered his position on relations between the two communities on Cyprus; he had agreed to recognize a separate zone in the northern part of the island for all Turkish Cypriots. Makarios was hugely popular, and given his stature and influence, he probably could have made the bitter but necessary compromise acceptable to the Greek majority. His passing produced a political vacuum, and no other leader could achieve what he might have done.

American officials viewed this as an unfortunate setback. Clifford wrote to the president expressing his concern that the archbishop's death might lessen the possibility of reaching an agreement on Cyprus. Henry Kissinger, now a private citizen, had had his share of problems with Makarios during his eight years in the Nixon and Ford administrations. He, too, reflected on the demise of the Cypriot leader: "I felt that with the by then somewhat chastened archbishop had also died the best hope for a rapid negotiated settlement of Cyprus. . . . Makarios more than any other Cypriot leader had the imagination to accept reality and the prestige to lead his compatriots in the direction of his necessities. I can imagine the sardonic gleam in the archbishop's eyes were he aware how many of his erstwhile critics missed him and his complicated, occasionally devious maneuvers. Makarios was, after all, a big man in a world not blessed with an excess of them."[59]

The United States sent an impressive delegation to the funeral, including Chief Justice Warren Burger, President Carter's sister Ruth, Clark Clifford, John Brademas, and Paul Sarbanes. Although the chief justice served as the formal head of the delegation, Clifford was its de facto leader and the one on whom the press focused. He publicly expressed his great respect for the departed leader and his sense of loss. When the group visited the body lying in state, Clifford "patted the frail yellow hand of Makarios." As one American official observed, "it was the grand gesture."[60]

At a press conference, Clifford said he was deeply honored to know that Makarios had considered him a friend. He had been impressed by the archbishop's moderation during the February talks. In responding to a question about "the other side," meaning the Turkish Cypriots, Clifford said he had invited them to attend the news conference, but they had obviously chosen not to come.[61]

The Turkish Cypriots responded sharply, criticizing Clifford's "eulogy" for Makarios, which was wholly undeserved, they said. Makarios had plotted the destruction of their community to achieve enosis. Clifford's speech, they charged, had been intended to soothe his Greek friends at their expense.[62]

There was discussion in Washington that Clifford's comments in Nicosia might have antagonized Ankara and weakened his influence on the Cyprus issue. (Turkey had neither sent a representative to the funeral nor expressed its condolences.) A recent article in the *Washington Post* had emphasized Clifford's harsh tone with US diplomats regarding Turkey and Cyprus in February. He had said Turkey was "dreaming" if it thought President Carter would try to push the DCA through Congress without major Turkish concessions on Cyprus. And then Ambassador Macomber had been recalled in June, a gesture, it was said, to the Greek lobby.[63]

Although developments in the first half of 1977 might have seemed threatening to Turkey's interests, this turned out to be the high-water mark of the Carter administration's attempt to link Cyprus and the DCA. By the fall of that year, in light of events in Ankara and Nicosia, the White House was slowly backing away from its previous position. As the likelihood of an early resolution receded, Cyprus declined in importance for the administration, just as Clifford had warned. For instance, when the vice president's staff drew up a list of foreign policy issues for 1978, Cyprus was listed under "candidates for de-emphasis." Clifford, too, expressed the general consensus when he told Carter, "We will still have an interest in Cyprus—but as a matter of fact, Cyprus is just one small piece of the chessboard—it is Turkey and Greece and our efforts to prevent trouble between them that matter."[64]

The administration was moving forward on a number of foreign policy issues, and Cyprus paled in significance. At the top of the list mentioned above, under "highest presidential priority," were the Panama Canal treaties, SALT II negotiations, and the Middle East—in that order. Cyprus would be dealt with hereafter at the secretarial level.[65]

6

The Embargo Must Go

Throughout the fall and winter of 1977–1978, the administration wrestled with the problem of what to do about US-Turkish relations. Another American delegation visited the region in September, and Secretary Vance stopped briefly in Ankara in January. There were also numerous high-level meetings with Turkish officials in Washington, New York City, and Brussels. Gradually, the Americans concluded that they could not postpone a decision on the stalled DCA much longer. According to one report, "We can no longer claim to be an administration studying the problem." The president did not want to push the agreement unless passage in Congress could be assured, but no one could give him that assurance. It appeared that the White House would have to support the DCA in Congress and that this would result in a battle.[1]

Ronald Spiers, the newly appointed US ambassador to Turkey, urged action. He remarked that Turkey "is more important than either Greece or Cyprus." He had already announced publicly to the Turkish media that "the embargo has not made a solution easier . . . it has made it more difficult."[2]

An Administration in Limbo

Congressmen Brademas and Rosenthal and Senators Sarbanes (newly elected) and Eagleton met again with Clark Clifford in early October 1977 to discuss the situation in Cyprus. It became clear that the administration was organizing a campaign to obtain congressional approval of the four-year DCA, which had been negotiated with Ankara eighteen months earlier. Clifford's visitors from the Hill continued to argue that Turkey had done nothing to warrant being rewarded with such a long-term military agreement. Clifford reminded them that it was unreasonable to expect to get everything they wanted from Turkey before lifting important elements of the restrictions on Ankara.[3]

After the meeting, Senator Eagleton penned a note to his new foreign policy adviser, Ann Proctor (Brian Atwood had accepted a position in the State Department). "In listening to Clifford," he wrote, "you heard from one of the GREAT MASTERS." But little had been achieved.[4]

Clifford reported that the meeting was largely friendly and more conciliatory than he had anticipated. There was none of the sharp language typical of earlier meetings with Kissinger—after all, they were all Democrats. Yet it was clear that the White House expected Congress to bend to its will. It would only be a matter of time before the administration revealed its plans. Clifford ended the meeting by remarking ominously, "The administration wants the DCA, I want the DCA."[5]

At a meeting a few days later, officials from the State and Defense Departments advised them to say nothing publicly about the DCA but to watch for positive movement from the Turks. Sarbanes remarked that he hoped the administration was not preparing to send the DCA to the Hill and that it would consult Congress before doing so. Matthew Nimetz, counselor of the Department of State, assured him that the administration was not considering the DCA at the moment and would definitely consult Congress beforehand. After the meeting broke up, Sarbanes and Brademas agreed that there would be a major fight over the DCA.[6]

While these early discussions with the administration were taking place, another serious issue arose that adversely affected congressional relations with officials in the Departments of Defense and State. Apparently, ever since the arms embargo had gone into effect in early 1975, the Turkish government had been taking advantage of a loophole to purchase US arms through the NATO Maintenance and Supply Agency (NAMSA) in Luxembourg. Thus, with the connivance of US officials, Turkey's purchases had gone from $0 to $28 million between 1975 and 1976, and this was continuing under the new administration. These purchases had not been counted as part of the ceiling on arms sales to Turkey set by Congress when it partially lifted the ban. Defense and State officials delayed responding to the queries of the pro-embargo leaders, and several very tense meetings took place. In one, Brademas told James Siena, deputy assistant secretary of defense, that they had been "flimflammed," and he should be ashamed. Not satisfied with either Siena's or Nelson Ledsky's (State) response, Brademas and his colleagues planned to meet with David McGiffert, assistant secretary of defense for international security affairs and Siena's superior.[7]

The matter dragged on. Congressman Les Aspin (D-WI), who had expertise in defense matters and a penchant for criticizing wasteful Pentagon practices, released a statement on September 26 detailing the NAMSA affair and his attempts to get the Pentagon to cooperate in closing the loophole. That same day, the Gang of Four issued its own statement, claiming that the NAMSA incident was a "clear circumvention of American law" and that they were awaiting a response from McGiffert's office. That response finally came on November 2, but it proved unsatisfactory, basically reaffirming what Siena had argued back on September 20. In the future, Turkey's purchases through NAMSA would be counted against the limit on all arms unless they were part of a partnership arrangement within NATO, which accounted for only a small portion of the purchases. None of these drawn-out discussions warmed relations or strengthened trust between the administration and the pro-embargo group in Congress.[8]

Eagleton's new staffer, Ann Proctor, expressed her pessimism and frustration in early December, telling the senator that she thought they had reached a dead end on the Cyprus issue. She wondered how Congress could back away from its position on the cutoff of aid, having taken a moral stand. And it seemed unlikely that Turkey would make any positive moves once the DCA was approved.[9]

A representative of the Cypriot government had contacted Proctor, complaining that US officials at the United Nations were regularly taking Turkey's side and downplaying the importance of the Cyprus issue. The United States was one of only six countries, including Turkey, that had voted in favor of a UN resolution not to keep the Cyprus issue "under constant review." It had abstained on the remainder of the resolution, designed to encourage the resumption of talks between representatives of the Greek and Turkish communities on Cyprus. The resolution passed, 116–6. Archbishop Iakovos criticized the US abstention, asking sardonically, "Is abstention the way to defend human rights? Is abstention a new form of diplomacy which the present administration is initiating in world affairs?"[10]

Clearly, it was time for the Gang of Four to meet again with the administration's top policymakers. They talked separately with Vice President Mondale and Secretary of State Vance at the end of January, but little progress was made. Early in February the congressmen wrote to President Carter to ascertain his intentions regarding Cyprus. They had repeatedly been assured that there would be a link between the supply of arms to Turkey and a solution on

Cyprus. Now, certain actions by the administration seemed to challenge that understanding. The Department of Defense, for example, had used the NATO supply agency in Luxembourg to channel weapons to Turkey, evading legal restrictions on its arms purchases. And Ambassador Spiers continued to speak publicly against the embargo, which encouraged Turkish intransigence. They hoped Carter still intended to bring peace and justice to Cyprus, as he had promised.[11]

There were important differences of opinion within the administration, and this was reflected in the advice the president received. Although the White House was still considering the DCA, the State Department's congressional liaison team and the president's assistant for congressional liaison sent a memo to Carter, setting out the cautious path the administration would have to take if it wanted to move forward with the agreement. In particular, it would need to be solicitous of the Greek American community and pro-embargo members of Congress, explaining why the administration had decided to proceed. When Paul Henze of the NSC staff read this memorandum, he was furious and wrote to Brzezinski, "I am appalled by the weakness of this paper." He accused the authors of pandering to the Greek lobby rather than making the strongest possible case to ensure success, and he urged the national security adviser to call a Special Coordinating Committee meeting on the subject. Brzezinski agreed but indicated that there were other priorities, adding, "But nothing open should be done until Panama is behind us!"[12]

Actually, the Carter administration was doing a much better job of keeping in touch with members of Congress than its predecessor had done. One of the chief complaints in the Ford years had been that the White House and Kissinger's State Department failed to provide adequate and accurate information and that they often "sent low-level actors to brief the Hill." In the new administration, both the assistant secretary of state for congressional relations, Douglas Bennet, and his deputy, Brian Atwood, had long experience as congressional aides and had maintained their personal connections on Capitol Hill. This made it easier for them to liaise with their former staff colleagues in promoting the administration's policies. Sometimes, of course, this also made them suspect among senior career officers at the State Department and officials like Henze, who came from very different backgrounds and often thought that legislators were "uninformed, opportunistic, controlled by special interests and altogether unsuitable to the prudent management of the national interest."[13]

Bennet and Atwood were both aware of this potential problem. It was for this reason that, when the time came to campaign to lift the embargo, Atwood assigned the chief role in the State Department to his deputy, Nelson Ledsky, who had formerly served as country director for Turkey, Greece, and Cyprus. Atwood rejected that role for himself because he thought he had been too close to the issue while serving on Eagleton's staff. As Atwood later recalled, Ledsky was "the guy who deserves credit for finding the votes."[14]

Ledsky initially knew nothing about congressional relations, but he was pleased to be working with Bennet and Atwood. He was responsible for European and African issues, and he also became the State Department liaison on internal committees and interagency task forces. No one from the State Department was supposed to appear before Congress without being accompanied by someone from the Congressional Relations Bureau. This requirement was respected while Cyrus Vance served as secretary of state.[15]

The vice president was particularly concerned about the possibility of a break with the pro-embargo forces in Congress. He urged Clark Clifford to meet discreetly with them and keep them informed as the administration worked out its strategy. Mondale also met with them often, and his aides singled out Senator Paul Sarbanes for special attention. The Maryland senator, who chaired the Senate Foreign Relations Committee's Subcommittee on Latin America, had impressed the vice president's staff with his handling of the Panama Canal treaty debates. They suggested that Mondale bring the senator to Carter's attention during his weekly luncheon with the president. Then, perhaps Carter could invite Sarbanes and Senator Frank Church and their wives to dine at the White House after the second Panama Canal treaty vote to thank them. "Paul," they noted, "is emerging as one of the brightest and most capable members of the [Senate Foreign Relations] committee. He is worth cultivating."[16]

As majority whip, John Brademas met with President Carter and two of his aides on February 13, 1978. Although the purpose was to discuss the upcoming legislative agenda, the premeeting memo prepared for Carter reemphasized the importance of Cyprus to the Indiana congressman. Frank Moore, assistant to the president for congressional liaison, reminded Carter that Brademas "is the *only* member of the leadership who is consistently on the floor urging Democratic members to support Administration positions on bills."[17]

Some NSC staff doubted that the State Department would be suitably tough on the DCA and should take a less prominent part in future negotiations, but Matthew Nimetz played a key role in maintaining the administration's ties to congressional opposition. He had made several trips to the eastern Mediterranean and was well versed in all the details of the crisis. He met with Brademas and Sarbanes on February 28 to explain how the administration's thinking was developing. The legislators warned again that if the administration moved ahead with the DCA, there would be a "bloody battle." The president needed their support on a number of difficult questions before Congress, and they hinted that such support might not be forthcoming. Nimetz cautioned them to consider a future investigation over "Who lost Turkey?"[18]

Referring to the approaching battle, Proctor wrote, "It looks like it could be quite messy." The press realized that the president had much at stake. Referring to Brademas, one journalist observed that Carter "is opposed by one of the shrewdest of his own legislative leaders in the House." Graham Hovey, foreign policy reporter for the *New York Times*, commented that the tone of the opposition had changed, and now they seemed "to imply that the president himself and the other administration officials have indulged in devious and misleading behavior."[19]

Administration policy was in limbo. Secretary Vance had been impressed with Ecevit during their meetings in Ankara in January. The prime minister had stressed that solving the Cyprus problem was a priority, yet it was becoming clearer each day that the Turkish government was unwilling to put forward adequate proposals in a timely fashion to satisfy the opposition in Congress and within the Greek American community. Lee Hamilton's subcommittee on Europe and the Middle East expected the administration to submit its request—whatever that might be—by early April. That would be the deadline if Congress were to take action in the current session.[20]

For some time, many members of the House International Relations Committee, including Hamilton, had been eager for the administration to state its position. On February 14 chairman Clement Zablocki sent Vance a letter signed by a majority of his committee indicating their "sympathetic consideration" for both a Greek and a Turkish DCA, "providing the president gives his unequivocal support to such action."[21] Zablocki had opposed the embargo from the beginning, and his views had not changed when he became chair at the beginning of 1977. As the longest-serving Democrat on the committee, he had expected to move unchallenged into the chairmanship after Doc Morgan's retirement, but he faced a surprising attempt to block his election. Committee member Benjamin Rosenthal had issued a memorandum claiming that Zablocki was out of step with the foreign policy views of a majority of the Democratic caucus and should not be chosen to head this important body. Zablocki, characterizing the memorandum as "replete with falsehoods, distortions and innuendos," rallied his supporters. He easily won the chairmanship, but Rosenthal's action left a bitterness between the two men. At the time, the media claimed that Rosenthal's actions had been rooted in the fact that Zablocki often took an independent line regarding Israel, and the Israel lobby wanted a stronger supporter in this key position. Whatever Rosenthal's motives, he and Zablocki were likely to clash in the coming battle over the DCA.[22]

Carter faced a dilemma. If he brought the DCA forward, he would likely lose the support of both Greek Americans and key Democratic members of Congress, who would charge that he had failed to uphold his campaign promises, and the administration might well lose. If he did not seek congressional approval of the DCA, he would antagonize Turkey and widen the breach between the two allies. The president finally came to a decision in late March 1978. Vance, Brzezinski, and Secretary of Defense Harold Brown had recommended that quick action be taken to restore ties with Turkey before irreparable damage was done. They offered Carter a series of choices. The one they favored, and the president supported, was to move to have the embargo lifted without further delay. There would be fallout, they knew, with a segment of Congress and with the Greek American community, but it was a case of choosing the least bad alternative. This plan might backfire, especially if the Turks were unhelpful, but it seemed that this would be the best course for the administration.

The administration had backed away from the DCA for a number of reasons. For one thing, it had aroused opposition from senators and congressmen, who disliked such a long-term agreement covering a four-year period. Getting the embargo lifted seemed to be an easier task. As time passed without action, Prime Minister Ecevit himself had raised questions about the stalled agreement, suggesting that it was becoming obsolete. He had asked the secretary of state in January whether he thought the embargo should be lifted before the DCA was taken up in Congress.[23]

By maintaining constant pressure on the administration, the Gang of Four could take some credit for the final abandonment of the two-year-old Turkish DCA. Officials in the vice president's office and in the State Department had expressed doubt about the outcome if there were a vote on the measure. The president wanted a clear victory, so he decided not to proceed with the DCA.

Carter Takes a Stand

The opposition had little time to enjoy its partial victory. It had correctly assumed that the administration was about to change course. For the White House, Cyprus had become less significant; bolstering US-Turkey relations was now uppermost in the president's mind. Reports from Ankara indicated a decline in the effectiveness of Turkish military units. Real harm was being done to NATO's southeastern flank. If passage of the DCA seemed improbable, the White House had no choice but to seek a lifting of the embargo. There would, of course, be determined opposition, but that was a fight the administration believed it could win.

Washington was also concerned by the warming of relations between Ankara and Moscow. In December 1975 Premier Alexei Kosygin had made a second state visit to Turkey, and Prime Minister Ecevit was planning to reciprocate in the early summer of 1978. Continued estrangement between Washington and Ankara could lead to a long-term advantage for the Soviet Union.

The president met with Sarbanes and his associates on March 24 to announce the decision, as his advisers had recommended. The administration was especially mindful of the new senator's important role in passage of the Panama Canal treaties, and it wanted to stay in close contact with him on the Cyprus issue. The pro-embargo leaders appreciated being consulted, even if they did not agree with the president's new policy.[24]

The administration had learned a great deal during the long debate over ratification of the Panama Canal treaties (September 1977–April 1978). It would repeatedly draw on this experience in the coming months. Between April and August, the White House put together a detailed lobbying effort, relying on a range of resources, to achieve the lifting of the Turkish arms embargo. Gone was the divided counsel and hesitancy that had characterized the previous fall and winter. At least for the moment, everyone seemed to be in agreement. When Frank Moore sent the president a sober analysis of the challenges that lay ahead, Carter responded with typical derring-do: "Frank—Against these odds it will take a lot of planning & work—Let's go."[25]

Once the president prioritized an issue, as he did with the embargo, it received his complete attention. He might even put other issues on hold. That was his style. He could also be rigid if he thought he was right—as he clearly did in this case. Carter often impressed congressmen in meetings, but he did not always understand the predicaments his demands placed them in. In one meeting, a member of Congress observed that Carter was asking them to do the impossible by giving them one big issue after the other. They needed time to educate their constituents on controversial topics. They could handle one or two issues in a two-year term, "but we can't do it three or four times," he said. The president replied, "Well, if I can do it, you can do it."[26]

As soon as Carter had made his decision, he sent Deputy Secretary of State Warren Christopher to Ankara to explain why he had taken this course and how events would unfold. Earlier, Ecevit had threatened to boycott the NATO meeting in Washington in May if no action had been taken by then. Everything now depended on a successful vote in Congress.[27]

Throughout the spring and summer, the administration repeatedly stressed that the Turkish prime minister needed to be a strong advocate for repeal of the embargo. Secretary Vance even sent Ambassador Spiers to Brussels to emphasize this point again, just as the Turkish leader was about to depart for the United States. The American diplomat advised him, "What you say over the next ten days in Brussels, Washington and New York could well make the difference between success and failure."[28]

During the NATO heads-of-state meeting, Carter, Vance, and Brzezinski met with Ecevit and his advisers to discuss the status of US-Turkey relations. The president reassured him that Turkey was a high priority for the United States. The upcoming vote was critical, and he urged the prime minister to take every opportunity, when meeting with American political representatives and the media, to emphasize the constructive character of Turkey's position. Carter noted that he had faced similarly difficult votes on Panama and the Middle East, where the opposition had seemed insurmountable. In those cases, the administration had prevailed through careful planning and organization.[29] The administration also tried to orchestrate Rauf Denktash's comments when he visited the United States. Vance praised his constructive statements, many of which drew on material the State Department had provided. Denktash said he wanted to be helpful.[30]

By early April, the administration had revealed its position publicly. At a White House leadership breakfast on April 5, the president told the assembled congressional Democrats of his decision to seek to lift the embargo. "I realize this is not a popular position," he noted, but it was time "to break the

Cartoon in the *Washington Star*, April 7, 1978, criticizing Carter for supplying arms to Turkey. (©2019 Patrick Oliphant/Artists Rights Society, New York)

stalemate." He had already thoroughly discussed his decision with John Brademas. The following day, Secretary of State Vance, Secretary of Defense Brown, and General David Jones, chairman-designate of the Joint Chiefs of Staff, reported to the House International Relations Committee that the administration "had concluded it was in the national interest . . . to repeal, unconditionally, the arms embargo against Turkey." The White House was also going to renegotiate the DCA with Turkey.[31]

Matthew Nimetz gave a briefing on April 17 for the Senate Foreign Relations Committee staff, spelling out the details. He revealed that the administration had decided to scale back the DCA to cover only a single year rather than four years. The arms embargo would be lifted, and the United States would make a $50 million loan to Turkey to help with its economic problems. US NATO allies as well as Israel believed that it was necessary to maintain Turkish strength. This policy might seem similar to that of previous administrations, Nimetz remarked, but whereas they had been cynical on Cyprus, the Carter administration was not. There could be no progress there, however, without lifting the embargo.[32]

The congressional staffers present indicated little support for the administration's new policy, and staffers' views could prove decisive, as they provided important input on policy issues. In the Senate, they often attended meetings with administration officials, sitting in for their bosses. They then reported back to their respective senators, providing background and suggesting policy options. They were well informed and exercised considerable influence. According to Brian Atwood, it was somewhat different in the House. "Senators let their staff run things; House members pretty much do it themselves." The staffs of the various House committees, however, were well informed. Clifford Hackett, chief of staff for the Committee on Foreign Relations, for example, was widely respected for his depth of knowledge on all the details related to the Turkish arms embargo.[33]

According to Nelson Ledsky, staff members put together pieces of legislation and drafted and redrafted them to satisfy the majority of the committee members. Key staffers such as Michael Van Dusen, staff director of the Subcommittee on Europe and the Middle East chaired by Lee Hamilton, often spoke on behalf of their principals. "Talking to [Van Dusen]," reported Ledsky, "was just as effective as talking to Hamilton. . . . When he spoke on an issue, I could count on that position being Hamilton's."[34]

The Gang of Four, minus Eagleton, met again with Vice President Mondale, his adviser on national security Dennis Clift, and deputy national security adviser David Aaron to discuss the embargo. In the two months since their last meeting with Clifford, it had become clear that this was now a major foreign policy issue for the Carter administration. The Senate had narrowly ratified the Panama Canal treaties, and now it was time to focus on other problems. Indeed, in a televised news conference in early May, the president would declare that lifting the embargo was "the most immediate and urgent foreign policy decision" facing Congress.[35]

In this meeting, the two sides remained far apart. Mondale and his aides argued for the resumption of intercommunal talks in Cyprus, even in the absence of an adequate Turkish response. Brademas claimed the administration had gotten itself into a bind by seeking an end to the embargo without first seeing the Turkish proposals. He stated that the mood in the House was against them, and he accused the administration of incompetence in the handling of this issue. Sarbanes added that if the embargo were lifted and nothing happened, Cyprus would be forgotten. As tensions in the room mounted, Mondale "sharply rejected the suggestion that the administration's principal goal was ending the embargo, not getting the talks resumed."[36]

Generally, the vice president was very skillful at lessening antagonisms. When the president declined to meet with Archbishop Iakovos, for example, Mondale met with him instead and did his best to calm the archbishop's concerns about the new policy. Mondale told Iakovos that "he knew that the Administration's position was disappointing," but he promised to do all they could "to maintain and merit the trust which now exists." Iakovos responded in a similar tone, remarking that the Greek American community trusted the administration, and "we pray your efforts will be fruitful."[37]

Ethnic Opposition Reenergized

The Greek American community had sensed the changing attitude of the administration. At a conference on human rights called by the State Department at the end of February 1978, Mary Mantis of MFC asked why the United States had failed to use its leverage to help implement the UN refugee resolution on Cyprus passed in November 1974. Assistant Secretary of State Charles Maynes responded that the United States had been significantly involved in implementing that UN resolution. A faculty member from George Washington University, Nicos Kyriacopoulos, challenged that assessment and wondered why the State Department consistently advocated increased aid to Turkey when that country regularly violated human rights on Cyprus.[38]

In April a leading Greek American newspaper in New York City, *Proini* (Morning), published a series of statements on its front page questioning Carter's supposed commitment to human rights: "Human Rights a la Carter: Dispossess 200,000 Cypriots . . . Get $1 Billion" and "Mr. Carter 200,000 Refugees Like Your Speeches on Human Rights." Centered on the page was a cartoon showing a fallen figure labeled "Cyprus" with a knife in his back; standing over him was a disheveled figure identified as "Attila." From the right, a hand reached out (the United States) to offer another dagger to "Attila." The caption read: "No God-fearing person would supply daggers to criminals."[39]

At the same time, another letter campaign began, blanketing the House membership and referring to the Carter administration's hypocrisy as far as human rights were concerned. The letter warned that 1978 was an election year, and "many surprises are in store." On May 3 the House Foreign Affairs Committee voted narrowly (18–17) to lift the embargo. Four out of five California congressmen on the committee voted in favor of lifting the embargo, but the Northern California Friends of Cyprus singled out Leo Ryan, who represented its members' district, for strong criticism. The group pointed out that Ryan had changed his vote from a year earlier and claimed the embargo would work if the administration supported it. The UHAC placed an announcement in twenty-eight major newspapers across the country, asking readers to "Stop Carter's Sale of Guns to Turkey!" It advised them to send telegrams to their representatives in Congress.[40]

Nevertheless, these groups had an uphill battle against the media, which seemed to be lining up with the administration. In a *Washington Post* article, journalist John Goshko analyzed the source of influence of the Greek American minority, which had modeled itself on the Jewish lobby. He cited three factors that explained the Greek Americans' effectiveness: they were concentrated in a few key states (he mentioned New York, Massachusetts, Illinois, and Maryland); they were very successful professionals and businesspeople; and the Greek Orthodox Church kept them together, even when they moved out of the old ethnic neighborhoods. Most important, however, was the Greek Americans' buildup of support in Congress. Here, Goshko cited the "Big Four," who were "adept practitioners of the in-fighting and horse trading that are marks of congressional effectiveness." Even now, he noted, Speaker Tip O'Neill and majority leader Jim Wright (D-TX) would not openly support repeal of the embargo. Through all this, the quartet had effectively projected "an image of moderation and reasonableness."[41]

The *New Yorker* published a less complimentary piece on June 5, suggesting that Congressman Rosenthal was kowtowing to a large bloc of Greek Americans in his district and that Turkey might not have broken the law when it used US arms to invade Cyprus. A similar theme, emphasizing constituent pressures, appeared in an editorial in the *St. Paul Dispatch and Pioneer Press* titled "Lift the Embargo." The editor noted that "the reason for embargoing the Turks is the same as for not embargoing the Israelis, constituent pressures." Under the heading "Mend Fences with the Turks," the same editor claimed that the embargo "was a destructive, dangerous mistake and should be corrected."[42]

Members of the MFC responded immediately to each of these pieces. Homer Mantis defended Rosenthal to the editor of the *New Yorker*, saying that the New York congressman had opposed supplying arms to the Greek junta in the late 1960s, even though many of his constituents had not. Rosenthal had an unwavering commitment to the principle that US interests would not be served by alliances bought with military aid. Mantis also wrote to the editor of the *St. Paul Dispatch,* reminding him of the lessons learned from the Vietnam experience—that giving arms to undemocratic regimes did not enhance American security. And no one, he wrote, contended that "Turkey did not use US arms in its invasion."[43]

Clarke Chambers also wrote to the *St. Paul Dispatch* to clarify that Carter had promised in 1976 and 1977 that his administration would not restore aid to Turkey until significant progress had been made on Cyprus. Now he was pressing for an end to the embargo without any such progress. Mary Mantis, who had attended the human rights conference in February as well as a recent gathering of prominent Greek American leaders at the White House, criticized the *Dispatch* for its general lack of coverage of the Cyprus problem.[44] Editor William Sumner pushed back, writing, "I am sure you and professor Chambers can regale us with horror stories in regard to Cyprus. I am equally certain I could get some on the other side." This kind of response had seldom been encountered earlier. Sumner finished by suggesting that Mantis send him a short article stating her viewpoint.[45]

When President Carter met with the visiting Greek prime minister, Karamanlis expressed little support for lifting the embargo. He remarked that the solution to the problem lay in Ecevit's hands. "He is the man who conquered the island," he pointed out. When Karamanlis appeared before the House International Relations Committee at the request of Chairman Zablocki, he said much the same thing. And later, when the embargo vote was about to take place, he wrote to Carter warning that Turkey would become more intransigent and Greek public opinion more embittered toward the United States.[46]

Perhaps Karamanlis spoke so forcefully because of the declining fortunes of his party in Greece. In the 1977 elections, his New Democracy Party lost forty-nine seats, most of them going to the Panhellenic Socialist Movement led by Andreas Papandreou. Although Karamanlis's party retained a comfortable majority, the long-term trend seemed to favor the left. The prime minister was aware that Greek public opinion had shifted since the return to democracy in 1974. Greeks generally favored a more independent foreign policy, especially with regard to Greece's relationship with the United States. This may have accounted for his determination to take a tough line with the American president.[47]

Yet it appeared that some of the force had gone out of the Greek American offensive. The lobbying of Congress in mid-1978 seemed less intense compared with the Ford years. Perhaps the embargo and Cyprus had been debated for too long, and the public was more willing to accept the new administration's claims that the embargo had failed, Cyprus was not being helped, and important security arrangements with Turkey were being damaged. In addition, new issues had arisen in the Middle East, including delicate negotiations between Egypt and Israel and a worrisome situation developing in neighboring Iran. These captured the attention of both the public and the administration. Many believed the time had come to put the embargo issue to rest after four years of agitation.

The board of the Minnesota Friends of Cyprus had already noted a lack of press coverage on the third anniversary of the Turkish invasion in August 1977 and of other Cyprus-related events in the Twin Cities. This had spurred its letters-to-the-editor campaign, which achieved limited results. MFC membership and resources were declining, indicating that interest was fading, even within the Greek American community.[48]

On June 22, 1978, the president hosted 100 Greek American leaders—among them Mary Mantis—at the White House. This was a crucial meeting, as Congress moved toward a decisive vote on the embargo. Archbishop Iakovos had declined to attend, concerned that his presence might be misinterpreted as support for the administration's policy. In replying to the invitation, he wrote, "I strongly believe that peace cannot be promoted by sending arms to a 'well-known' ally that has little regard for human rights and certainly less for peace. . . . I find it inappropriate to attend a discussion and briefing on a matter of policy which has already been crystallized by the administration and to which I conscientiously object."[49]

Given this preliminary statement by the foremost leader of the Greek American community, the administration had to be prepared for a storm of criticism from those who accepted the invitation to the White House. Deputy Secretary of State Warren Christopher, Clark Clifford, and General George Allen of the US Air Force each spoke at some length. Christopher told the group that he expected a chain reaction to take place once the embargo had been lifted. Ecevit had been returned to power and seemed determined to make progress on Cyprus; he would be handicapped if the embargo continued. Then Clifford talked about his fifty-year love affair with Greece. After eighteen months of working on this issue, he was convinced that the embargo was a hindrance, not an aid, to a settlement. General Allen emphasized how important Greece and Turkey were to NATO. The military strength of both countries had diminished, and steps needed to be taken to restore the southeastern flank of the alliance.[50]

Finally, President Carter talked of his friendship with many members of the group and how important it was to share ideas. He spoke in support of ending the embargo. And then he admitted, with characteristic candor, "I have learned a lot since I have become president, which I did not know as a candidate." Carter claimed that he had not broken his word but merely differed with those assembled on how peace for Cyprus could best be achieved.[51]

The inveterate critic George Christopher spoke first for the Greek Americans, noting that he had embraced Carter the candidate, who had promised justice for Cyprus. Now, he said, he would have to retrace his steps to the Republican Party. The embargo had failed because first Ford and Kissinger and now this administration had not supported it. "Where have we addressed human rights on Cyprus?" he asked. Finally, he challenged those who criticized Greek Americans for opposing administration policy, calling his people "the finest group of Americans."[52]

Others spoke more briefly but in a similar vein, emphasizing human rights violations. Nick Petris, the influential California state senator, remarked that Carter's policy on human rights had been inspiring at first, but it had been "diminished by selective application." The president responded by observing that human rights on Cyprus had been violated for a long time before the present crisis. "Perhaps, there have been violations on the other side," he suggested. Here, of course, he was referring to Greek Cypriot actions toward the Turkish Cypriot minority, a topic that officials had previously avoided.[53]

Essentially, no new arguments came forth from either side. Most of the statements only reiterated what had been said many times before during the previous and current administrations. Only one new theme appeared—a concern for human rights—which everyone now felt obligated to include in his or her remarks. Ironically, this was due in part to the president's own agenda.

Carter faced a dilemma: he did not want to be seen as abandoning his earlier promises, but he believed the embargo must be lifted. In the long run, he knew he would be proved right.

Doing Battle

The Carter administration had set a course that looked remarkably similar to that of its predecessor. In fact, the president telephoned Gerald Ford and asked him to lobby key Republican senators to vote for repeal of the embargo, as the measure would not pass without strong bipartisan support. Ford agreed. The call from the White House must have given him some satisfaction, although members of his party bristled at the thought of contributing to another foreign policy success for Carter.[54]

The Republicans in Congress—responding to the rejection of Richard Nixon and the so-called imperial presidency and hoping to hang on to vulnerable seats in the upcoming off-year elections—had narrowly supported the embargo in the fall of 1974, but by the summer of the following year, they had turned against it. Their loyalty to the Ford administration, even if somewhat conflicted, was not surprising. That they continued to support the Carter administration on this issue requires some explanation. It was not an easy decision for John Rhodes and his caucus members. The minority leader accused the Democrats of playing politics with the Cyprus issue. They had, he complained, "rammed" the embargo through Congress. And "during the campaign," Carter himself had "played the sleaziest kind of politics with the Cyprus situation." The Democrats had passed the measure and taken the political credit, "and now [they] are asking Republicans to furnish votes to help repeal it." According to the House Republican leadership, this forced a Hobson's choice on the minority members: either emulate the Democrats and play politics, or "consider the importance of our NATO alliance." They would, of course, choose the latter. Rhodes could never sacrifice principle for political expediency, he explained, when doing so would weaken the whole defense structure of the Free World.[55]

Former minority whip Robert Griffin, who served on the Senate Foreign Relations Committee, continued to oppose the embargo under President Carter, reiterating that it had been "dictated by the political whims of 535 congressional 'Secretaries of State.'" He claimed that it was "'ineffective' and even 'counterproductive' as a means of trying to restore peace to Cyprus." Although Griffin was acutely aware of the opinions of his Greek American constituents in Michigan—his mail ran almost ten to one against lifting the embargo—he would continue to be guided by his own best judgment "on the merits of the issue."[56]

The White House selected a bipartisan group of fourteen supporters on Capitol Hill to lead the challenge to the embargo. The president would unleash the same kind of campaign that had succeeded in obtaining passage of the Panama Canal treaties in the Senate. This included briefing sessions for uncommitted legislators; lobbying by General Alexander Haig, commander of NATO forces in Europe, and other top military leaders, as well as by Ronald Spiers, US ambassador to Turkey; and working to secure the support of major veterans' organizations. The assistant secretary of state for congressional relations put together a packet showing overwhelming newspaper support countrywide for lifting the embargo.[57]

Clark Clifford took a very active and effective part in the Capitol Hill lobbying effort. He briefed relevant committees and groups of legislators at White House breakfasts; as the vote approached in each chamber, he contacted individual senators and representatives to press for their support. In responding to wavering congressmen, he drew on wisdom gained from long experience in government, telling them that "policy must continually be tested against reality. If a policy is not bringing the desired result, consideration should be given to changing it. That is certainly one of the lessons I learned from our Viet-Nam policy of the 1960s."[58]

The Senate voted first, on July 25. Although the administration felt comfortable about the likely outcome, its lobbyists (including the president himself) appealed individually to all but the sixteen senators most firmly opposed to repeal. The measure passed easily, 57–42, with a majority of Republicans in support and a majority of Democrats opposed.[59]

Senators voting with the majority supported the administration for a variety of reasons. They worried about the embargo's harmful effects on Turkey's military, on NATO, and on US-Turkish relations. Senator Robert Byrd, now majority leader, had recently returned from a visit to NATO allies as the president's personal representative. He reported to his colleagues that German officials strongly believed the embargo should be lifted. Chancellor Helmut Schmidt wondered whether Congress comprehended the full political effect of the embargo in the eastern Mediterranean. For Byrd, there seemed to be a constitutional as well as a practical issue. As he related to one constituent who complained about the Turkish embargo, "I have no direct authority whatever in the conduct of our foreign policy, the Constitution placing upon the President this responsibility. The situation in the Middle East is such an inflammatory one, changing from day to day, that consultation with the Senate is not possible on every development."[60]

The majority leader had organized a bipartisan group of senators to back the amended international security assistance bill, which now called for the lifting of the embargo. Byrd arranged for his colleagues and their staffs to meet with members of the Joint Chiefs of Staff and top administration officials. He focused his lobbying efforts on new senators "who had not been in Congress at the time of the earlier battles over Turkey." He was pleased by "the surprisingly large margin in the vote" on July 25.[61]

On the day after the vote, Dan Tate, the administration's liaison with the Senate, wrote to Byrd, praising his masterful handling of the embargo issue. Two days later, President Carter sent Byrd a formal thank-you note, adding at the bottom in his bold, distinctive handwriting, "Your leadership was crucial—J." They seemed to be on a winning trajectory.[62]

In spite of the victory in the upper chamber, members of the administration were concerned about the upcoming vote in the House. They needed to gain the support of younger, more liberal Democratic members, and for this, they counted on the vice president. According to Frank Moore, Mondale was "the best vehicle" for winning these votes.[63] They also wanted UN Ambassador Andrew Young to get involved, especially with the members of the Congressional Black Caucus. White House chief of staff Hamilton Jordan urged the president to give Young a nudge. Although they had already asked the ambassador to help, he had not yet met with the caucus.[64]

The administration faced an unusual predicament in the House of Representatives, where all the most prominent Democrats, including the Speaker, the majority leader, and the chief Democratic whip, planned to vote against lifting the embargo. As Rhodes would remark during the upcoming debate, "So, Mr. Speaker, I would be much less reluctant to vote to end the Turkish arms embargo if you and the Majority Whip would join me." Although the Senate had voted to lift the embargo by a comfortable margin, everyone knew that the House vote would be "very, very close." Many members were "reluctant to take the heat back home" without the support of their leadership.[65]

Supporters of the embargo did all they could to influence undecided congressmen. Greek American constituents met with a number of representatives to try to convince them to support the embargo. Under such pressure, Representatives Edwin Forsythe (R-NJ) and John Buchanan (R-AL) apparently agreed to keep the arms limitations in place. Another representative, Lamar Gudger (D-NC), expressed an interest in participating in the upcoming floor fight, but he needed to be briefed on the latest developments. The staffers agreed that it was important for non-Greeks to play vocal roles in the debate.[66]

In the relatively quiet hours before the battle in the House, Archbishop Iakovos wrote to John Brademas to thank him for all his efforts over the past four years. He referred to Brademas "as one of the greatest American statesmen of our time. Championing the law of the land and defending the inalienable rights of the wronged and oppressed." Iakovos wished him success in the days ahead.[67]

A group of twenty-one pro-embargo congressmen sent out a series of five letters to their colleagues, beginning on July 24, providing context for the upcoming vote. In one, they listed all the steps Congress had taken to "ease the pressure on Turkey," without any substantial response from Ankara. In another, they argued that if the embargo were lifted, the administration would use this as a wedge to exclude Congress from its rightful place in the foreign policy–making process. After referring to the tragedy in Vietnam and the abuses of Watergate, they claimed that surrendering to the administration now would be seen "as an abdication of our newly regained responsibility." Finally, they explained how the debate would proceed in the House. Fascell, Rosenthal, and Edward Derwinski (R-IL) would offer an amendment to the international security assistance bill that would strike section 16, which called for an end to the Turkish arms embargo. The bill would be presented for debate on Monday, July 31, and voting would take place on August 1. They urged support for their amendment.[68]

Before the vote, a debate appeared in the pages of *US News and World Report* between two Jewish congressmen, Stephen Solarz (D-NY) and Benjamin Rosenthal, both ardent supporters of Israel. Solarz favored lifting the embargo for all the reasons previously mentioned. The only new perspective was Rosenthal's comment that the law applied to all countries receiving US arms, which meant that Israel might face a similar cutoff if its forces stayed in Lebanon as long as Turkey's had in Cyprus.[69]

Brademas's office once again became the control center for the House debate. His assistant, Jim Morrey, provided him with a list of people to invite to a strategy meeting one week before the vote. Each person attending the meeting would receive a list of congressmen to contact regarding their votes. "At this point we have no way of gauging how much damage the administration has done. I'd like to take no chances," wrote the staff assistant. By the afternoon of Friday, July 28, they hoped to have a good idea of the likely vote in the House if all the whips did their work. Morrey suggested putting out a packet of Oliphant cartoons, critical of administration policy regarding Turkey and Cyprus, that UHAC had put together. "We might as well have some fun at this," he told his boss.[70]

Brademas took the floor on July 31, sensing that the mood of the House was against him. He would be surprised, he said, "if today the House voted to sustain its previous position." Nevertheless, he would present all the arguments they needed to hear. The president, who had talked so much about human rights, seemed to have lost his way, said Brademas, noting that "the view from the White House is different than the view from the campaign platform." He made it clear that he refused to be part of any compromise that was merely cosmetic. Finally, he thought the United States should stand by its principles: "might does not make right, bullies ought to be resisted, expediency does not justify abandonment of principles." He urged his colleagues on both sides of the aisle to stand with him.[71] It was an impassioned appeal, but the administration had done its work too well. The House voted narrowly, 205–208, not to approve the amendment. After four years of struggle, the cause had finally been lost.[72]

As in the Senate, a majority of House Democrats voted to maintain the embargo, and a majority of Republicans supported its repeal. The Republican majority was much smaller than in October 1975, presumably because many GOP members were reluctant to contribute to another success for the Carter administration. Nevertheless, Frank Moore's observation regarding the Panama Canal treaties was equally applicable to the lifting of the embargo. "We couldn't have done it without the Republicans," he remarked, "without the Republican establishment supporting it."[73]

Embargo supporters were unrepentant. Brademas saw the narrowness of the defeat as "a great moral victory." He noted that, "once again, as in the Senate, President Carter's position on this issue was rejected by a majority of his own party." Speaker O'Neill viewed the closeness of the vote as an assurance of "a continuing American commitment to a fair and just settlement of the Cyprus situation." Congress, he believed, "would not hesitate to restore the military embargo" should the Turkish government fail to make substantial progress toward a solution.[74]

Throughout the long effort with Congress, the State Department had not neglected the contending parties in the eastern Mediterranean. Staff had hoped the United Nations would sponsor a resumption of talks. US officials urged the Turkish Cypriots to be more flexible and told the Greek Cypriots that this might be "the last opportunity to negotiate for several years to come." These approaches brought no positive results. According to UN Secretary-General Waldheim, both sides had become "so preoccupied with the debate in the Congress . . . that the negotiation of a Cyprus settlement has become secondary." And so the matter rested.[75]

Mending Fences

The administration had little time to savor its victory before the situation in Iran began to unravel. Back in June, Paul Henze had referred to "riots in Iran" and other disturbances in the region, stressing the desirability of "keeping Turkey firmly on our side." The collapse of the shah would put new pressures on Ankara and lead many Turkish officials to wonder how much they could rely on US support in a crisis.[76]

The administration did, however, take a few moments to extend thanks and to celebrate. President Carter sent letters to a small group of legislators who had taken leading roles in the repeal. Madeleine Albright, then a midlevel official on the NSC staff, sent a warm note to Clifford, thanking him for his many presentations and his "crucial role" in achieving victory. (Clifford soon turned to other assignments, having accomplished his mission.) Stephen Solarz, one of only four Jewish congressmen to vote for repeal, hosted a party for the victors at his home.[77]

Soon, a bipartisan group of eleven congressmen showed the remarkable pragmatism of American politics. Having just ended a hard-fought battle over repeal of the arms embargo, these former opponents, including Lee Hamilton, Clement Zablocki, and Paul Findley on one side and John Brademas, Benjamin Rosenthal, and Dante Fascell on the other, wrote to the president, urging him to pursue an early initiative to settle the dispute on Cyprus. They assured him of their full support.[78]

Prime Minister Ecevit, however, made it clear that Turkey did not want the Cyprus issue to be internationalized. The United States, he argued, should not become directly involved in Greek-Turkey problems. Instead, Washington should encourage negotiations from the sidelines. Soon after President Carter signed the legislation lifting the embargo in October, the Turks reopened the four intelligence-gathering bases to the Americans.[79]

Although some Greek American activists had urged him to do so, Carter was unlikely to take up the Cyprus issue using personal diplomacy, as he had recently done with Israel and Egypt at Camp David. There were far too many other issues demanding his attention and offering better chances of success. Now that amicable relations were being restored with Turkey, the president would not endanger that fragile relationship by pressing Ankara on Cyprus.

After August 1, however, the White House did take steps to restore ties to the disaffected Greek American community. Andrew Manatos drafted a memorandum pointing out the danger of Greek Americans returning to the Republican Party. He argued that although they felt betrayed, it might be possible to reverse this drift. According to another official, the Greek American community wanted to see whether Carter would use "as much influence with Turkey in settling Cyprus as he did in influencing Congress in lifting the embargo." A meeting with Sarbanes and Brademas in the near future would be important to assure them of the president's determination to pursue "a just and lasting solution in Cyprus."[80]

Following the signing of the Camp David Accords on September 17, resolving many of the differences between Egypt and Israel, some Greek Americans encouraged President Carter to give similar personal attention to the Cyprus problem. Henze was adamantly opposed to coddling the Greek lobby, as he so bluntly put it, or to any idea of "a Camp David type" involvement by Carter. The administration must avoid the past mistake of letting Brademas and Sarbanes "call the shots." Only national security concerns should determine policy.[81]

Henze also complained to Brzezinski that the president should not meet with Archbishop Chrysostomos, Makarios's spiritual successor, who was a hard-liner on Cyprus matters. This could send the wrong message just as Cypriot president Spyros Kyprianou and Turkish Cypriot leader Rauf Denktash were about to resume talks. Henze marveled at "the ingeniousness of the Greeks and Armenians in taking advantage of the president's good nature and religious predilections." He also reported a brief conversation with the archbishop at a reception at the Cyprus embassy. Chrysostomos had remarked, "'Oh, you are from the NSC staff—that is a collection of enemies of Cyprus.'" Henze doubted that Carter would gain many Greek American votes as a result of a photo session with the archbishop, and he concluded that the president needed to demonstrate "a statesmanlike preoccupation with fundamentals." Henze seemed to persuade Brzezinski, who recommended to Anne Wexler, the president's assistant for public liaison, that the planned meeting be dropped.[82]

President Carter, however, did not take that advice. He met Chrysostomos along with Archbishop Iakovos, and they had a brief, substantive discussion about Cyprus. It was important for the administration to welcome these leading churchmen to the White House if it wanted to regain some support in the Greek American community. The president had to think politically, Henze's comments notwithstanding.

Henze, who seemed determined to promote US-Turkey relations, weighed in again in November 1979 when he wrote to Brzezinski, assessing the president's response to Ambassador Spiers. Carter had told Spiers that the Turks were consistently negative and needed to give more. Henze characterized this reply as "depressing and petulant," showing a "shallow understanding of the realities of our relationship toward an indispensable ally." These were exceptionally harsh words to put to paper; one wonders how the national security adviser responded.[83]

Clearly, the unity that had prevailed within the administration up to the repeal of the embargo had evaporated. Once again, the vice president tried to smooth out differences, even though he was not comfortable opposing many of his former congressional colleagues. Mondale asked Sarbanes and Brademas to review his proposed comments for a Greek National Television interview celebrating the fifth anniversary of the return of democracy to Greece in July 1979. Earlier, he had met with the two legislators to discuss developments on Cyprus. He knew they had been working in their respective chambers to oppose additional grant aid for Turkey. Although many senators had been reluctant to oppose Sarbanes, the influential junior senator from Maryland, majority leader Byrd had convinced sixty-three of his colleagues to support $50 million in additional military grant aid for Turkey. Brademas, however, managed to thwart the Senate's largesse, winning an overwhelming majority of votes (303–107) in the House in opposition to the increase. It took three months to resolve the differences between the two houses. Ironically, it was Brian Atwood, formerly on Eagleton's staff and now part of the Carter administration, who arranged the meeting between Byrd and Zablocki, where the compromise was reached.[84]

Mondale also met with several Greek American leaders, who urged the administration to take a new initiative. There seemed to be a window of opportunity that the White House should not ignore. Mondale sent a memorandum to Carter urging him to meet with Andy Athens, chairman of UHAC, for whom he had great respect. The vice president spoke to Greek American groups in New England in May, and in June he spoke in Chicago at a banquet celebrating the twentieth anniversary of the enthronement of

Archbishop Iakovos. In a speech that contained many pleasantries, Mondale did not shy away from the most sensitive topic. He assured the audience that "none of us will rest until the day of justice has come for all of the people of Cyprus."[85]

In the year following the lifting of the embargo, President Carter courted the two most important representatives of the Greek American community. In April he met with leaders of AHEPA, and in September the White House staged a Greek American festival on the South Lawn to celebrate Archbishop Iakovos's twentieth anniversary as primate of the Americas. The following June, Iakovos was awarded the Presidential Medal of Freedom for his progressive religious ideas related to human rights and the ecumenical movement.[86]

The importance of the ethnic vote captured the attention of most politicians and their advisers but left many in a quandary. According to Stephen Aiello, special assistant to the president for ethnic affairs, the ethnic vote had been a major factor in Ford's loss to Carter in 1976 and was now playing a role in Carter's run for reelection; many ethnic voters had recently crossed party lines in primaries or supported Ted Kennedy in protest. The administration, he argued, needed to include more ethnics in its campaign structure. Some political observers, however, still questioned whether an ethnic viewpoint on a particular issue always equated with the national interest. According to Michael Van Dusen, Congressman Hamilton's staff director, ethnic political pressure could be beneficial, but it could also have negative effects when lobbying groups became fixated on a particular cause and would not change their views in spite of strong countervailing evidence.[87]

Apparently, some of the Greek American organizations had decided to make their peace with the administration. Brademas was surprised at the warm reception Carter received from Iakovos and leaders of AHEPA at its annual dinner in late February 1980. Unlike President Ford's brief address four years earlier, Carter delivered a long speech brimming with praise for the accomplishments of Greek Americans and for the profound legacy of Greek culture. He extolled the educational accomplishments of Paul Sarbanes and John Brademas, both Rhodes scholars. All this brought forth loud applause. Carter even mentioned the troubled island of Cyprus, pointing out how hard his administration had worked to bring peace there. He reached out to the Greek American community as effectively as he possibly could.[88]

Prime Minister Karamanlis was not so quick to settle his differences with the administration. One year after the lifting of the embargo, he sent a tough letter to Carter stating that Turkey's Cyprus policy had not changed, just as he had predicted. Now, the administration and Congress were in an embarrassing position, he noted. The prime minister seemed to take satisfaction in the fulfillment of his prophecy.[89]

This letter prompted a remarkable shift in thinking by Greece's newly arrived ambassador John Tzounis. Privately, he claimed that Karamanlis's policy had backfired, angering the White House and many in Congress. The prime minister's decision to support the legislative branch against the executive had resulted in deep anti-Greek attitudes among senior officials. Tzounis planned to present his views to Foreign Minister Georgios Rallis (1978–1980) and then meet with Karamanlis himself.[90]

As the 1980 presidential election approached, Greek American opponents spoke out against the Carter administration. In the primaries, many had supported Ted Kennedy, but when he lost the nomination, they turned to the Republican nominee, who had criticized Carter for reneging on his pledges regarding Cyprus. To no one's surprise, George Christopher encouraged them to vote for Ronald Reagan. President Carter, he said, had "betrayed three million Greek Americans."[91] The administration countered by arguing that a Republican administration had caused the problems in the first place. The Carter campaign pointed out that Reagan had already asked Henry Kissinger for advice on the presidential debates, and the former secretary of state had an abysmal record on the Cyprus issue. Further, by building defenses against the Soviet Union, Reagan would "greatly exalt Turkey because of Turkey's strategic location."[92]

Greek American friends of the Carter administration were few. Chris Spirou, Andy Athens, and Andy Manatos urged the administration to take some action, even late in the campaign, to show its concern about issues of importance to the Greek American community. Spirou, a New Hampshire legislator, encouraged meetings between Secretary of State Edmund Muskie and leaders of the community. He warned that without this show of concern, he could no longer lobby for the president's reelection.[93]

In a White House meeting, Brademas and the president seemed to agree that the recent military coup in Turkey was "munificent." The congressman suggested that it presented an excellent opportunity to bring Greece back into the NATO military command. Such a step could be extremely helpful in states with large numbers of Greek American voters, such as New York and Illinois. Carter replied that he was already working on this.[94]

Speaker Tip O'Neill (center) and John Brademas (right) greeting the Speaker of the Cyprus House of Representatives on Capitol Hill, 1980. (Courtesy Burns Library, Boston College)

The Carter White House did what it could to restore good relations with the Greek American community. Anne Wexler emphasized how important this could be in the election. "The importance of this effort," she wrote, "to the continuance of our presence in this building cannot be overemphasized." In what was the equivalent of a Hail Mary pass, she organized a meeting at the White House for 100 Greek American leaders from all over the country just a few days before the election. Even more surprising, perhaps, was the fact that Brzezinski was the featured speaker.[95]

In mid-1979 the national security adviser had sent a memorandum to the president that Henze would have approved of. Brzezinski argued that "*de facto* partition in the framework of political stalemate" had settled on Cyprus. The issue had waned in importance in both Greece and Turkey. Congress had only complicated the problem, according to Brzezinski, and it was difficult to see "how any move made by the United States . . . could help now."

The United States should keep a low profile, he advised, and let the United Nations take the lead. Although his views had apparently not changed since then, it is unlikely that he conveyed this sobering message to the Greek American leaders gathered at the White House less than a week before the election.[96]

Brademas had much more to worry about than Carter's reelection. Due to gerrymandering by the Republican-controlled legislature in Indianapolis in 1968, areas of strong Democratic support in his Third District had been replaced by Republican counties. Now he faced a tough race against John Hiler, a twenty-seven-year-old businessman. As one journalist phrased the situation, "The House's Golden Greek Is a Republican Target This Year." Brademas lost the election by a remarkable 10 percent margin, and after twenty-two years of service, he left the House of Representatives. Although several factors influenced the outcome, including the Reagan landslide, high unemployment related to the recession, disenchantment with big government, and out-of-state funding for Hiler, one wonders how much Brademas's leadership on the Cyprus issue and the Turkish embargo contributed to his defeat.[97]

Like his predecessor, Carter failed in his bid for a second term, losing decisively to Reagan in the November election. He had, however, begun the process of restoring harmonious relations with Turkey. In his final presidential communication to the Turkish government on January 17, 1981, Carter wrote, "I take particular satisfaction from the knowledge that sustained efforts in Ankara and Washington have put the Turkish-American relationship back on a solid foundation." This success would enhance security in the region in the troubled times that lay ahead. He made no mention of Cyprus.[98]

Historians have begun to reassess the Carter administration's foreign policy, challenging the first generation of scholars who argued that, overall, it produced a series of failures, including SALT II, Nicaragua, the disaster in the Horn of Africa, and, above all, the collapse of the shah's government in Iran. More recent studies, especially those by Professor Nancy Mitchell, have argued persuasively that Carter and his policies have been misunderstood, that he was always a cold warrior and "was in fact waging a more complex, preemptive, and diffuse Cold War." Trying to address too many issues in his first year in office—more than he could hope to settle—opened him to criticism that he was naïve, weak, and incompetent. Mitchell has focused on Carter's successes in Africa, including the administration's efforts to help resolve the Rhodesian crisis and its indirect support of Somalia in its war against Ethiopia, a Soviet client state. Others have added the Panama Canal treaties, the establishment of full diplomatic relations with the People's Republic of China, and the Camp David Accords. And now, I think, we can add the lifting of the Turkish arms embargo to that list of successes. Even though we cannot know precisely what the final assessment of Carter's foreign policy will look like, it will surely be more positive than originally suggested.[99]

Conclusion

Scholars have long viewed the Turkish arms embargo as a prime example of the antagonistic relationship between Congress and the executive during the transformative decade of the 1970s. During this time, it is said, legislators acted—with disastrous results—to usurp the president's prerogative to make and conduct foreign policy. In hindsight, this episode represents a rare occasion when a series of critical factors aligned to temporarily tilt the advantage toward the insurgents. And even though it did not herald a permanent transformation in governance, it did have lasting significance.

In addition to a number of critical factors—among them a weakened presidency, a botched coup attempt, an aggressive and determined ally, and an epidemic of drug abuse—personalities contributed to the deepening of the crisis. As skillfully as Secretary of State Kissinger could woo foreign leaders and their diplomatic representatives, he possessed an uncanny ability to antagonize domestic opponents, who often found him arrogant and sought to check his unbridled domination of American foreign policy. Several seasoned, determined, and resourceful Capitol Hill characters joined forces in a timely manner to achieve their surprising victory. They could rely, at least for a time, on the support of colleagues who were impatient for a greater voice in international affairs.

The embargo movement drew supporters from a variety of backgrounds—defenders of human rights, legal constitutionalists, advocates of ethnic revival, antidrug crusaders, and even Turkophobes—uniting them in a common cause. Included in this group were many senior legislators, who typically would not be expected to offer such a blatant challenge to executive authority. Given their divergent interests, any success they achieved would likely be temporary, lasting long enough to obtain only short-term objectives.

The importance of the ethnic factor in the 1970s cannot be overemphasized. In the mid-1970s political leaders found important ethnic and religious allies among Greek, Armenian, and Jewish Americans in communities across the country, proving once again how effective well-organized minorities can be. Their religious and fraternal organizations exercised remarkable influence at both ends of Pennsylvania Avenue.

Because the Cyprus crisis came on the heels of the Watergate scandal and the undoing of the Nixon presidency, it proved relatively easy to rally forces that were rooted in respect for the law to challenge Turkey's violation of its bilateral arms agreement. "If not now, when?" became a common refrain.

Still, even a weakened President Ford had at his disposal many tools to thwart Congress. It was therefore no trifling success that the pro-embargo forces remained focused and determined, despite attempts to divide and overwhelm them. Even under Ford's successor, who enjoyed large majorities in both houses of Congress, the pro-embargo forces came within three votes of delivering a major defeat to Carter at the hands of his fellow Democrats.

The scourge of drug addiction fed a desire to punish those responsible for the spread of this modern epidemic. This desire was fed by fear, which government policy and popular film culture magnified. In this rush to judgment, Turkey became the principal target of American wrath, even though the evidence did not support the accusation.

Perhaps we should look at the embargo not as an example of a system in crisis but as an example of one that worked exceedingly well. The struggle for and against Turkish sanctions proved the efficacy of essential elements of our democracy. When it finally ended, Americans could take well-deserved satisfaction in the process.

Congress had reestablished its bona fides as a partner—albeit a junior one—in the development of foreign policy. Congress had done what it was supposed to do, confronting the executive when justified. The House and Senate may have overreacted initially, but good sense prevailed. All the well-developed internal mechanisms— committees, staffs, hearings—had functioned as they ought to. Any future administration would ignore Capitol Hill at its peril, and yet, this very experience may have served as a salutary check on any subsequent congressional challenges to foreign policy.

The executive, too, had orchestrated its own campaigns to convince Congress to alter course, lobbying groups of lawmakers at White House briefings, providing expert testimony to congressional committees, and buttonholing individual senators and representatives. These measures took time and involved substantial give-and-take, but they eventually achieved success.

The counteroffensive against the embargo would have taken much longer to succeed absent bipartisan support. Members of the minority party showed their mettle, putting nation above party interests. Their tough decisions deserved more approbation than they received at the time.

We also witnessed remarkable input from segments of society well beyond Washington. Individual activists and groups lobbied elected representatives with amazing effectiveness. Their voices became diminished only over time, when the negative impact of the embargo became more apparent.

The media played a key role in the crisis, at first supporting the embargo movement with telling cartoons, well-researched articles, and thoughtful editorials. Later, press opinion shifted in response to a growing recognition of the harmful effects of the embargo on US interests.

And what about the international aspects of the crisis that threatened US relations with Greece and Turkey? Here, too, US leaders found an acceptable, if awkward, way forward. They gathered information regarding drugs, refugees, policies, and politics, all the while encouraging foreign leaders to work toward solutions.

Most important, however, was Turkey's attitude. Throughout the embargo years, the Turkish government rejected compromise when it believed its basic interests were being threatened. It showed intense resistance, using every means available. Successive governments in Ankara refused to yield to American pressure on either Cyprus or the cultivation of opium poppies. Because of its strategic location, bordering both Iran and the USSR, Washington had to approach Turkey thoughtfully. Greeks, Greek Cypriots, and their supporters in the United States became frustrated when they realized that Washington would not continue to press Ankara indefinitely to withdraw from Cyprus. Realpolitik eventually carried the day, with only a perfunctory nod to moral claims.

Over the next four decades, Washington did not forget this lesson. Yet today, US-Turkey relations stand at a low point due to differing interpretations of security. Washington has once again increased the pressure on Ankara to bend to its will, and the Erdogan government refuses to yield. Some rethinking of tactics seems overdue.

Epilogue

De Facto Partition

During the Reagan administration the Cyprus issue continued to fade, although the new president took care to reach out to the Greek American community. The president met with Archbishop Iakovos early in his first term, listening politely to his concerns. A picture of the two smiling leaders appeared on the front page of the *Hellenic Times.* Another familiar voice was that of George Christopher, who had helped mobilize Greek American support for candidate Reagan. Early in 1983 he wrote to the president, criticizing the administration's decision to increase aid to Turkey without any progress on Cyprus. He went on to accuse the president of a "complete reversal" of his campaign promises. When Christopher discovered that his nemesis Henry Kissinger had visited Ankara in an apparently semiofficial capacity, he wrote a worried letter to national security adviser William Clark, seeking clarification. Clark responded promptly, indicating that Kissinger's trip had been wholly private and assuring Christopher that the administration continued to support UN-sponsored talks in Cyprus.[1]

In spite of general reassurances, supporters of Cyprus in Congress struggled to maintain US assistance for the island. In August 1981 Lee Hamilton, chair of the Subcommittee on Europe and the Middle East, asked Secretary of State Alexander Haig to explain why, for the second time that year, the administration had decided to reprogram funds earmarked for Cyprus. Concerned legislators campaigned repeatedly to maintain a level of $15 million a year for refugee aid. In 1986 the Reagan administration threatened to divert most of the money earmarked for Cyprus to Ireland to support the peace initiative there. Eagleton and Sarbanes, still in the Senate, challenged the move. With the bipartisan support of eight other senators, they explained to

President Reagan and Archbishop Iakovos at the White House, November 1981. (Courtesy Reagan Presidential Library)

Secretary of State George Shultz why this was such a bad decision. The administration relented and took the funds from Sudan instead. Long before this time, of course, the Gang of Four had ceased to exist. Brademas had gone on to serve as the very successful president of New York University (1981–1992). Rosenthal had died in Washington on January 11, 1983, at the relatively young age of sixty.[2] He did not live to see the closing of the door to compromise in Cyprus. On November 15, 1983, the Turkish Cypriots declared the independence of their portion of the island. Henceforth it would be called the Turkish Republic of Northern Cyprus. The following month Turkey became the only nation to recognize the new state.

One knowledgeable observer, Constantinos Lordos, a member of the Cypriot House of Representatives, had feared such a move. Writing to Senator Tsongas in April 1982, he had warned that "with every passing day the two communities are drifting further apart." They had been living as total strangers without any personal contact. Thus, they became prey to "rumor, misunderstanding and mistrust." Although Lordos remained optimistic about a settlement, he could not have been surprised by this outcome.[3]

Protesting the declaration establishing the Turkish Republic of Northern Cyprus, New York City, November 18, 1983. Left to right: Eleni Kazantzakis; Peter Cardiges, supreme president of AHEPA; Andrew Athens, chairman of UHAC (partially obscured); Metropolitan Silas; Linas Kojelis, Public Liaison Office of the White House; Archbishop Iakovos; Mayor Edward Koch; Philip Christopher, Pancyprian Association of America. (Courtesy Greek Orthodox Archdiocese of North and South America)

Reaction to this development in the United States was predictable. The Greek American community held demonstrations of protest across the country. One of the largest took place in New York City, with prominent religious and political figures attending. Archbishop Iakovos was joined by Cyprus president Spyros Kyprianou, New York City mayor Ed Koch, a representative from the Reagan administration and another from Governor Mario Cuomo's office, New York Republican senator Alfonse D'Amato, and leaders of all the important Greek American organizations.[4]

Clement Zablocki, still chair of the House International Relations Committee, wrote to the Turkish ambassador, Sukru Elekdag, to warn that Turkey's decision to recognize the new republic might jeopardize US military assistance. Measures were being initiated in the House to reduce or even eliminate these funds. Zablocki did not know whether these measures could be defeated or what his own position might be. He urged the Turkish government "to reconsider its action and support intercommunal talks."[5]

The ambassador had recently written an op-ed for the *Washington Times* titled "Greece and Turkey Should Be Friends." Interestingly, not once did he refer to the Cyprus issue, as if this no longer affected relations between the two NATO allies. This was the preferred position of the Turkish government and of many of its supporters in the United States.[6]

Rauf Denktash, president of the newly declared republic, quickly sent an exculpatory letter to select members of Congress, justifying the actions of the Turkish Cypriot parliament. Hoping, no doubt, to forestall any official backlash from Washington, he placed the decision in the context of an inalienable right of his people, repeatedly referring to the American Declaration of Independence. This step would not, he remarked, in any way affect the establishment of a genuine federation of equal partners on the island. He ended by calling for "an equitable, objective and constructive attitude" toward the republic on the part of the United States.[7]

Turkey's recognition of the new republic strained relations with the Reagan administration, prompting Foreign Minister Ilter Turkmen's mission to Washington and an exchange of letters between Tukey's president Kenan Evren and President Reagan. The Americans opposed the Turkish Cypriot decision and asked Ankara to do all it could to have it rescinded. The Turkish president expressed his dismay "to see that what has happened in Cyprus is portrayed as a serious rift between our two countries." Evren observed that there was such a broad range of shared interests between the two allies that he could not understand how events "in the tiny island" could put everything else at risk. He hoped that Reagan would personally "enable everybody concerned to see the present problem in its true dimensions" and would refrain from taking any measures to impair the Turkish-American friendship.[8]

As chief of the General Staff of Turkey, General Evren had led a successful coup d'etat on September 12, 1980. Frustrated by a bankrupt economy, increasing violence between left- and right-wing groups, and the rising influence of Islamic fundamentalism, the military finally took action. The officers would hold power until the restoration of democracy in November 1983. Members of the European Union strongly criticized the seizure of power, but Washington showed more understanding. The generals initiated a course correction in Turkey's foreign policy, moving the country closer to the United States than either Ecevit or Demirel would have thought prudent. Evren served as appointed president until November 1989. In Turkey, rumors persisted that the United States had been involved in plotting the coup d'etat, but to this day, all evidence remains circumstantial.[9]

It was certainly easier for the United States to deal with the military government in Ankara. It enabled Greece to resume full membership in NATO in October 1980, after an absence of more than six years. This pleased Karamanlis, now serving as president in Athens. Members of the Carter administration could trumpet this success to the disaffected members of the Greek American community.

Congressmen and senators would make threats from time to time, leveling many of the same charges as their predecessors and warning of limiting or even cutting off US assistance. These threats would elicit concerned letters from the Turkish embassy and high-level administration meetings, where most would agree that "Congress is the problem." The State Department and the Department of Defense would vow to do a better job of getting across the vital message that, with all the turmoil in the region, "Turkey's strength and well-being" were vital to Western interests. Given Turkey's enhanced strategic position, the likelihood of any punitive measures seemed remote. Further, the experience of what had happened during the embargo provided a note of caution for would-be activists.[10]

Turkish officials could draw their own conclusions from events. In spite of American bluster, they must have believed that they could push Washington, without serious consequences. US officials concentrated increasingly on Southwest Asia and the importance of Turkey in that region. The Soviet invasion of Afghanistan, the Iranian revolution, security concerns in the Persian Gulf, civil war in Lebanon, and the Iran-Iraq War all called for closer US Turkish cooperation, making it highly unlikely that Washington would confront Ankara over Cyprus. In the 1980s only Israel and Egypt received more US military and economic aid than Turkey.[11]

The arms embargo provided an important lesson for the Turkish government as well. In the future, it would arrange to hire lobbyists in Washington to present its arguments whenever sensitive bilateral issues arose. The recent controversy (2017) over then–national security adviser Michael Flynn's lobbying efforts on behalf of Prime Minister Erdogan's government provides a good example of how successful Ankara has become in this regard.

Today, Americans pay little attention to what happens on the island of Cyprus; there are too many other pressing issues in the eastern Mediterranean region, including Israel-Palestine, Turkey and the Kurds, and civil war in Syria. All these events are being played out in the neighborhood of Cyprus and are seemingly far more urgent than the fate of the divided island. In the 1960s and 1970s Cyprus regularly appeared on front pages of major newspapers across the country. Many Americans were focused on that medium-sized island, believing that if its long-running interethnic problem could be solved, it might provide momentum for the resolution of other divisive issues, such as the civil war in Lebanon, and thus contribute to lasting peace in the region.

Political differences between the two ethnic communities on Cyprus are far from resolved. This raises the possibility that Greece and Turkey will be drawn in, and those two nations happen to be the defenders of NATO's southeastern flank. Rising tensions could prove disastrous for the military alliance. In addition to differences over Cyprus, Athens and Ankara continue to engage in their own direct disputes over islands in the Aegean and hydrocarbon reserves in those waters. With the recent discovery of oil and gas reserves in the territorial waters of Cyprus, the divided island is making news again. Whether these discoveries will help or hinder reunification has yet to be determined.

The de facto partition of Cyprus took place well over forty years ago, and life on the island has not stood still. Over the decades, there has clearly been more change on the Greek Cypriot side, where the economy has flourished. In 2004 the Republic of Cyprus became a member of the European Union, and this membership has contributed substantially to its economic growth. As a member of the EU, Cyprus has the ability to veto Turkey's full membership in the organization, for any expansion must receive the unanimous support of existing members. The Turkish Republic of Northern Cyprus remains something of a backwater; it is still recognized only by Turkey and is hindered by international sanctions. Most of its contacts abroad are filtered through the Republic of Turkey. Its population has grown in part due to emigration from Anatolia. Its per capita gross domestic product stands at about half that of the Republic of Cyprus.

There have been occasional discussions between leaders of the two communities, but disagreements abound. These concern security of the island, the continued occupation of the north by the Turkish army, the disposition of abandoned property on either side of the dividing line, and the place of the settler population in a federal state. Perhaps the closest the island came to reunification was the 2004 Anan Plan, named for the then–UN secretary-general. This plan would have set up a federal government with limited powers and shared rule, such as Archbishop Makarios seemed to be on the verge of endorsing before his untimely death in August 1977. In the 2004 referendum, the Turkish Cypriot community voted overwhelmingly (65 percent) in support of the plan, while the Greek Cypriot community rejected it by an especially large majority (76 percent). Now, of course, the discovery of hydrocarbons in offshore waters might add a new and potent reason for disagreements to continue.

Successive US administrations have taken care not to appear to want a settlement more than the parties themselves. Developments in the 1970s led to a unique time in the history of American foreign policy. Congressional activism resulting from the Watergate scandal and the Vietnam War created a distrustful relationship between Congress and the White House, but that did not become the norm. Even in those heady days of the Watergate radicals, leaders in both houses of Congress felt uncomfortable pressing their advantage over the executive branch in foreign policy making. One might reasonably suggest that the harm done to US-Turkey relations by the arms embargo provided a cautionary lesson for future members of Congress.

As for the Greek and Armenian ethnic lobbies, which were so critical to the initial success of the embargo movement, their power ebbed soon after reaching its peak in the late summer of 1975. In contrast, the pro-Israel lobby group AIPAC has maintained its influence over the years by successfully making its case to the American public that Washington and Tel Aviv share mutual security and cultural interests. Few American politicians would argue that Cyprus or even Greece is more important to US security than the Republic of Turkey. Even during the Ford administration, embargo proponents failed to convince Americans of that proposition. Rather, it was a combination of concerns—legal, political, and humanitarian—that succeeded in producing a perfect storm that, for a brief time, thwarted the wishes of both Republican and Democratic administrations.

Acknowledgments

This study benefited from the support of numerous archivists, librarians, and scholarly colleagues over the past decade. Without this support, such work would be almost impossible, and I extend heartfelt thanks to all of them. I would like to note in particular the assistance of archivists Elizabeth Druga (Ford Presidential Library), Sara Mitchell (Carter Presidential Library), Michael Pinckney (Reagan Presidential Library), Maura Coonan (Immigration History Research Center), John M. Zarrillo (New York University Archives), Anthony Sampas (University of Massachusetts, Lowell), Andrew Isidoro (Burns Library, Boston College), Erin Sidwell (Library of Congress), and Katie Rudolph (Denver Public Library). I would also like to thank the librarians at Grand Valley State University (GVSU), who helped me obtain some obscure publications. Scholars K. C. Johnson, Douglas Little, Ekavi Athanassopoulou, and Fatih Tokatli offered thoughtful comments on all or part of the manuscript, as did the two anonymous readers for the University Press of Kentucky. Many former colleagues at GVSU, especially John Constantelos and David Zwart, contributed important insights. I am grateful to the Center for Scholarly and Creative Excellence and the Padnos International Center at GVSU, which funded several research trips to archives. Thanks also to J. Brian Atwood, then dean of the Hubert H. Humphrey School of Public Affairs at the University of Minnesota, who interrupted his busy schedule for a lengthy interview, and to Susan Gahan, also at the University of Minnesota, who kindly accepted a short-term research mission at the IHRC. Finally, thank you to the editorial staff at the University Press of Kentucky: Melissa Hammer, who guided me through the approval stage, and her successor Natalie O'Neal, who brought me to the finish line, kindly answering myriad questions and providing helpful suggestions, and Sarah Olson, who expertly guided the process of turning my manuscript into a book.

Appendix

The International Debate over Human Rights Violations

On January 23, 1977, the *Sunday Times* of London published excerpts from a hitherto secret report by the European Commission of Human Rights, focusing on allegations made by the government of Cyprus against Turkey. The commission had concluded that Turkey was guilty of violating seven articles of the European Convention on Human Rights and forwarded its findings to the member nations of the Council of Europe for a determination of whether to apply sanctions.

The report cited numerous serious human rights violations, many of which related to the Turkish army and concerned the period from the Turkish invasion to the end of 1975. The appearance of the report set off two years of intense discussions and negotiations among all parties to determine the proper course of action. European governments trod carefully; they did not want to antagonize Ankara unduly, but they also needed to uphold their good reputation on human rights.

Turkey submitted a lengthy rebuttal, denying all allegations and charging that they were nothing more than attempts by Greeks and Greek Cypriots to blacken its international reputation. All the evidence of human rights violations came from Greek Cypriots, it claimed, and was not credible. The Turkish public generally assumed that this was "just another in a long series of anti-Turkish efforts by Greek Cypriots."[1]

Inevitably, the United States became deeply involved in the discussion. The Carter administration was clearly mindful of the recent strained relations with Ankara and the US failure to convince Turkey to resolve the Cyprus situation. Furthermore, to the extent that relations between Cyprus and Turkey worsened because of these allegations, the likelihood of a general settlement on the island also diminished.[2]

The United States and its European allies agreed that human rights conditions had improved dramatically by the end of the first year of the Turkish occupation. Although they never doubted that human rights violations occurred on Cyprus during the period of intense fighting, American officials believed that Turkey was not solely responsible. Rather, these acts reflected "long-standing intercommunal hatreds" that did not represent deliberate policy, nor had they continued to the present.[3]

In early 1978 the State Department mentioned the commission's report in its annual nation-by-nation human rights report to Congress. The Turkish ambassador protested, and Assistant Secretary George Vest replied in part that the "Department had tried to take into consideration Turkish sensitivities to [the] extent possible." However, the commission's report was now in the public domain, and they could not ignore it.[4]

Finally, in January 1979, the Council of Europe completed action on the original complaints by Cyprus, reaching a decision that was, according to the State Department, "as good a mix of the political exigencies and the human rights system aspects as could be found." The council urged the resumption of intercommunal talks under UN auspices and agreed to declassify four relevant texts, including the controversial 1976 commission report itself. (The EC-nine states only reluctantly accepted the release of the human rights document, which they considered "lacking in balance.") Apparently, the decision satisfied none of the contending parties.[5]

Notes

Abbreviations

AAD	Access to Archival Databases, National Archives, Suitland, MD
BCP	John Brademas Congressional Papers, New York University, New York City
CLH	Center for Lowell History, University of Massachusetts, Lowell
FRUS	*Foreign Relations of the United States*
GPO	Government Printing Office
GRFPL	Gerald R. Ford Presidential Library, Ann Arbor, MI
IHRC	Immigrant History Research Center, University of Minnesota, Minneapolis
JCPL	Jimmy Carter Presidential Library, Atlanta, GA
Memcon	memorandum of conversation
MFC	Records of the Minnesota Friends of Cyprus, IHRC
MHS	Minnesota Historical Society, St. Paul
NLC	National Library Carter
NSA	national security adviser
RAC	Remote Archives Capture
RG	Record Group
RRPL	Ronald Reagan Presidential Library, Simi Valley, CA
SHSM	State Historical Society of Missouri, Columbia
SS	secretary of state

Preface

1. Some of the most important early studies are Richard C. Campany Jr., *Turkey and the United States: The Arms Embargo Period* (New York: Praeger, 1986); Thomas M. Franck and Edward Weisband, *Foreign Policy by Congress* (New York: Oxford University Press, 1979); Clifford Hackett, "Ethnic Politics in Congress: The Turkish Embargo Experience," in *Ethnicity in U.S. Foreign Policy,* ed. Abdul A. Said (New York: Praeger, 1977); Ellen B. Laipson, *Congressional-Executive Relations and the Turkish Arms*

Embargo, Congress and Foreign Policy Series no. 3 (Washington, DC: GPO, 1981); Hoyt Purvis and Steven J. Blake, eds., *Legislating Foreign Policy* (Boulder, CO: Westview Press, 1984); Paul Y. Watanabe, *Ethnic Groups, Congress, and American Foreign Policy: The Politics of the Turkish Arms Embargo* (Westport, CT: Greenwood Press, 1984). I have been especially interested in and influenced by the exceptional work of Robert David Johnson, *Congress and the Cold War* (Cambridge: Cambridge University Press, 2005), which appeared approximately twenty years after the earlier works. Only a small part of his fine study of Congress is devoted to the crisis with Turkey.

2. After the initial Greek-inspired coup d'etat in Nicosia and the Turkish invasion that followed, the role of Athens in resolving the crisis was less significant than developments in either Ankara or Cyprus.

3. At the beginning of the Ninety-Fifth Congress in January 1977, the Democrats held 292 seats in the House and 61 in the Senate.

4. Unfortunately, the papers of Senator Paul Sarbanes at Johns Hopkins University have not yet been opened for research. He was a key figure in Congress during this episode.

1. Background to Crisis

1. A few observers claimed that Greece had also illegally introduced US arms into Cyprus, but their argument found little support. Democracy had just returned to Athens with the fall of the junta. After seven years of harsh military rule (1967–1974), the Americans seemed unlikely to chastise the new government for actions initiated by the right-wing officers.

2. As an indication of this developing interest, in March 1946 the US government returned the remains of former Turkish ambassador Munir Ertugun, who had died in Washington during the war, on board the renowned battleship USS *Missouri.* This singular honor impressed the Turkish government and the Turkish people. Bruce R. Kuniholm, *The Origins of the Cold War in the Near East: Great Power Conflict and Diplomacy in Iran, Turkey, and Greece* (Princeton, NJ: Princeton University Press, 1980), 335–37.

3. Ekavi Athanassopoulou, *Turkey–Anglo-American Security Interests, 1945–1952: The First Enlargement of NATO* (Portland, OR: Routledge, 1999), 163–68, 174–80, 176. Dean Acheson, *Present at the Creation: My Years in the State Department* (New York: W. W. Norton, 1969), 195–96, 563–64.

4. According to a recent study, however, the government in Ankara only gradually accepted an "activist foreign policy" toward Cyprus. During the late 1940s and 1950s, the media and the public campaigned for a change from passive acceptance of the status quo on the island. Eventually, the government policy shifted, partly in response to this popular nationalist impulse. Umut Uzer, *Identity and Turkish Foreign Policy: The Kemalist Influence in Cyprus and the Caucasus* (New York: I. B. Tauris, 2011), 116, 117, 143–45.

5. Mustafa Aydin, "Determinants of Turkish Foreign Policy: Changing Patterns and Conjunctures during the Cold War," *Middle Eastern Studies* 36, no. 1 (January 2000): 121.

6. Document 59, in US Department of State, *FRUS, 1964–1968,* vol. 16, *Cyprus; Greece; Turkey* (Washington, DC: Office of the Bureau of Public Affairs, 2000).

7. Nasuh Uslu, *The Turkish-American Relationship between 1947 and 2003: The History of a Distinctive Alliance* (New York: Nova Science Publishers, 2003), 172–73.

8. *Enosis* refers to the movement to unite Cyprus and Greece. Double enosis would result in partition of the island, with the Turkish Cypriots joining Turkey and the Greek Cypriots joining Greece.

9. I gave almost no attention to the harsh rule of the military junta in Athens that had taken power two years before our visit.

2. Killing America's Children

1. James W. Spain, "The United States, Turkey and the Poppy," *Middle East Journal* 29 (Summer 1975): 298–99. Spain later served as US ambassador to Ankara in 1980–1981. In 1974 the poppy-growing area in Turkey had shrunk to only six provinces and four towns of Konya province, all in the southwestern part of the country. This was a reduction from forty-two provinces in 1961. Jorrit Kamminga, "Opium Poppy Licensing in Turkey: A Model to Solve Afghanistan's Illegal Opium Economy?" in International Council on Security and Development, *Afghanistan Reports* (January 2011), 12–16. According to a September 7, 1975, article in the *Baltimore Sun,* "2 per cent of the illicit heroin reaching this country comes from Turkish poppies." Heroin is a highly processed form of opium. It takes approximately ten pounds of opium to produce one pound of heroin.

2. https://www.rogerebert.com/reviews/midnight-express-1978; emphasis added.

3. Eugene Rossides, an American of Greek Cypriot heritage and one of the most forceful members of the committee, argued for a hard line against Turkey. "We are at war," he proclaimed. "If the Turks refuse to go along with us in this crusade against heroin, we have to consider them enemies rather than allies." See Edward Jay Epstein, *Agency of Fear: Opiates and Political Power in America* (New York: Putnam, 1977), 86–91. A CIA report had estimated that Turkey was responsible for only 3 to 8 percent of the illicit opium produced globally. Kamminga, "Opium Poppy Licensing in Turkey," 16; Uslu, *Turkish-American Relationship,* 223. See US Department of State, *FRUS, 1969–1976,* vol. E-1, *Documents on Global Issues, 1969–1972* (Washington, DC: Office of the Historian, Bureau of Public Affairs, 2005), docs. 148–227, for the development of the campaign against Turkey.

4. Kamminga, "Opium Poppy Licensing in Turkey," 24–26. See also Kyle T. Evered, "'Poppies Are Democracy!' A Critical Geopolitics of Opium Eradication and Reintroduction in Turkey," *Geographical Review* 101, no. 3 (2011): 299–315, which includes reflections from Turkish poppy farmers.

5. James Spain attributed the decline to better local control in poppy-growing areas far to the east of Turkey. Spain, "The United States, Turkey and the Poppy," 304.

6. SS to US Embassy, Ankara, March 22, 1974, RG 59, Central Foreign Policy Files, 1973–1976, AAD.

7. SS to US Embassy, Ankara, April 11, 1974, AAD. Passman was a consistent opponent of foreign aid in any form, which he claimed amounted to taking from the poor in rich countries and giving to the rich in poor countries.

8. SS to US Mission, UN, May 13, 1974, AAD. Senator Mondale had become greatly concerned about the growing opioid epidemic in the country. Email to author, May 16, 2019.

9. US Embassy, Ankara, to SS, April 12, 1974, AAD.

10. Memcon, April 15, 1974, in US Department of State, *FRUS, 1969–1976,* vol. 30, *Greece; Cyprus; Turkey, 1973–1976* (Washington, DC: Office of the Historian, Bureau of Public Affairs, 2007), doc. 201. Unsurprisingly, humor can improve relationships with counterparts. Self-deprecating humor is especially effective in this respect: it not only increases likability but also elevates counterparts' status by inviting them into the "in crowd," granting them permission to laugh both with you and at you, despite your opposing roles. An occasional joke about yourself can create an environment of collaboration, as long as it does not go too far. https://www.linkedin.com/pulse/using-humor-negotiations-michael-robertson/.

11. Memcon, April 15, 1974.

12. US Embassy, Ankara, to SS, May 6, 1974, AAD.

13. Spain, "The United States, Turkey and the Poppy," 302; SS to US Embassy, Ankara, May 28, 1974, AAD.

14. Document 204, July 2, 1974, in *FRUS, 1969–1976,* vol. 30.

15. Document 204, July 2, 1974.

16. US Congress, House Committee on Foreign Affairs, *Turkish Opium Ban Negotiations: Hearing before the Committee on Foreign Affairs,* 93rd Cong., 2nd sess., July 16, 1974, 5, 7.

17. US Congress, *Turkish Opium Ban Negotiations,* 38. The Ad Hoc Committee on Narcotics knew that there was considerable "leakage" of Indian opium into illicit markets, even if the congressman did not. Epstein, *Agency of Fear,* 87.

18. US Congress, *Turkish Opium Ban Negotiations,* 51, 56.

19. US Congress, *Turkish Opium Ban Negotiations,* 205.

20. It is worth noting that these critical votes took place well before the new "radical" members of the so-called Watergate Congress (the Ninety-Fourth) took office in January 1975.

3. Making Turkey Pay

1. Observations based on the author's visit to Paphos, September 1969.

2. Henry Kissinger, *Years of Renewal* (New York: Simon & Schuster, 1999), 218.

3. Greek, Turkish, and Cypriot affairs had been transferred earlier in 1974 to the European Division within the State Department, and many of those with experience in the eastern Mediterranean countries had been transferred elsewhere. Thus, when the crisis began that summer, expertise was lacking. Document 91, July 17, 1974, in *FRUS, 1969–1976*, vol. 30. According to Nelson Ledsky, a new arrival at the Office of Southern European Affairs, Bureau of European Affairs, he had never been to any of the countries he was asked to cover, and his "background in Greece, Turkey and Cyprus matters was woefully inadequate and out of date." Interview with Ambassador Nelson Ledsky, June 28, 2003, Association for Diplomatic Studies and Training, Foreign Affairs Oral History Project, Georgetown University.

4. Kissinger, *Years of Renewal,* 217–18. Kissinger telephoned British foreign secretary James Callaghan on the evening of July 20, immediately after the Turkish attack. In response to Callaghan's question about what he would do if the fighting continued, the secretary of state replied that the United States "would cut off aid to the Turks, and indeed to the Greeks if they took up arms. The U.S. would not act as an open supply line for this fighting." This is puzzling, given Kissinger's stout opposition to sanctions against Turkey. Was this perhaps a bit of bravado that the secretary of state had no intention of actualizing? Was he genuinely—if only briefly—angry at the Turks? Whatever his intentions at that moment, he soon turned to other remedies. British Foreign and Commonwealth Office to British Embassy, Ankara, July 20, 1974, in *Nuclear Weapons and Turkey since 1959,* Briefing Book 688, ed. William Burr (National Security Archive, George Washington University, Washington, DC).

5. Kissinger, *Years of Renewal,* 209–10, 228–29.

6. Campany, *Turkey and the United States,* 52; Uzer, *Identity and Turkish Foreign Policy,* 117, 144; Uslu, *Turkish-American Relationship,* 216; US Embassy, Ankara, to SS, July 30, August 10, 1974, AAD.

7. Saloutos diary, August 30–September 17, 1974, box 79, 2355, Theodore Saloutos Papers, IHRC.

8. US Embassy, Ankara, to SS, August 19, 1974, AAD.

9. US Embassy, Ankara, to SS, August 24, 1974, AAD.

10. Robert L. Beisner, *Dean Acheson: A Life in the Cold War* (New York: Oxford University Press, 2006), 633, 635, 647.

11. Karine V. Walther, *Sacred Interests: U.S. Foreign Relations in the Islamicate World, 1821–1921* (Chapel Hill: University of North Carolina Press, 2015), 62, 66, 72.

12. "Dear Friends," n.d., Donald M. Fraser, Congressional Office Files, box 36, MHS. The attempt to cut off US arms to Greece did not succeed. As chair of the House Foreign Affairs Subcommittee on International Organizations and Movements, however, Fraser had taken the lead in organizing hearings on human rights violations, including those in Greece. Given the reform of House rules in 1970, subcommittee chairs now exercised more authority and had larger staffs to assist them. Sarah B. Snyder, *From Selma to Moscow: How Human Rights Activists Transformed U.S. Foreign Policy* (New York: Columbia University Press, 2018), 148–53, 244.

13. Flyer, n.d., box I: 36, MC 168, BCP. In Turkey, the operation was also called the Cyprus Peace Offensive. Turks view Attila as a hero with an important place in their history, so using his name would not have seemed unusual. Many Turkish parents proudly name their sons after the king of the Huns.

14. Kavadas to Spence, August 22, 1974, box I: 22, MC 168, BCP.

15. Spiro Romvos to Brademas, October 2, 1974, box I: 33, MC 168, BCP; Basil Rodes to Ford, n.d., ibid.; Gloria Mary Zulumian to Kissinger, February 26, 1975, box 163B, Paul Tsongas Collection, CLH.

16. *Ahepan,* January–February 1975, 13.

17. Embassy of Cyprus, November 20, 1974, box I: 33, MC 168, BCP; Iakovos to Brademas, December 9, 1974, box I: 32, MC 168, BCP. In the Greek Orthodox Church, a priest may be married if the marriage occurs before his ordination.

18. *Ahepan,* November 1974, S-7. See also the appendix.

19. US Embassy, Ankara, to SS, August 21, 1974, AAD; US Embassy, Athens, to SS, July 25, 1974, AAD; US Embassy, Nicosia, to SS, October 1, 1974, AAD.

20. *Ahepan,* October 1974, 12; *Turkish Daily News,* March 1, 1975. One is reminded of President George W. Bush's reference, following the 9/11 attacks, to a "crusade" against terrorism. This sparked fears of a modern crusade against Islam, or a clash of civilizations. Bush quickly clarified his meaning. See also James F. Goode, *Negotiating for the Past: Archaeology, Nationalism, and Diplomacy in the Middle East, 1919–1941* (Austin: University of Texas Press, 2007), 21–23.

21. I remember well a newspaper headline in 1999 in the *Turkish Daily News* that encapsulated this Turkish regional perspective: "Secretary of State Albright," it read, "has arrived in Ankara after her recent trip to the Middle East[!]"

22. Greek-American Co-ordinating Committee of Illinois and Indiana, August 26, 1974, box V: 16, MC 168, BCP.

23. Press release, July 22, 1974, box I: 23, MC 168, BCP.

24. Watanabe, *Ethnic Groups, Congress, and American Foreign Policy,* 145–46.

25. Watanabe, *Ethnic Groups, Congress, and American Foreign Policy,* 146–47.

26. Memorandum, July 26, 1974, box I: 22, MC 168, BCP. Evidence of such a conspiracy has never come to light. Perhaps Iakovos meant only that US policies and inaction had enabled Turkish action.

27. Brademas et al. to Karamanlis, July 26, 1974, box II: 30, MC 168, BCP.

28. Goldbloom to Fraser, February 16, 1971, Donald M. Fraser, Congressional Office Files, box 36, MHS. It appears that none of the Greek American congressmen actively opposed the junta.

29. Memorandum, July 29, 1974, box I: 22, MC 168, BCP.

30. Announcement by Greek Orthodox Archdiocese, July 30, 1974, box I: 22, MC 168, BCP. UN Security Council Resolution 353, passed unanimously on July 20, called for the immediate withdrawal of all foreign military personnel from Cyprus and for Turkey, Greece, and Britain to enter negotiations aimed at returning peace and constitutional government to the island.

31. Proceedings, Order of AHEPA, 52nd Supreme Convention, Boston, August 18–24, 1974, 305, 316.

32. Proceedings, 86.

33. Proceedings, 113–14.

34. *Ahepan,* March–April 1975, 10.

35. Matthew Frye Jacobson, *Roots Too: White Ethnic Revival in Post–Civil Rights America* (Cambridge, MA: Harvard University Press, 2006), 26, 212; Salim Yaqub, *Imperfect Strangers: Americans, Arabs, and U.S.–Middle East Relations in the 1970s* (Ithaca, NY: Cornell University Press, 2016), 60.

36. Saloutos diary, IHRC. Roybal cited Otto Passman, chair of the Foreign Operations Subcommittee, who had a favorite project in Taiwan and was willing to swap votes in support of his program.

37. Umut Uzer challenges this notion, writing that "nobody wanted independence for Cyprus as their first preference." He argues that there was no Cypriot cultural identity at the time and that those on the island thought of themselves as either Greeks or Turks "who happened to reside in Cyprus." Uzer, *Identity and Turkish Foreign Policy,* 113–14.

38. Founded in 1890, the ARF was an Armenian nationalist and socialist political party also known as the Dashnaks. Much of the city of Smyrna (called Izmir by the Turks) was burned in the closing days of the Greek-Turkish War, when most of the Greek and Armenian residents fled elsewhere for safety.

39. Saloutos diary, IHRC.

40. Brademas to Rev. Constantine Mathews, August 3, 1974, box V: 16, MC 168, BCP; Brademas to Prof. J. Robert Nelson, August 3, 1974, box II: 02, MC 168, BCP.

41. Letter to members of House, August 14, 1974, box I: 22, MC 168, BCP.

42. Barbara Keys, "Congress, Kissinger and the Origins of Human Rights Diplomacy," *Diplomatic History* 34, no. 5 (2010): 823–51.

43. Memorandum of meeting with SS, August 15, 1974, box II: 02, MC 168, BCP.

44. Brademas, handwritten notes, February 3, 1975, box I: 34, MC 168, BCP.

45. "JB's Encounter with President Ford," October 12, 1974, box I: 33, MC 168, BCP.

46. "JB's Encounter with President Ford."

47. Interview with Brian Atwood, May 29, 2014, Minneapolis.

48. Atwood interview.

49. Atwood interview.

50. Atwood interview.

51. Watanabe, *Ethnic Groups, Congress, and American Foreign Policy,* 117.

52. Watanabe, *Ethnic Groups, Congress, and American Foreign Policy,* 112, 127. Eagleton is referring to Kissinger's support for General Pinochet in Chile and for the Karachi government in the bloody war against the secession of East Pakistan (Bangladesh) in 1971.

53. Franck and Weisband, *Foreign Policy by Congress,* 42.

54. Brademas to Eagleton, September 16, 1974, box II: 30, MC 168, BCP; *Ahepan,* November 1974, 11.

55. Brademas, handwritten notes, October 20, 1974, box I: 32, MC 168, BCP.

56. Greek-American Ethnic Groups, n.d., box 3, Myron Kuropas Files, GRFPL; draft letter, n.d., box I: 22, MC 168, BCP.

57. *Newsweek,* October 21, 1974, 43.

58. See Johnson, *Congress and the Cold War,* 199–231.

59. The vote on October 11 was 106 to 44, and the vote on December 11 was 98 to 73.

60. Timmons to Ford and Jones to Scowcroft, September 24, 1974, box 22, Presidential Handwriting File, GRFPL.

61. Document 211, September 26, 1974, in *FRUS, 1969–1976,* vol. 30.

62. Kissinger to Ford, October 7, 1974, box 2, Presidential Name File, National Security Adviser's Files, GRFPL.

63. Scowcroft to Kissinger, October 30, 1974, box 16, NSA–Trip Briefing Book, RAC Program, GRFPL; Ford, Kissinger, and Scowcroft, NSA Memcons, December 3, 1974, box 7, GRFPL; Kissinger, Schlesinger, and Scowcroft, NSA Memcons, November 14, 1974, ibid.

64. With a caretaker government in Ankara from September to March, even if Kissinger had acted more resolutely, his chances of success were slight.

65. Van Voorst to Conway, December 27, 1974, box "Storeroom," series 1: Legislation, 94th Congress, Wayne Hays Papers, MSS Collection 96, Ohio University Archives, Athens, OH. Few in Washington knew of this arrangement, but as the following quotes indicate, the Greek media assumed that Hays was representing the secretary of state: "Kissinger Man Mediates on Cyprus—Congressman Hays in Athens and Ankara" (*Vima*), "The Flying Foreign Minister (Kissinger) this time mobilized Democrat Congressman Hays to serve his objectives" (*Avghi*). Press summary and translation, Athens, January 3–4, 1975, box 23, folder 2, series 1, Hays Papers.

66. Brademas, Sarbanes, and Makarios, Memcons, January 9, 1975, box II: 30, MC 168, BCP.

67. Brademas et al. to Kissinger, January 28, 1975, box II: 30, MC 168, BCP.

68. Document 172, February 1, 1975, in *FRUS, 1969–1976,* vol. 30.

69. Document 172, February 1, 1975.

70. Eagleton seemed to be responding in part to a confidential memorandum written by his chief foreign policy adviser Brian Atwood. Minutes of telephone conversation between Eagleton and Brademas, February 3, 1975, box I: 34, MC 168, BCP.

4. Turning Congress

1. NSA Memcons, February 6, 1975, box 9, GRFPL.

2. NSA Memcons, February 6, 1975.

3. NSA Memcons, February 6, 1975.

4. Max Friedersdorf to Ford, February 7, 1975, Presidential Handwriting File, box 22, GRFPL. Although the proposal to name Rusk went nowhere, it underlines the level of antagonism toward the secretary of state.

5. Bi-Partisan Congressional Leaders, February 20, 1975, Ron Nessen Papers, box 294, GRFPL.

6. Bi-Partisan Congressional Leaders, February 20, 1975.

7. Ford and Kissinger, NSA Memcons, February 25, 1975, box 9, GRFPL; Ford, Kissinger, and Scowcroft, NSA Memcons, February 21, 1975, ibid.

8. Brademas to Morris Katz, January 13, 1976, box I: 23, MC 168, BCP.

9. Green to Brademas, February 25, 1975, box V: 19, MC 168, BCP; Green to Brademas, March 22, 1975, box II: 03, MC 168, BCP.

10. Creasey to Rosenthal, March 2, 1975, box 3, Benjamin Rosenthal Papers, Queens College, City University of New York. Creasey's wife was a Greek Cypriot.

11. Koch to Iakovos, February 25, 1975, box II: 30, MC 168, BCP; Iakovos to Koch, December 2, 1975, box I: 32, MC 168, BCP.

12. "Note Regarding Cyprus-Israeli Relations," July 10, 1975, folder 4523, Thomas Eagleton Papers, SHSM.

13. Shiffman to Rosenthal, March 11, 1975, box 3, Rosenthal Papers; Rosenthal to Shiffman, April 3, 1975, ibid. Dimitrios Bitsios served as minister of foreign affairs from 1974 to 1977.

14. Washington to US Delegation Secretary, July 10, 1975, AAD; Franck and Weisband, *Foreign Policy by Congress,* 193.

15. Memo to file, September 12, 1975, box I: 30, MC 168, BCP.

16. Memorandum, July 26, 1977, box 1, Rosenthal Papers. In June 1975 Archbishop Makarios had visited several Arab states, including Syria, Iraq, Egypt, and Libya, to seek backing for the withdrawal of Turkish forces from Cyprus. Congressional Research Service Issues Brief, July 14, 1975, box 16, Robert C. Byrd Congressional Papers, Robert C. Byrd Center for Legislative Studies, Shepherdstown, WV.

17. Rosenthal to Alexandrakis, August 2, 1977, box 1, Rosenthal Papers. Under socialist prime minister Andreas Papandreou (1981–1989, 1993–1996), Greece moved even closer to the PLO, straining relations with Israel. "Notes on Visit of Knesset Delegation," [1982?], box 70C, Paul Tsongas Collection, CLH.

18. Paul Dawson, chairman, n.d., box 79, Theodore Saloutos Papers, IHRC. This was apparently the same badly organized rally that Saloutos criticized in his diary.

19. 60th Bulletin, March 1975, box 78, Saloutos Papers.

20. *Los Angeles Times* ad, April 24, 1975, box 76, Saloutos Papers. Two months earlier, a fellow Hoosier of Armenian descent had written to congratulate Brademas on his forthright stand. "Remember sixty years ago Turkey committed genocide on the Armenian people. She must not be allowed to get away with such acts in this day and age." V. K. Babayan to Brademas, February 11, 1975, box I: 33, BCP.

21. Armenian Bicentennial, April 24, 1976, box 7, Myron Kuropas Files, GRFPL. Morgenthau served as US ambassador to the Ottoman Empire from 1913 to 1916.

22. George S. Harris, "Turkish-American Relations since the Truman Doctrine," in *Turkish-American Relations: Past, Present and Future,* eds. Mustafa Aydin and Cagri Erhan (New York: Routledge, 2004), 77. The terror came to an end by the

mid-1980s. By then, the public had taken note of the Armenian cause, and the deaths of civilian bystanders had resulted in negative publicity. Michael M. Gunther, "Armenian Terrorism: A Reappraisal," *Journal of Conflict Studies* 27, no. 2 (2007): 8. The PLO and Armenian terrorists had been cooperating, especially in Lebanon. This provided an added incentive for Ankara and Tel Aviv to work together. The United States has not officially recognized the Armenian genocide, although resolutions to that effect have been introduced in recent years in both houses of Congress. The White House has consistently opposed such a measure, in part because of its presumed harmful effect on US-Turkish relations.

23. Memcon, March 5, 1975, box II: 30, BCP.

24. Ford, Scowcroft, Brademas, et al., NSA Memcons, March 21, 1975, box 10, GRFPL. The future status of Famagusta, on the east coast of the island and possessing the deepest harbor, has come up repeatedly in negotiations over the years. The Varosha district of the city was the main tourist center on Cyprus prior to Turkish occupation.

25. NSA Memcons, March 27, 1975, box 10, GRFPL.

26. Ford, Scowcroft, Brademas, et al., NSA Memcons, March 21, 1975.

27. Campany, *Turkey and the United States,* 43–48.

28. *Chicago Tribune,* February 11, 1975; Athens to Brademas, February 12, 1975, box II: 30, BCP; *Baltimore Sun,* September 7, 1975.

29. Athanassiades to Brademas, April 10, 1975, box V: 19, BCP.

30. AHEPA Chapter 89 to Ford, April 30, 1975, Name File, box 10, WHCF, GRFPL.

31. Ford, Kissinger, and AHEPA delegation, NSA Memcons, April 25, 1975, box 11, GRFPL.

32. Cusack to Brademas, April 21, 1975, box V: 19, BCP.

33. UHAC letter, May 23, 1975, box II: 03, BCP; Brademas to Dr. Tegeris, June 11, 1975, ibid.

34. "Byrd's-Eye View," August 2, 1978, box 16, Byrd Congressional Papers.

35. Ford, Kissinger, Karamanlis, et al., NSA Memcons, May 29, 1975, box 12, GRFPL.

36. Ford and Kissinger, NSA Memcons, May 26, 1975, box 12, GRFPL.

37. Document 228, June 19, 1975, in *FRUS, 1969–1976,* vol. 30.

38. Document 229, June 23, 1975, in *FRUS, 1969–1976,* vol. 30. Andreas Papandreou was an early supporter of the Palestinian cause; he delivered the keynote address at the annual convention of the then-militant Association of Arab American University Graduates in the early 1970s. Yaqub, *Imperfect Strangers,* 69.

39. Ford, Kissinger, Bi-Partisan House Leadership, NSA Memcons, June 26, 1975, box 13, GRFPL.

40. Arthur Haritos et al. to Honorable John Rhodes, May 8, 1975, and Rhodes to Haliotis et al., May 20, 1975, ML: 25/21, Issues Cyprus, John J. Rhodes Papers, Arizona State University, Tempe. The writers had sent copies of their letter to all members of the Arizona congressional delegation as well as to Senator Scott, the

Greek embassy and government officials in Athens, and President Makarios. Rhodes copied his reply to them all.

41. This was often said about the Jewish lobby in the United States and Israel as well. Ford, Kissinger, Bi-Partisan House Leadership, NSA Memcons, June 26, 1975.

42. Ford, Kissinger, Bi-Partisan House Leadership, NSA Memcons, June 26, 1975.

43. Clift to Baroody, July 8, 1975, Subject File, box 24, WHCF, GRFPL; Ford and Pappas, NSA Memcons, July 15, 1975, box 13, GRFPL; Tim Weiner, *Legacy of Ashes* (New York: Doubleday, 2007), 330–31; McCrary to Marsh, July 22, 1975, Presidential Name File, box 2, NSA Files, GRFPL.

44. Marsh to Ford, July 22, 1975, John Marsh Files, box 41, GRFPL.

45. "Press Release, Embassy of Greece," July 23, 1975, folder 4522, Eagleton Papers.

46. UHAC letter, July 17, 1975, box I: 33, BCP.

47. Chirgotis to Brademas, June 20, 1975, box I: 33, BCP; minutes, July 16, 1975, box 1, MFC; Instructions to Delegates, n.d., ibid.

48. Oberstar to Ford, July 25, 1975, Subject File, box 24, WHCF, GRFPL. Most of the Republican congressmen who continued to support the embargo came from states in the Northeast and the Midwest.

49. Homer Mantis to Fraser, July 21, 1975, box 2, MFC.

50. Mary Mantis to Schull, July 29, 1975, box 2, MFC.

51. M. Mantis to editor, *Minneapolis Star,* February 6, 12, 1975, box 1, MFC; *Orthodox Observer,* July 23, 1975, box 9, MFC; Ford, Kissinger, AHEPA, NSA Memcons, April 25, 1975, box 11, GRFPL; Trevor Rubenzer and Steven B. Redd, "Ethnic Minority Groups and US Foreign Policy: Examining Congressional Decision Making and Economic Sanctions," *International Studies Quarterly* 54 (2010): 755–77.

52. Debaters' points, July 13, 1975, box II: 30, BCP; "Checklist," July 13, 1975, ibid.

53. Other items on Brademas's list included the following: draft a letter to House members signed by opponents of the Scott bill, especially members who had voted against the bill in committee; draft editorials for the *Washington Star, Washington Post,* and *New York Times;* consult with Eugene Rossides about more lobbying of House members; arrange for appearances on the three morning shows *Today, CBS News,* and *AM America;* discuss with colleagues the tactics for the debate on the House floor; and get someone to speak with freshman Republican representatives. "Checklist," July 13, 1975.

54. Van Fleet to Brademas, July 14, 1975, box I: 33, BCP; Zumwalt statement, July 18, 1975, folder 4522, Eagleton Papers.

55. "Ball-Vance Statement," July 10, 1975, folder 4522, Eagleton Papers. In the 1960s each of them had tried, without success, to fashion a compromise between the two Cypriot communities.

56. James Avrett to Brademas, July 28, 1975, box I: 36A, BCP; Dera Bridges to Brademas, July 23, 1975, ibid.; Thorne Griscom to Tsongas, July 25, 1975, box 156D, Tsongas Collection.

57. Goldwater to Kokalis, May 19, 1975, box 79, Saloutos Papers; Save Cyprus Council letter, June 18, 1975, box 76, Saloutos Papers.

58. Saloutos to Kourides, August 6, 1975, box 13, Saloutos Papers; Athens to Saloutos, August 13, 1975, ibid.

59. "Ethnic Politics," n.d., box 20, Saloutos Papers.

60. Document 51, July 30, 1975, in *FRUS, 1969–1976,* vol. 30. By the mid-1970s, direct lobbying of Congress by foreign governments had become more common. The steps taken by the Greek embassy pointed to this growing phenomenon. This development would complicate policymaking for future administrations as it did for Ford.

61. Document 51, July 30, 1975.

62. Document 183, July 31, 1975, in *FRUS, 1969–1976,* vol. 30.

63. Jack Marsh, interview by Richard Norton Smith, 2008, Gerald R. Ford Oral History Project, GRFPL.

64. Ford to Bob, August 1, 1975, box 12, Byrd Congressional Papers; Kissinger to Bob, August 7, 1975, ibid.

65. Memo to file, September 4, 1975, box I: 31, BCP.

66. Memo to file, September 10, 1975, box I: 31, BCP.

67. Memo to file, September 10, 1975.

68. Memo to file, September 12, 1975, box I: 31, BCP.

69. Brademas et al. to Karamanlis, July 26, 1974, box II: 30, BCP. Kissinger had studied Metternich's diplomacy closely and saw the Austrian chancellor as something of a model. According to Robert Dallek, "Kissinger saw parallels between Metternich's time and his own. . . . Only a reliance on balance-of-power diplomacy could defend the interests of nations hoping to preserve an existing world order. . . . Kissinger never changed his mind about the primacy of power over justice or abstract moral good." Robert Dallek, *Nixon and Kissinger: Partners in Power* (New York: Harper, 2007), 45–46.

70. *Baltimore Sun,* September 7, 1975; memo to file, September 8, 1975, box 1: 31, BCP.

71. Max Friedersdorf to President, September 10, 1975, box C27, Presidential Handwriting File, GRFPL; James E. Connor to Max Friedersdorf, September 11, 1975, ibid.; Madden to Morgan, September 11, 1975, ML-LC: 13/8, Legislative Committees: International Relations: Turkey, Rhodes Papers. Before the summer recess, Madden, under considerable pressure from the Greek American lobby, had repelled efforts to bring the Senate bill to the floor. Franck and Weisband, *Foreign Policy by Congress,* 192.

72. *Baltimore Sun,* September 7, 1975; memo to file, September 8, 1975, box I: 31, BCP.

73. Memo to file, September 12, 1975, box I: 31, BCP.

74. Memo to file, September 18, 1975, box I: 31, BCP.

75. Memo to file, September 19, 1975, box I: 31, BCP.

76. "Statement on Senate Joint Resolution 247," General Subject Files, 1951–1983, series FA-3.1, box 3, Clement J. Zablocki Papers, Marquette University Library, Milwaukee, WI; Zablocki to Andrew A. Nicolaides, n.d., Zablocki Papers.

77. "Congressional Leadership Meetings with the President: Republican," March 3, 1976, box 9, Marsh Files, GRFPL; "Dear Colleague," July 23, 1975, ibid.; "Dear Colleague," September 30, 1975, MPP2, box 159, Lee H. Hamilton Congressional Papers, Indiana University Archives, Bloomington.

78. "Authorization of Appropriations for the Board for International Broadcasting and Partial Lifting of the Turkish Arms Embargo," in *Hearing before the Committee on International Relations on S. 2230, September 17, 1975* (Washington, DC: GPO, 1975), 12; Ford, Rockefeller, Rogers Morton, and Republican Congressional Leaders, NSA Memcons, September 24, 1975, box 15, GRFPL.

79. Campany, *Turkey and the United States,* 81.

80. NSA Memcons, September 12, 1975, box 15, GRFPL.

81. Document 185, September 24, 1975, in *FRUS, 1969–1976,* vol. 30.

82. Document 237, September 25, 1975, in *FRUS, 1969–1976,* vol. 30; Congressional Bi-Partisan Leadership, September 25, 1975, box 9, Marsh Files, GRFPL.

83. "Turkish Arms Embargo," October 1, 1975, box 28, Theodore C. Marrs Files, GRFPL.

84. Luns, Ford, Kissinger, and Scowcroft, NSA Memcons, September 24, 1975, box 15, GRFPL; "Congressional Leadership Meetings with the President: Republican," September 23, 1975, box 9, Marsh Files, GRFPL.

85. "Congressional Leadership Meetings with the President: Republican," September 23, 1975.

86. Congressman John Rhodes radio program, July 28, 1975, MSS 5: JR Press Office Files, 1953–1983, Rhodes Papers.

87. "Dear Friend," March 5, 1975, and Griffin to Bob, March 7, 1975, box 190, 682D, Senator Robert P. Griffin Papers, Clarke Historical Library, Central Michigan University, Mount Pleasant.

88. Mosher to Rhodes, July 23, 1975, ML, Legislative Committees, 1975: 13/8, Rhodes Papers.

89. Press release, October 1, 1975, box 3, Rosenthal Papers.

90. Johnson, *Congress and the Cold War,* 180.

91. Of those voting, 84 percent of Republicans and 43 percent of Democrats now supported the administration. Even "Skip" Bafalis broke with his Greek American colleagues to support the measure. For whatever reason, 5 percent fewer Democrats voted in October than in July (287 versus 273); Republican numbers remained roughly the same (142 versus 140).

92. Ford to Karamanlis, October 4, 1975, AAD; Ford to Demirel, October 6, 1975, AAD.

93. Only a month later, on November 4, Ford initiated the so-called Halloween massacre, a major reorganization of his cabinet. His recent success on the embargo question must have added to his confidence as he took this significant step.

94. SS to US Consul, Istanbul, July 31, 1974, AAD.

95. Broadside, n.d., box 9, MFC.

96. Document 208, August 21, 1974, in *FRUS, 1969–1976,* vol. 30.

97. US Embassy, Ankara, to SS, September 12, 1974, AAD.

98. SS to US Embassy, Ankara, September 20, 1974, AAD.

99. SS to US Mission, UN, October 17, 1974, AAD.

100. SS to US Embassy, Brussels, December 12, 1974, AAD; US Embassy, Ankara, to SS, November 21, 1974, AAD.

101. Uslu, *Turkish-American Relationship,* 248.

102. SS to US Embassy, Brussels, December 12, 1974, AAD.

103. *Hellenic-American Reporter,* March 22, 1975, box 78, Saloutos Papers.

104. *New York Times,* July 21, 1975. The ad cleverly recalled the 1963 blockbuster film *From Russia with Love,* which was set in Istanbul.

105. SS to US Embassy, Ankara, June 6, 1975, AAD.

106. Statement by Admiral Zumwalt, July 18, 1975, folder 4522, Eagleton Papers.

107. "Checklist," July 13, 1975. Brademas had also urged Rangel to get Bill Attwood, the editor at *Newsday* (Long Island, NY), to revive some of that paper's attacks on the heroin issue. SS to US Embassy, Ankara, June 3, 1975, AAD; *New York Times,* July 19, 1975.

108. James Cannon to President Ford, July 30, 1975, box 51, James M. Cannon Papers, GRFPL.

109. Cannon to Ford, July 30, 1975.

110. Memcon, July 31, 1975, in *FRUS, 1969–1976,* vol. 30, doc. 233; SS to US Embassy, Ankara, August 1, 1975, AAD.

111. US Embassy, Ankara, to SS, October 15, 1975, AAD; Ford to Senator McClellan, December 8, 1975, White House Press Releases, box 19, GRFPL.

112. A fourth caucus member, Ralph Metcalfe (D-IL), did not vote in October; he had supported the embargo in July. Almost all Democrats representing urban districts in the North and West continued to support the embargo.

113. US Embassy, Ankara, to SS, November 5, 1976, AAD. Turkey's tattered reputation was not so easily repaired. The negative impact of the 1978 film *Midnight Express* lingered for years. Today, few even remember the opium crisis of forty-five years ago. Some scholars have recently suggested that Afghanistan, currently the world's largest supplier of opium, should follow the Turkish model. See, for example, Kamminga, "Opium Poppy Licensing in Turkey."

5. "They Have Made a Mess of Cyprus"

1. Ford, Kissinger, and Caglayangil, NSA Memcons, March 24, 1976, box 18, GRFPL.

2. Eagleton to Staats, March 30, 1976, and Eagleton to Ihsan Caglayangil, March 30, 1976, folder 4523, Thomas Eagleton Papers, SHSM.

3. Kissinger to Ford, September 10, 1975, Presidential Name File, box 2, NSA Files, GRFPL; McCrary and Ford, NSA Memcons, September 10, 1975, box 2, GRFPL.

4. Lavadas to Kuropas, January 24, 1976, Subject File, box 16, WHCF, GRFPL; Kopan to Kuropas, February 6, 1976, box 3, Myron Kuropas Files, GRFPL. In the fall election, Ford would carry Illinois and lose Massachusetts.

5. *Greek Star,* February 12, 1976, box 2, Kuropas Files, GRFPL; Baroody to Ford, May 7, 1976, box C40, Presidential Handwriting File, GRFPL.

6. Remarks to Heritage Group leaders, May 11, 1976, box C40, Presidential Handwriting File, GRFPL.

7. Christopher, important notice, May 17, 1975, box 3, Kuropas Files, GRPFL.

8. Eve Griffin to Baroody, n.d., box 7, Kuropas Files, GRFPL; Kuropas to Marsh, April 5, 1976, ibid.

9. *Ahepan,* March–April 1976, 6–7.

10. Kuropas to Baroody, August 30, 1976, Subject File, box 16, WHCF, GRFPL.

11. *Greek Star,* September 23, 1975, box 76, Theodore Saloutos Papers, IHRC.

12. Editor, *Light,* n.d., box I: 23, BCP.

13. "American Turkish Association," October 31, 1976, box 78, Saloutos Papers.

14. Denktash to Carter, August 20, 1976, Subject File, box 16, WHCF, GRFPL.

15. George S. Harris, "Turkey's Foreign Policy: Independent or Reactive?" in *Diplomacy in the Middle East: The International Relations of Regional and Outside Powers,* ed. L. Carl Brown (New York: I. B. Tauris, 2004), 266–67; American Consul, Istanbul, to SS, September 6, 1977, AAD.

16. "Cyprus and the Bases Agreement with Turkey," June 22, 1976, folder 4381, Eagleton Papers.

17. Eagleton to Brzezinski, September 1, 1976, folder 4381, Eagleton Papers.

18. Karoazes to Kuropas, April 5, 1976, Subject File, box 16, WHCF, GRFPL; Demirel to Ford, April 25, 1976, AAD.

19. Ford to Demirel, May 6, 1976, AAD.

20. Mildred Leonard to the President, August 12, 1976, Carter, Jimmy, File, box 16, Richard B. Cheney Papers, GRFPL.

21. Gerald R. Ford, *A Time to Heal* (New York: Harper & Row, 1979), 302.

22. Memo to file, November 23, 1976, Carter Administration: 5, John J. Rhodes Papers, Arizona State University, Tempe.

23. Cunningham to members, December 14, 1976, box 9, MFC. Former Democratic whip John McFall had become caught up in the Koreagate scandal.

24. Minutes, January 5, 1977, box 1, MFC.

25. Brademas to Dan Cheever, November 21, 1975, box II: 30, BCP.

26. M. Mantis to W. Anderson, July 2, 1978, box 2, MFC; Anderson to M. Mantis, July 14, 1978, ibid.; Sarbanes letter, August 29, 1978, ibid. Even as late as June 1979, first-term congressman Arlen Erdahl (R-MN) informed Chambers that he would be supporting measures to deny military assistance to Turkey until Ankara made a more sincere effort to negotiate concerning Cyprus. Erdahl to Chambers, June 12, 1979, ibid.

27. Manatos to Eagleton, November 1976, folder 4381, Eagleton Papers.

28. Ford, Kissinger, and Scowcroft, NSA Memcons, November 4, 1976, box 21, GRFPL.

29. Caglayangil to McGhee, November 19, 1976, box 17, Clark Clifford Papers, Library of Congress, Washington, DC.

30. Eagleton et al. to Carter, December 14, 1976, folder 4381, Eagleton Papers.

31. Document 5, February 10, 1977, in US Department of State, *FRUS, 1977–1980,* vol. 21, *Greece; Cyprus; Turkey* (Washington, DC: GPO, 2014).

32. A State Department contact read a number of embassy cables to Brian Atwood over the phone. In one, Ambassador Macomber, bête noire of the embargo supporters, lobbied the outgoing administration to push the Carter team to pursue ratification of the DCA no later than March 1977. Atwood to Eagleton, November 10, 1976, folder 4381, Eagleton Papers; Ford and Kissinger, NSA Memcons, January 4, 1977, box 21, GRFPL.

33. Document 84, January 21, 1977, in *FRUS, 1977–1980,* vol. 21.

34. Jimmy Carter to Clark Clifford, May 6, 1976, box 17, Clifford Papers.

35. Clifford to Muskie, June 16, 1975, box 35, Clifford Papers.

36. Document 5, February 10, 1977.

37. Denis Clift to Mondale, February 14, 1977, Donated Historical Material—Mondale, Walter F., box 108, folder 4, RAC Program, JCPL.

38. Jac Lechelt, *The Vice Presidency in Foreign Policy: From Mondale to Cheney* (El Paso, TX: LFB Scholarly Publishing, 2009), 38, 41.

39. Document 5, February 10, 1977.

40. Some in Ankara even wondered whether Greece was plotting to restore the old Byzantine Empire and combine all Greeks into one political unit, referred to as the "Megali idea." Aydin, "Determinants of Turkish Foreign Policy," 120; Kemal Yamak, *Golgede Kalan Izler ve Golgelesen Bizler* [Traces of shadows and shadows] (Istanbul: Dogan Kitap, 2006), 266; Jonathan Alford, ed., *Greece and Turkey: Adversity in Alliance* (New York: Palgrave Macmillan, 1984), 59; Uzer, *Identity and Turkish Foreign Policy,* 143, 145.

41. Document 7, in *FRUS, 1977–1980,* vol. 21.

42. Document 8, in *FRUS, 1977–1980,* vol. 21.

43. Kubisch to SS, February 22, 1977, AAD. Thanks to Athanasios Antonopoulus for bringing this telegram to my attention.

44. Document 8, in *FRUS, 1977–1980,* vol. 21.

45. Document 8.

46. Document 10, in *FRUS, 1977–1980,* vol. 21.

47. Carter to Clifford, March 4, 1977, Office of Staff Secretary, Handwriting File, Presidential Files, box 10, JCPL.

48. Document 89, note, in *FRUS, 1977–1980,* vol. 21.

49. Document 91, in *FRUS, 1977–1980,* vol. 21.

50. Document 94, in *FRUS, 1977–1980,* vol. 21.

51. See Uslu, *Turkish-American Relationship,* 184–87; Campany, *Turkey and the United States,* 52; Suha Bolukbashi, *The Superpowers and the Third World: Turkish-*

American Relations and Cyprus, vol. 15 of Exxon Education Foundation Series on Rhetoric and Political Discourse (Lanham, MD: University Press of America, 1988), 190.

52. Cy to President, April 19, 1977, Plains File, box 128, folder 12, RAC Program, JCPL. In a compromise move, congressional leaders had agreed to an absolute maximum of $125 million for cash or credit sales for fiscal years 1976 and 1977.

53. Denis Clift to Richard Moe, April 22, 1977, Donated Historical Materials—Mondale, Walter F., box 107, folder 2, RAC Program, JCPL.

54. "Voting Record on Cyprus Legislation," March 1, 1978, box II: 06, BCP.

55. "Turkish Troops on Cyprus," interagency intelligence memorandum, March 28, 1977, General CIA Records, CREST Database.

56. Greg to Eagleton, April 26, 1977, folder 4523, Eagleton Papers.

57. Greg to Eagleton, April 26, 1977.

58. Carras to Brademas, June 8, 1977, box I: 32, BCP. Paul Findley served as Republican congressman from Illinois from 1960 to 1982.

59. Document 42, in *FRUS, 1977–1980,* vol. 21; Kissinger, *Year of Renewal,* 238.

60. Nicosia—mourning, August 7, 1977, box 16, Clifford Papers; interview with Brian Atwood, May 29, 2014.

61. US Embassy, Nicosia, to SS, August 10, 1977, box 17, Clifford Papers.

62. Turkish Cypriot Journalists Association, August 10, 1977, and Ozer Hatay, Turkish-Cypriot Historical Society, August 10, 1977, box 17, Clifford Papers.

63. Ankara to SS, August 26, 1977, AAD; *Washington Post,* April 20, 1977; SS to Ankara, April 21, 1977, AAD.

64. Vice Presidential Papers, 153.L.19.6F, Walter Mondale Papers, MHS; document 16, in *FRUS, 1977–1980,* vol. 21. Here, Clifford was referring to ongoing tensions over territorial waters in the Aegean.

65. Vice Presidential Papers, 153.L.19.6F, Mondale Papers.

6. The Embargo Must Go

1. Document 98, in *FRUS, 1977–1980,* vol. 21.

2. Documents 108 and 110, in *FRUS, 1977–1980,* vol. 21. Spiers was reprimanded for his comments to the press.

3. "Summary of Meeting," October 13, 1977, box I: 42, BCP. Sarbanes won handily against incumbent John Glenn Beall Jr.; it was not a good year for Republicans. The Democrat had solid support from the Greek American community in Maryland (25,000), but more importantly, perhaps, Sarbanes had gained favorable attention through his service on the House Watergate Committee, offering the first article of impeachment against President Nixon. The congressmen had met earlier in the week with Turkey's foreign minister Ihsan Caglayangil to exchange views about Cyprus and US policy toward Turkey.

4. Eagleton to Ann, October 12, 1977, folder 4381, Thomas Eagleton Papers, SHSM.

5. "Summary of Meeting," October 13, 1977.

6. Eagleton to Ann, October 12, 1977; Ann to Eagleton, October 20, 1977, folder 4381, Eagleton Papers.

7. Rick and Ed to Eagleton et al., August 5, 1977, folder 4523, Eagleton Papers; Hackett to Eagleton et al., September 20, 1977, ibid.; Ann to Eagleton, September 20 and 28, 1977, ibid.

8. "Aspin Reveals Loophole in Turkish Arms Ceiling," September 26, 1977, folder 4523, Eagleton Papers; "Joint Statement," September 26, 1977, ibid.; Brademas to Eagleton and Sarbanes, November 2, 1977, ibid.

9. Proctor to Eagleton, December 5, 1977, folder 4381, Eagleton Papers.

10. Proctor to Eagleton, November 14, 1977, folder 4381, Eagleton Papers; Religious News Service, December 2, 1977, box 17, Clark Clifford Papers, Library of Congress, Washington, DC. Twenty nations abstained, including Israel and six NATO members, in addition to the United States.

11. Congressmen to Carter, February 8, 1978, box I, Benjamin Rosenthal Papers, Queens College, City University of New York.

12. Document 111, in *FRUS, 1977–1980,* vol. 21; Henze to Brzezinski, March 8, 1978, National Security Affairs, Brzezinski Material, Country File, box 75, JCPL. All too familiar with his assistant's forceful approach to issues, Brzezinski placed a double line under the word "But." The Special Coordinating Committee was one of two NSC committees set up by Carter in 1977. It was chaired by the national security adviser and considered any matter involving several departments. In early March 1978 the administration faced significant challenges in obtaining Senate ratification of the first Panama Canal treaty. Franck and Weisband, *Foreign Policy by Congress,* 275–86.

13. Laipson, *Congressional-Executive Relations and the Turkish Arms Embargo,* 16; Franck and Weisband, *Foreign Policy by Congress,* 267.

14. Interview with Brian Atwood, May 29, 2014.

15. Interview with Nelson Ledsky, June 28, 2003.

16. Denis Clift, memoranda for the vice president, November 3 and 10, December 9 and 19, 1977, March 20, 1978, NLC-133-109-2-8-3, NLC-133-109-2-18-2, NLC-133-109-3-17-2, NLC-133-109-3-39-8, NLC-133-50-6-12-9, JCPL; Dick Moe to VP Mondale, talking points for luncheon with the president, March 20 and April 7, 1978, Walter Mondale Papers, MHS. On Sarbanes, see also Frank Moore Oral History, 2002, JCPL.

17. Frank Moore to President Carter, February 13, 1978, NLC-126-11-22-1-4, JCPL.

18. Document 110, in *FRUS, 1977–1980,* vol. 21.

19. Proctor to Eagleton, June 15, 1978, folder 4523, Eagleton Papers; "Carter's High-Stakes Foreign Policy Test," June 15, 1978, ibid.; *New York Times,* June 15, 1978, ibid.

20. Vance to Brzezinski, January 12, 1978, NLC-16-42-4-51-8, JCPL.

21. Zablocki et al. to Vance, February 14, 1978, General Subject Files, 1951–1983, series FA-3.1, box 3, folder 1, Clement J. Zablocki Papers, Marquette University, Milwaukee, WI.

22. Zablocki to "Dear Colleague," January 17, 1977, Chairman's Election Files, 1976–1977, FA-1.2, box 1, Zablocki Papers. Apparently, some observers concluded that Zablocki was neither a masterful parliamentarian nor an intellectual leader in the House. Johnson, *Congress and the Cold War,* 269.

23. SS to President, Ankara, January 22, 1978, AAD.

24. Moe to Mondale, talking points for luncheon with the president, March 20 and April 7, 1978.

25. Moore to Carter, May 17, 1978, Staff Offices, Ethnic Affairs, Aiello, box 40, JCPL.

26. Atwood interview.

27. Document 113, in *FRUS, 1977–1980,* vol. 21.

28. SS to US Mission, NATO, May 24, 1978, NLC-16-112-1-48-7, JCPL.

29. Document 116, in *FRUS, 1977–1980,* vol. 21.

30. Warren Christopher to Carter, May 23 and 24, 1978, NLC-128-13-8-16-0, NLC-128-13-8-17-9, JCPL.

31. "White House Notes," April 5, 1978, box 9, Eleanor Kelley Files, Staff Files, subseries B, series II, Tip O'Neill Papers, Burns Library, Boston College; "Archived Issue Brief," January 16, 1979, folder 4523, Eagleton Papers.

32. Proctor to Eagleton, April 17, 1978, folder 4523, Eagleton Papers.

33. Hackett would later author an important study of this issue (*The Congressional Foreign Policy Role,* 1979). Atwood interview.

34. Ledsky interview. When Hamilton became chair of the Committee on Foreign Affairs in 1993, Van Dusen served as his chief of staff.

35. Memo to file, April 27, 1978, box I: 32, BCP; *Washington Post,* June 20, 1978.

36. Memo to file, April 27, 1978.

37. Memcon, April 20, 1978, NLC-133-50-2-10-5, JCPL. The letter that Iakovos left for the president took a much harsher tone. Iakovos to Carter, April 16, 1978, National Security Affairs, Staff Material, Horn/Special, box 2, JCPL.

38. M. Mantis, report on conference, February 27, 1978, box 6, MFC.

39. *Proini,* April 14, 1978, box V: 25, BCP.

40. "Congressman," April 15, 1978, box V: 25, BCP; "Editorial," May 3, 1978, ibid. Six months later and just a few days after his reelection, Ryan was murdered in the Jonestown massacre in Guyana. Although the Democrats lost seats in both houses of Congress in November, they still enjoyed comfortable majorities (Senate, 58–41; House, 277–158).

41. *Washington Post,* June 20, 1978.

42. *New Yorker,* June 5, 1978; *St. Paul Dispatch and Pioneer Press,* April 6 and June 19, 1978.

43. H. Mantis to editor, June 17, 1978, box 2, MFC; H. Mantis to editor, April 7, 1978, ibid.

44. Chambers to editor, n.d., box 2, MFC; M. Mantis to Sumner, July 2, 1978, ibid. Mary Mantis and her associates had complained earlier to the *Minneapolis Star* about its inadequate coverage of international events and sought a meeting with its editor, Harold Chucker. M. Mantis et al., February 6 and 12, 1975, box 1, MFC.

45. Sumner to M. Mantis, July 5, 1978, box 2, MFC.

46. Documents 175, 177, 179, in *FRUS, 1977–1980,* vol. 21.

47. See Van Coufoudakis, "Greek Foreign Policy since 1974: Quest for Independence," *Journal of Modern Greek Studies* 6, no. 1 (May 1988): 60, 63.

48. Minutes, August 1977, box 1, MFC; minutes, July 8, 1978, ibid.

49. M. Mantis, report, June 22, 1978, box 1, MFC; Iakovos to Anne Wexler, June 20, 1978, box 2, MFC.

50. Memo to file, June 22, 1978, box I: 34, BCP.

51. Memo to file, June 22, 1978.

52. Memo to file, June 22, 1978.

53. Memo to file, June 22, 1978.

54. This move showed Carter's determination. One year earlier he had bitterly criticized Ford at a White House leadership meeting for breaking tradition when the former president spoke out almost immediately against the new administration. "Speaker's Notes," April 19, 1977, box 9, Eleanor Kelley Files, Staff Files, subseries B, series II, O'Neill Papers; Frank Moore to Carter, July 12, 1978, Office of Congressional Liaison, Beckel, box 233, JCPL; Frank Moore, "Meeting with Congressmen on Turkey/Greece," July 12, 1978, Office of Congressional Liaison, Moore, box 49, JCPL; Frank Moore, "Meeting with Speaker O'Neill, Jim Wright and Dan Rostenkowski," July 11, 1978, ibid.

55. Remarks of the Honorable John J. Rhodes of Arizona in the House of Representatives, August 1, 1978, MSS5, Press Office Files, 1953–1983, John J. Rhodes Papers, Arizona State University, Tempe.

56. "Talking Points," July 20, 1978, and "Draft Turkey Letter," n.d., Mid/Near East, Aid to Turkey, box 190, 682D, Senator Robert P. Griffin Papers, Clarke Historical Library, Central Michigan University, Mt. Pleasant.

57. *New York Times,* June 2, 1978; Proctor to Eagleton, June 5, 1978, folder 4523, Eagleton Papers; Proctor to Eagleton et al., June 15, 1978, ibid.; Douglas Bennet to Eagleton, June 28, 1978, ibid.

58. Clifford to Honorable Timothy Wirth, June 7, 1978, box 16, Clifford Papers.

59. "Current Senate Vote Analysis," June 28, 1978, Office of Congressional Liaison, Moore, box 49, JCPL.

60. Report of European trip, June 3–July 9, 1978, International Travel, box 1, Robert C. Byrd Congressional Papers, Robert C. Byrd Center for Legislative Studies, Shepherdstown, WV; Byrd to Leonard Bott, April 19, 1978, box 16, Byrd Congressional Papers.

61. Summary of trip to Middle East, October 1979, International Travel, box 1, Byrd Congressional Papers.

62. Dan Tate to Robert C. Byrd, July 26, 1978, box 39, Byrd Congressional Papers; Carter to Byrd, July 28, 1978, box 54, Byrd Congressional Papers. Earlier, Byrd had received similar letters of gratitude from Carter for his vigorous support of the Panama Canal treaties. Carter to Byrd, March 22, April [n.d.], 1978, ibid.

63. "Elements of a Congressional Strategy," May 5, 1978, Office of Congressional Liaison, Moore, box 49, JCPL; Frank Moore to Carter, May 31, 1978, ibid.; "Meeting with Congressmen on Turkey/Greece," June 1, 1978, ibid.

64. Jordan to Carter, July 5, 1978, Hamilton Jordan's Confidential Files, Office of the Chief of Staff Files, box 37, JCPL. Only three members of the caucus would vote to lift the embargo.

65. Remarks in House of Representatives, August 1, 1978, MSS5, Press Office Files, Rhodes Papers; Moore to Carter, July 28, 1978, Office of Congressional Liaison, Moore, box 49, JCPL; Moore to Carter, June 24, 1978, Office of Congressional Liaison, Beckel, box 233, JCPL. The administration won majority leader Jim Wright's support at the last moment. The Speaker did not vote on August 1.

66. Memos to Brademas, June 14 and 20, 1978, box I: 34, BCP.

67. Iakovos to Brademas, June 28, 1978, box V: 25, BCP.

68. "Dear Colleague," July 1978, box 1, Rosenthal Papers.

69. *US News and World Report,* July 31, 1978, 29–30. Israeli forces would remain in Lebanon for eighteen years (1982–2000), long after Rosenthal died. There was no cutoff of US arms. Rosenthal had also sent a letter to the State Department, asking for information about Indonesia's use of US weapons in East Timor.

70. Morrey to Brademas, July 21 and 25, 1978, box II: 06, BCP.

71. Comments in the House, July 31, 1978, box II: 06, BCP.

72. Democrats voted 141–130; Republicans, 64–78. Big-city Democrats continued to support the embargo overwhelmingly. Interestingly, Rangel and Chisolm, who had supported a partial lifting of the embargo in October 1975, now voted to keep it in place.

73. Moore Oral History.

74. "Brademas Statement," August 1, 1978, and "Speaker's Letter," August 4, 1978, box 6, Bills Not Sponsored, Legislative Files, subseries 4, subseries E, series III, O'Neill Papers. Given the narrowness of the vote to lift the embargo, one is tempted to speculate about the outcome had it been delayed beyond 1978. After the successful Iranian revolution and overthrow of the shah's regime in early 1979, Turkey's policies toward the Islamic regime in Tehran differed considerably from those of the United States. Ankara refused the American request to impose sanctions on Iran, and bilateral trade expanded rapidly. Who can predict how Congress might have voted had the embargo still been in place at that time?

75. Department of State Briefing Paper, May 1978, NLC-133-79-3-18-4, JCPL; Warren Christopher to Carter, April 22, 1978, NLC-128-13-7-15-2, JCPL.

76. Henze to Ralph Walter, June 29, 1978, National Security Affairs, Staff Material, Horn/Special, box 2, JCPL.

77. Albright to Clifford, August 2, 1978, box 16, Clifford Papers.

78. Lee Hamilton et al. to the President, September 27, 1978, MPP2, box 160, Lee H. Hamilton Congressional Papers, Indiana University Archives, Bloomington; Warren Christopher to Lee Hamilton, October 17, 1978, ibid.

79. Mary Jane to Byrd, notes for press conference on Middle Eastern trip, December 8, 1978, box 39, Byrd Congressional Papers.

80. Document 25, in *FRUS, 1977–1980,* vol. 21; Vicki Mongiardo to Anne Wexler, August 2, 1978, Staff Offices, Ethnic Affairs, Aiello, box 41, JCPL; Carter to Lee Alexander, August 4, 1978, Staff Offices, Ethnic Affairs, Aiello, box 40, JCPL.

81. Document 26, in *FRUS, 1977–1980,* vol. 21.

82. Document 68, in *FRUS, 1977–1980,* vol. 21; Henze to Brzezinski, April 24, 1979, National Security Affairs, Staff Material, Horn/Special, box 3, JCPL; Brzezinski to Wexler, n.d., ibid.; Henze to Brzezinski, May 21, 1979, ibid. Some on the NSC staff opposed Henze's recommendation; see Robert Hunter to Brzezinski, April 24, 1978, ibid. An analysis by the State Department's Bureau of Intelligence and Research mirrored Henze's view, saying that the archbishop would use any positive response in the United States to further his own political ambitions at home. Christopher to Lee Hamilton, May 16, 1979, MPP2, box 161, Hamilton Congressional Papers.

83. Document 145, in *FRUS, 1977–1980,* vol. 21.

84. Denis Clift to Mondale, July 24, 1979, NLC-133-14-2-18-6, JCPL; Richard Moe to Mondale, insert for vice president's lunch with the president, March 30 and April 9, 1979, Mondale Papers; Purvis and Blake, *Legislating Foreign Policy,* 59–66.

85. Andrew Athens to Carter, March 13, 1979, Mondale Papers; Moe to Mondale, April 2 and May 24, 1979, ibid.; remarks of Vice President Mondale, June 9, 1979, Staff Offices, Ethnic Affairs, Aiello, box 40, JCPL.

86. Gretchen Poston to Landon Butler, July 19, 1979, Chief of Staff, Butler, box 90, JCPL; Mongiardo to Wexler, August 6, 1979, ibid.; Medal of Freedom citation, June 9, 1980, Staff Offices, Ethnic Affairs, Aiello, box 13, JCPL.

87. Aiello to Hamilton Jordan, n.d., Staff Offices, Ethnic Affairs, Aiello, box 49, JCPL; Van Dusen to Hamilton, October 12, 1979, MPP2, box 161, Hamilton Congressional Papers.

88. Talking points, January–June 1980, vice president's lunch with the president, 153.J.8 4F, Foreign Policy Materials from the JCPL, Mondale Papers.

89. Document 193, in *FRUS, 1977–1980,* vol. 21.

90. Document 195, in *FRUS, 1977–1980,* vol. 21. In spite of his bold words, there is no evidence that the ambassador took further action, and it would have been unusual for a Greek diplomat to approach the prime minister.

91. Philip Christopher to Chris Spirou, August 24, 1979, Staff Offices, Ethnic Affairs, Aiello, box 41, JCPL; Spirou to Aiello, June 17, 1980, Staff Offices, Ethnic

Affairs, Aiello, box 13, JCPL; "Reagan and Bush News Release," September 26, 1980, box 14B, Paul Tsongas Collection, CLH; *Hellenic Times,* July 3–9, 1980, Office of Anne Wexler, Special Assistant to the President, Anne Wexler's Subject Files, box 20, JCPL.

92. Talking points, 1980, Staff Offices, Ethnic Affairs, Aiello, box 41, JCPL; David Aaron to Anne Wexler, talking points, September 16, 1980, Office of Anne Wexler, Special Assistant to the President, Anne Wexler's Subject Files, box 20, JCPL.

93. Spirou to Aiello, June 17, 1980; Aiello to Muskie, June 27, 1980, Staff Offices, Ethnic Affairs, Aiello, box 13, JCPL; Moe to Vice President, June 11, 1980, Mondale Papers. Cyrus Vance had resigned as secretary of state on April 28, 1980, in response to the attempted military rescue of the American hostages in Tehran, a measure he had consistently opposed. Muskie served from May 8, 1980, until the end of the administration. As a senator, he had supported the embargo.

94. Speaker's notes, White House leadership meeting, September 17, 1980, box 9, Eleanor Kelley Files, Staff Files, subseries B, series II, O'Neill Papers. Greece returned to NATO in October 1980.

95. Document 207, in *FRUS, 1977–1980,* vol. 21; meeting with Greek American leaders, October 29, 1980, Staff Offices, Ethnic Affairs, Aiello, box 13, JCPL.

96. Brzezinski to Carter, n.d., National Security Affairs, Staff Material, Horn/ Special, box 3, JCPL.

97. Brademas to Rick, March 21, 1978, box I: 32, BCP; UHAC to Dear Friend, September 30, 1978, box 2, MFC; Yiannis P. Roubatis, *Greek Accent,* box 2, MFC.

98. Document 161, in *FRUS, 1977–1980,* vol. 21.

99. Nancy Mitchell, "The Cold War and Jimmy Carter," in *The Cambridge History of the Cold War,* vol. 3, eds. Melvyn P. Leffler and Odd Arne Westad (New York: Cambridge University Press, 2010); Nancy Mitchell, *Jimmy Carter in Africa: Race and the Cold War,* Cold War International History Project (Stanford, CA: Stanford University Press, 2016).

Epilogue

1. *Hellenic Times,* November 12–19, 1981, Max Green Files, 1985–1988, box 11, White House Staff Member and Office Files, RRPL; Christopher to Reagan, February 8, 1983, box 14B, Paul Tsongas Collection, CLH; Christopher to Clark, July 14, 1983, and Clark to Christopher, n.d., European and Soviet Affairs Directorate Records, RAC, box 6, RRPL.

2. Hamilton to Haig, August 12, 1981, MPP2, box 163, Lee H. Hamilton Congressional Papers, Indiana University Archives, Bloomington; Fox to Lugar, September 28, 1986, folder 4382, Cyprus 1974–1986, Thomas Eagleton Papers, SHSM; Pressler to Schultz, July 31, 1986, ibid.; Fox to Eagleton, September 29, 1986, ibid.

3. "The Case for Famagusta," enclosure, Lordos to Senator Tsongas, April 28, 1982, box 14A, Tsongas Collection.

4. News release, November 30, 1983, Max Green Files, 1985–1988, box 11, White House Staff and Office Files, RRPL.

5. Zablocki to Sukru Elekdag, November 16, 1983, Foreign Affairs Committee, 1949–1983, series FA-1.2, box 1, Clement J. Zablocki Papers, Marquette University Library, Milwaukee, WI.

6. *Washington Times,* April 21, 1983. As Paul Henze wrote in late 1979, "Cyprus is not a central issue in either Greece or Turkey." Henze to ZB, December 20, 1979, NLC-6-26-8-27-0, JCPL.

7. Denktash to Dear Honorable Senator, January 5, 1984, folder 4382, Eagleton Papers.

8. Evren to Reagan, and Reagan to Evren, December 12, 1983, Head of State File, Records, 1981–1989, Executive Secretariat, NSC, RRPL. There is some evidence that elements of the Turkish government, especially the Foreign Ministry, were upset by the timing of the declaration of independence, which came just days before the restoration of civilian rule in Ankara. Jed C. Snyder, *Defending the Fringe: NATO, the Mediterranean, and the Persian Gulf,* SAIS Papers in International Affairs no. 11 (Boulder, CO: Westview Press, 1987), 55–56.

9. Erik K. Zurcher, *Turkey: A Modern History* (New York: I. B. Tauris, 2004), 268–69; Mehmet Akif Okur, "The American Geopolitical Interests and Turkey on the Eve of the September 12, 1980, Coup," *CTAD* 11, no. 21 (Spring 2015): 199–222.

10. "Greece-Turkey-Cyprus: Major Congressional Issues," November 3, 1987, Alison B. Fortier Files, box 5, RRPL; Sukru Elekdag to Frank Carlucci, March 26, 1987, Alison B. Fortier Files, box 6, RRPL; Fritz Ermark to Carlucci, March 24 and April 7, 1987, ibid.

11. Uslu, *Turkish-American Relationship,* 100. For details on this development, see Ekavi Athanassopoulou, *Strategic Relations between the US and Turkey, 1979–2000* (New York: Routledge, 2014), 14–17.

Appendix

1. US Embassy, Ankara, to SS, January 20, 1977, AAD.
2. SS to Embassy, Ankara, June 22, 1977, AAD.
3. SS to Ankara, October 26, 1977, AAD.
4. SS to Ankara, February 10, 1978, AAD.
5. US Consul, Strasbourg, to SS, January 22, 1979, AAD.

Bibliography

Presidential Libraries

Jimmy Carter Presidential Library, Atlanta, GA

Frank Moore Oral History, 2002
National Security Affairs
  Brzezinski Material, Country File
  Staff Material, Horn/Special
Office of Anne Wexler, Special Assistant to the President
  Anne Wexler's Subject Files
Office of the Chief of Staff Files
  Landon Butler
  Hamilton Jordan's Confidential Files
Office of Congressional Liaison
  Beckel
  Moore
Office of Staff Secretary, Handwriting File, Presidential Files
Remote Archives Capture Program
  Donated Historical Material—Mondale, Walter F.
  Plains File
Staff Offices, Ethnic Affairs, Aiello

Gerald R. Ford Presidential Library, Ann Arbor, MI

James M. Cannon Papers
Richard B. Cheney Papers
Myron Kuropas Files
Theodore C. Marrs Files
John Marsh Files
National Security Adviser's Files
  Memoranda of Conversations
  Presidential Name File

Ron Nessen Papers
Presidential Handwriting File
White House Central File
  Subject File
White House Press Releases

Ronald Reagan Presidential Library, Simi Valley, CA

European and Soviet Affairs Directorate Records, Remote Archives Capture
Alison B. Fortier Files
Head of State File, Records, 1981–1989, Executive Secretariat, NSC
White House Staff and Office Files
  Max Green Files, 1985–1988

Other Archival Sources

Arizona State University, Tempe

John J. Rhodes Papers

Burns Library, Boston College

Tip O'Neill Papers

Robert C. Byrd Center for Legislative Studies, Shepherdstown, WV

Robert C. Byrd Congressional Papers

Center for Lowell History, University of Massachusetts, Lowell

Paul Tsongas Collection

Clarke Historical Library, Central Michigan University, Mount Pleasant

Senator Robert P. Griffin Papers

CREST Database

General CIA Records

Immigrant History Research Center, University of Minnesota, Minneapolis

Records of the Minnesota Friends of Cyprus
Theodore Saloutos Papers

Indiana University Archives, Bloomington

Lee H. Hamilton Congressional Papers

Library of Congress, Washington, DC

Clark Clifford Papers

Marquette University Library, Milwaukee, WI

Clement J. Zablocki Papers

Minnesota Historical Society, St. Paul

Donald M. Fraser, Congressional Office Files
Vice Presidential Papers, Walter Mondale Papers

National Archives, Suitland, MD

Access to Archival Databases

New York University, New York City

John Brademas Congressional Papers

Ohio University Archives, Athens, OH

Wayne Hays Papers

Queens College, City University of New York

Benjamin Rosenthal Papers

State Historical Society of Missouri, Columbia

Thomas Eagleton Papers

Books and Articles

Acheson, Dean. *Present at the Creation: My Years in the State Department.* New York: W. W. Norton, 1969.

Alford, Jonathan, ed. *Greece and Turkey: Adversity in Alliance.* New York: Palgrave Macmillan, 1984.

Athanassopoulou, Ekavi. *Strategic Relations between the US and Turkey, 1979–2000.* New York: Routledge, 2014.

———. *Turkey–Anglo-American Security Interests, 1945–1952: The First Enlargement of NATO.* Portland, OR: Routledge, 1999.

"Authorization of Appropriations for the Board for International Broadcasting and Partial Lifting of the Turkish Arms Embargo." In *Hearing before the Committee on International Relations on S. 2230, September 17, 1975.* Washington, DC: Government Printing Office, 1975.

Aydin, Mustafa. "Determinants of Turkish Foreign Policy: Changing Patterns and Conjunctures during the Cold War." *Middle Eastern Studies* 36, no. 1 (January 2000): 152–86.

Beisner, Robert L. *Dean Acheson: A Life in the Cold War.* New York: Oxford University Press, 2006.

Bolukbashi, Suha. *The Superpowers and the Third World: Turkish-American Relations and Cyprus.* Vol. 15 of Exxon Education Foundation Series on Rhetoric and Political Discourse. Lanham, MD: University Press of America, 1988.

Burr, William, ed. *Nuclear Weapons and Turkey since 1959.* Briefing Book 688. National Security Archive, George Washington University, Washington, DC.

Campany, Richard C., Jr. *Turkey and the United States: The Arms Embargo Period.* New York: Praeger, 1986.

Coufoudakis, Van. "Greek Foreign Policy since 1974: Quest for Independence." *Journal of Modern Greek Studies* 6, no. 1 (May 1988): 55–79.

Dallek, Robert. *Nixon and Kissinger: Partners in Power.* New York: Harper, 2007.

Epstein, Edward Jay. *Agency of Fear: Opiates and Political Power in America.* New York: Putnam, 1977.

Evered, Kyle T. "'Poppies Are Democracy!' A Critical Geopolitics of Opium Eradication and Reintroduction in Turkey." *Geographical Review* 101, no. 3 (2011): 299–315.

Ford, Gerald R. *A Time to Heal.* New York: Harper & Row, 1979.

Franck, Thomas M., and Edward Weisband. *Foreign Policy by Congress.* New York: Oxford University Press, 1979.

Goode, James F. *Negotiating for the Past: Archaeology, Nationalism, and Diplomacy in the Middle East, 1919–1941.* Austin: University of Texas Press, 2007.

Gunther, Michael M. "Armenian Terrorism: A Reappraisal." *Journal of Conflict Studies* 27, no. 2 (2007): 109–28.

Hackett, Clifford. "Ethnic Politics in Congress: The Turkish Embargo Experience." In *Ethnicity in U.S. Foreign Policy,* ed. Abdul A. Said, 16–45. New York: Praeger, 1977.

Harris, George S. "Turkey's Foreign Policy: Independent or Reactive?" In *Diplomacy in the Middle East: The International Relations of Regional and Outside Powers,* ed. L. Carl Brown, 266–67. New York: I. B. Tauris, 2004.

———. "Turkish-American Relations since the Truman Doctrine." In *Turkish-American Relations: Past, Present and Future,* ed. Mustafa Aydin and Cagri Erhan, 66–88. New York: Routledge, 2004.

Jacobson, Matthew Frye. *Roots Too: White Ethnic Revival in Post–Civil Rights America.* Cambridge, MA: Harvard University Press, 2006.

Johnson, Robert David. *Congress and the Cold War.* Cambridge: Cambridge University Press, 2005.

Kamminga, Jorrit. "Opium Poppy Licensing in Turkey: A Model to Solve Afghanistan's Illegal Opium Economy?" In International Council on Security and Development, *Afghanistan Reports* (January 2011), 1–63. http://www.jorritkamminga.com/wpcontent/uploads/2016/04/A76_JK_Turkey_Report_0.pdf.

Keys, Barbara. "Congress, Kissinger and the Origins of Human Rights Diplomacy." *Diplomatic History* 34, no. 5 (2010): 823–51.

Kissinger, Henry. *Years of Renewal.* New York: Simon & Schuster, 1999.

Kuniholm, Bruce R. *The Origins of the Cold War in the Near East: Great Power Conflict and Diplomacy in Iran, Turkey, and Greece.* Princeton, NJ: Princeton University Press, 1980.

Laipson, Ellen B. *Congressional-Executive Relations and the Turkish Arms Embargo.* Congress and Foreign Policy Series no. 3. Washington, DC: Government Printing Office, 1981.

Lechelt, Jac. *The Vice Presidency in Foreign Policy: From Mondale to Cheney.* El Paso, TX: LFB Scholarly Publishing, 2009.

Mitchell, Nancy. "The Cold War and Jimmy Carter." In *The Cambridge History of the Cold War,* vol. 3, ed. Melvyn P. Leffler and Odd Arne Westad, 66–88. New York: Cambridge University Press, 2010.

———. *Jimmy Carter in Africa: Race and the Cold War.* Cold War International History Project. Stanford, CA: Stanford University Press, 2016.

Okur, Mehmet Akif. "The American Geopolitical Interests and Turkey on the Eve of the September 12, 1980, Coup." *CTAD* 11, no. 21 (Spring 2015): 199–222.

Proceedings, Order of AHEPA. 52nd Supreme Convention, Boston, August 18–24, 1974.

Purvis, Hoyt, and Steven J. Blake, eds. *Legislating Foreign Policy.* Boulder, CO: Westview Press, 1984.

Rubenzer, Trevor, and Steven B. Redd. "Ethnic Minority Groups and US Foreign Policy: Examining Congressional Decision Making and Economic Sanctions." *International Studies Quarterly* 54 (2010): 755–77.

Snyder, Jed C. *Defending the Fringe: NATO, the Mediterranean, and the Persian Gulf.* SAIS Papers in International Affairs no. 11. Boulder, CO: Westview Press, 1987.

Snyder, Sarah B. *From Selma to Moscow: How Human Rights Activists Transformed U.S. Foreign Policy.* New York: Columbia University Press, 2018.

Spain, James W. "The United States, Turkey and the Poppy." *Middle East Journal* 29 (Summer 1975): 295–309.

US Congress, House Committee on Foreign Affairs. *Turkish Opium Ban Negotiations: Hearing before the Committee on Foreign Affairs.* 93rd Cong., 2nd sess., July 16, 1974.

US Department of State. *Foreign Relations of the United States, 1964–1968.* Vol. 16, *Cyprus; Greece; Turkey.* Washington, DC: Office of the Bureau of Public Affairs, 2000.

———. *Foreign Relations of the United States, 1969–1976.* Vol. E-1, *Documents on Global Issues, 1969–1972.* Washington, DC: Office of the Historian, Bureau of Public Affairs, 2005.
———. *Foreign Relations of the United States, 1969–1976.* Vol. 30, *Greece; Cyprus; Turkey, 1973–1976.* Washington, DC: Office of the Historian, Bureau of Public Affairs, 2007.
———. *Foreign Relations of the United States, 1977–1980.* Vol. 21, *Greece; Cyprus; Turkey.* Washington, DC: Government Printing Office, 2014.
Uslu, Nasuh. *The Turkish-American Relationship between 1947 and 2003: The History of a Distinctive Alliance.* New York: Nova Science Publishers, 2003.
Uzer, Umut. *Identity and Turkish Foreign Policy: The Kemalist Influence in Cyprus and the Caucasus.* New York: I. B. Tauris, 2011.
Walther, Karine V. *Sacred Interests: U.S. Foreign Relations in the Islamicate World, 1821–1921.* Chapel Hill: University of North Carolina Press, 2015.
Watanabe, Paul Y. *Ethnic Groups, Congress, and American Foreign Policy: The Politics of the Turkish Arms Embargo.* Westport, CT: Greenwood Press, 1984.
Weiner, Tim. *Legacy of Ashes.* New York: Doubleday, 2007.
Yamak, Kemal. *Golgede Kalan Izler ve Golgelesen Bizler* [Traces of shadows and shadows]. Istanbul: Dogan Kitap, 2006.
Yaqub, Salim. *Imperfect Strangers: Americans, Arabs, and U.S.–Middle East Relations in the 1970s.* Ithaca, NY: Cornell University Press, 2016.
Zurcher, Erik K. *Turkey: A Modern History.* New York: I. B. Tauris, 2004.

Interviews

Atwood, Brian. May 29, 2014, Minneapolis, MN.
Ledsky, Ambassador Nelson. June 28. 2003. Association for Diplomatic Studies and Training, Foreign Affairs Oral History Project, Georgetown University.
Marsh, Jack. 2008. Interviewed by Richard Norton Smith, Gerald R. Ford Oral History Project.

Index

Studies in Conflict, Diplomacy, and Peace

Series Editors: George C. Herring, Andrew L. Johns, and Kathryn C. Statler

This series focuses on key moments of conflict, diplomacy, and peace from the eighteenth century to the present to explore their wider significance in the development of U.S. foreign relations. The series editors welcome new research in the form of original monographs, interpretive studies, biographies, and anthologies from historians, political scientists, journalists, and policymakers. A primary goal of the series is to examine the United States' engagement with the world, its evolving role in the international arena, and the ways in which the state, nonstate actors, individuals, and ideas have shaped and continue to influence history, both at home and abroad.

Advisory Board Members

Books in the Series

Truman, Congress, and Korea: The Politics of America's First Undeclared War
Larry Blomstedt

The Legacy of J. William Fulbright: Policy, Power, and Ideology
Edited by Alessandro Brogi, Giles Scott-Smith, and David J. Snyder

The Gulf: The Bush Presidencies and the Middle East
Michael F. Cairo

Reagan and the World: Leadership and National Security, 1981–1989
Edited by Bradley Lynn Coleman and Kyle Longley

A Diplomatic Meeting: Reagan, Thatcher, and the Art of Summitry
James Cooper

American Justice in Taiwan: The 1957 Riots and Cold War Foreign Policy
Stephen G. Craft

Soccer Diplomacy: International Relations and Football since 1914
Edited by Heather L. Dichter

Diplomatic Games: Sport, Statecraft, and International Relations since 1945
Edited by Heather L. Dichter and Andrew L. Johns

Nothing Less Than War: A New History of America's Entry into World War I
Justus D. Doenecke

Aid under Fire: Nation Building and the Vietnam War
Jessica Elkind

Enemies to Allies: Cold War Germany and American Memory
Brian C. Etheridge

Grounded: The Case for Abolishing the United States Air Force
Robert M. Farley

Foreign Friends: Syngman Rhee, American Exceptionalism, and the Division of Korea
David P. Fields

The Myth of Triumphalism: Rethinking President Reagan's Cold War Legacy
Beth A. Fischer

The American South and the Vietnam War: Belligerence, Protest, and Agony in Dixie
Joseph A. Fry

Lincoln, Seward, and US Foreign Relations in the Civil War Era
Joseph A. Fry

The Turkish Arms Embargo: Drugs, Ethnic Lobbies, and US Domestic Politics
James F. Goode

Obama at War: Congress and the Imperial Presidency
Ryan C. Hendrickson

Fourteen Points for the Twenty-First Century: A Renewed Appeal for Cooperative Internationalism
Edited by Richard H. Immerman and Jeffrey A. Engel

The Cold War at Home and Abroad: Domestic Politics and US Foreign Policy since 1945
Edited by Andrew L. Johns and Mitchell B. Lerner

US Presidential Elections and Foreign Policy: Candidates, Campaigns, and Global Politics from FDR to Bill Clinton
Edited by Andrew Johnstone and Andrew Priest

Paving the Way for Reagan: The Influence of Conservative Media on US Foreign Policy
Laurence R. Jurdem

The Conversion of Senator Arthur H. Vandenberg: From Isolation to International Engagement
Lawrence S. Kaplan

Harold Stassen: Eisenhower, the Cold War, and the Pursuit of Nuclear Disarmament
Lawrence S. Kaplan

America's Israel: The US Congress and American-Israeli Relations, 1967–1975
Kenneth Kolander

JFK and de Gaulle: How America and France Failed in Vietnam, 1961–1963
Sean J. McLaughlin

Nixon's Back Channel to Moscow: Confidential Diplomacy and Détente
Richard A. Moss

Breaking Protocol: America's First Female Ambassadors, 1933–1964
Philip Nash

Peacemakers: American Leadership and the End of Genocide in the Balkans
James W. Pardew

The Currents of War: A New History of American-Japanese Relations, 1899–1941
Sidney Pash

Eisenhower and Cambodia: Diplomacy, Covert Action, and the Origins of the Second Indochina War
William J. Rust

So Much to Lose: John F. Kennedy and American Policy in Laos
William J. Rust

The Sailor: Franklin D. Roosevelt and the Transformation of American Foreign Policy
David F. Schmitz

Foreign Policy at the Periphery: The Shifting Margins of US International Relations since World War II
Edited by Bevan Sewell and Maria Ryan

Lincoln Gordon: Architect of Cold War Foreign Policy
Bruce L. R. Smith

Thomas C. Mann: President Johnson, the Cold War, and the Restructuring of Latin American Foreign Policy
Thomas Tunstall Allcock